JASPER RIDLEY former barrister turned author. He is one of England's leading biographers, recent works include the lives of Henry VIII and Elizabeth I. His *Lord Palmerston* was winner of the James Tait Black prize for non-fiction. His most recent book *The Freemasons* was highly acclaimed.

Praise for *Bloody Mary's Martyrs*

'Jasper Ridley, the distinguished biographer, explains the issues clearly . . .'   John Pollock, biographer and historian

'Even if readers are already relatively familiar with this period of English history, Mr Ridley's new book will prove of significant interest. It is highly recommended.'
                    John E. Marshall, *The Banner of Truth*

'Ridley has crafted a well-written tale . . .'   *Choice*

By the same author

BLOODY MARY'S MARTYRS

The Story of England's Terror

Jasper Ridley

CARROLL & GRAF PUBLISHERS
New York

Carroll & Graf Publishers
An imprint of Avalon Publishing Group, Inc.
161 William Street
New York
NY 10038 2607
www.carrollandgraf.com

First published in the UK by Constable,
an imprint of Constable & Robinson Ltd, 2001

This edition first published in paperback in the UK by Robinson,
an imprint of Constable and Robinson Ltd, 2002

First Carroll & Graf edition, 2002

ISBN 0–7867–0986–3

Printed and bound in the EU

Library of Congress Cataloging-in-Publication Data is available on file.

To my son Benjamin Nicholas Ridley

CONTENTS

LIST OF ILLUSTRATIONS

Note on integrated illustrations from Foxe's *Book of Martyrs*

When Foxe published the first edition of his *Book of Martyrs* in 1563, it contained illustrations by an illustrator whose identity is unknown. Further illustrations appeared in the 1570 edition, which included most, but not all, of the illustations in the 1563 edition. These illustrations were obviously drawn from the illustrator's imagination, and in some cases differed from Foxe's account of the martyrdoms. The editors of the seventeeth- and eighteenth-century editions substituted new illustrations which sometimes varied from the 1563 and 1570 editions. I have included the illustrations from the 1732 edition and hope they are of interest to readers.

ACKNOWLEDGEMENTS

I wish to thank everyone who has helped me with this book, by giving me information, advice, editorial and clerical assistance, and in other ways: the Rev. Canon David Bishop; Geoffrey Copus; David Glazebrook; Ken Hall (the Essex County Archivist); Charles Hodgson; Dr Charles Littleton and Randolph Vigne of the Huguenot Society of Great Britain and Ireland; Krystyna Niedenthal; Maria Perry; Denise Sells; Dr Michael Smith; Dr Gabor Thomas (Research Officer of the Sussex Archaeological Society); Sharon Willett of Press Ahead; my publishers Constable and Robinson (Benjamin Glazebrook and Nick Robinson, and Tony Hall and Anna Williamson for their editorial assistance); my literary agents Curtis Brown of London (Peter Robinson and Mike Shaw and their assistants); the librarian and staff of the British Library; the East Sussex Record Office; the Kent County Library; the London Library; the Wiltshire and Swindon Record Office; and my wife Vera and my sons Benjamin and John.

Jasper Ridley
Tunbridge Wells
30 April 2001

CHAPTER 1

The Persecuting Church

IN ENGLAND IN THE REIGN of Queen Mary Tudor, for forty-five terrible months between 4 February 1555 and 10 November 1558, 283 Protestant martyrs – 227 men and 56 women – were burned alive. They have been remembered as martyrs for 400 years, and should be remembered today, though public recollection of them is beginning to fade. The Queen who was responsible for their suffering and death has gone down in history as 'Bloody Mary', and her Roman Catholic co-religionists still suffer, at least in some respects, because of what she did to the martyrs. It is impossible for a King or Queen of England to be a Roman Catholic or to marry a Roman Catholic; and Bloody Mary is indirectly responsible for the hatred of 'Papists' felt by the Protestants in Northern Ireland today. It was chiefly because the English and Irish Protestants remembered her martyrs that 130 years later, in 1688, they refused to accept a Roman Catholic king and to grant religious toleration to Roman Catholics. This led to the siege of Londonderry, the Battle of the Boyne, and the events of 1690 which are remembered with such disastrous results in Northern Ireland today.

The burning of Queen Mary's martyrs was the culmination of more than a century of religious conflict and persecution. The Roman Catholic Church which dominated Europe in the Middle Ages, like most organised religions, was an intolerant and persecuting Church. By the thirteenth century it had firmly established the law that heretics should be burned alive. Members of heretical sects who challenged the authority of the Church, like the Albigenses in the south of France and other sects of Cathars, were burned in such large numbers between the eleventh and thirteenth centuries that the sects were almost completely exterminated. Although various theories have been put forward as to why burning was adopted as the punishment for heresy, none of them can be substantiated. Burning alive was one of several cruel forms of capital punishment which was used by the Romans in ancient times and afterwards by the Christian states of medieval Europe. Men and women were burned alive for poisoning, arson and witchcraft as well as for heresy. Men who committed sodomy or bestiality were burned alive – in cases of bestiality, so was the animal – and women who committed high treason or murdered their husbands were also burned alive.

In the fourteenth century a new heresy appeared, inspired by the English priest and theologian John Wycliffe from Hipswell near Richmond in Yorkshire, who became a favourite of John of Gaunt, Duke of Lancaster, the fourth son of King Edward III. Wycliffe translated the Bible into English, and his translation, like those of the Protestant reformers 150 years later, led him and his followers, who were known as Lollards, to develop doctrines which challenged the most fundamental dogmas of the Catholic Church and the authority of the priesthood. His ideas were adopted by the Czech theologian, Jan Hus, who was denounced as a heretic and burned at Constance in Germany in 1415. Hus's followers in Bohemia launched a formidable insurrection led by a brilliant military leader, Jan Žižka. For fifteen years they ruled Bohemia and defied the armies of the Holy Roman Emperor until the conflict was ended by a compromise peace.

In England, three Acts of Parliament were passed in 1382, 1401 and 1414, giving statutory authority for burning heretics who had previously been burned under the English common law. The Act for the Burning of Heretics of 1401 enacted that when a person had been condemned as a heretic by the ecclesiastical courts, the King was to issue a warrant ordering the civil power – the sheriffs, and justices of the peace (JPs) – to burn the heretic alive. In the reigns of Henry IV and Henry V and the early years of Henry VI (between 1401 and 1440), sixteen heretics were burned in England and many more were imprisoned.

When a person was accused of heresy, he was dealt with by the procedure which was followed in the case of Mary Tudor's martyrs. He was arrested and brought before the court of the bishop of his diocese. Here he was tried either by the bishop himself or by the bishop's Ordinary, a judicial officer who was a qualified lawyer trained in the canon law of the Church. The accused heretic was given every encouragement to recant his heresy and was put under great psychological pressure to do so. If he refused to recant he was sentenced to be burned and was handed over to the sheriff of the county, the JPs and their officers, who carried out the sentence in public at the appointed time; but if he recanted he was sentenced to a lesser punishment – imprisonment for some months or years in a prison or monastery – and forced to wear a badge showing that he was a heretic. He was also forced to take part in the ceremony known as 'carrying his faggot'. The heretic was taken to the place of execution carrying a faggot of wood on his shoulder, and when the fire was lit he threw his faggot into the fire, so that only the faggot, and not the heretic, was burned. If he was an eminent and educated man, he was also required to preach a sermon confessing his error, repudiating his heresy and begging for the forgiveness of the Church.

After undergoing the sentence prescribed by the bishop, the repentant heretic was eventually forgiven and taken back into the Church and religious and public life; but if he afterwards again advocated heretical opinions, he was then a relapsed heretic and was not spared a second time. A relapsed heretic who was convicted of heresy by the ecclesiastical court was sentenced to be burned, and the sentence was carried out by the sheriff and JPs even if the heretic again recanted.

The persecution of Lollards continued throughout the fifteenth century. In the reign of King Henry VII, twelve heretics – ten men and two women – were burned between 1485 and 1509. The first to suffer was Joan Boughton, a very old widow whose daughter had married a knight. She was burned at Smithfield on 28 April 1494.

The Protestant movement intensified after Martin Luther in Germany in 1517 denounced the system by which the Pope granted dispensations to commit sins – sometimes to commit any sin in future – in return for gifts of money to pay for the cost of rebuilding St Peter's Basilica in Rome. Although the great majority of the English people were still loyal Catholics, sympathisers with Luther were to be found chiefly among those classes which always form the advance-guard of a new radical movement – the lower classes in the towns, especially the youth, and the intellectuals. Many theology graduates and students at Cambridge University were sympathetic to Luther's ideas. They met at the White Horse Inn in Cambridge, and began to be called 'Lutherans' instead of Lollards, though another name applied to them by their opponents was 'Protestants'. These Cambridge intellectuals and the artisans and youth of the towns of south-east England supplied most of the martyrs who thirty years later were burned in Mary's reign.

Oxford, unlike Cambridge, was a more orthodox Catholic university; but at least one Oxford man, William Tyndale, was a devoted Protestant. He graduated in theology at Magdalen Hall in Oxford, and became a priest. Soon afterwards he went abroad to join the Protestants in Germany. In Cologne he translated the New Testament into English from the Latin Vulgate Bible, and though no printer in Cologne dared to print it, he succeeded in having it secretly printed by Protestant supporters in the city of Worms in 1526. Tyndale then arranged for these Bibles to be smuggled into England. They were often hidden in bales of straw which the Protestants pretended were being sent to farmers in England. Most English people could not read or write, but some of them could, and those who were literate read Tyndale's English Bible aloud to their friends at secret Protestant meetings.

The English Catholic Establishment considered that an English translation of the Bible was a great threat to their authority. Before the Bible was translated priests read the Bible in Latin, told the people what the Bible said, and also taught them doctrines which are not to be found in the Bible, but had been developed in the writings of the early Christian theologians of the third, fourth and fifth centuries AD – St Augustine, Origen and St John Chrysostom – or had been orally handed down from the earliest times after the crucifixion of Jesus Christ. If the people could read the Bible in their native language, they could find out what the Bible really said, not what the Church told them that it said, and they could quote the authority of the Bible against the authority of the Church. Tyndale declared that by translating the Bible he hoped to make every ploughboy as knowledgeable in Scripture as the most learned clerk. This was exactly what most learned clerks did not wish to see.

The people who read Tyndale's Bible could discover that although Christ had appointed St Peter to be head of his Church, there was nothing in the Bible which said that the Bishops of Rome were St Peter's successors and that Peter's authority over the Church had passed to the Popes. Indeed, there was nothing in the Bible that said that Peter had ever been to Rome. As the Bible stated that God had ordered the people not to worship graven images, the images and pictures of the saints, and the stations of the cross, should not be placed in churches and along the highways.

The Protestants challenged at every point the special position of the priesthood. They taught that men would be saved and go to Heaven by their faith, by believing the true Christian doctrine, not by good works. The Catholic Church would not accept this, for 'good works' had come to mean giving lands and money to monasteries on condition that monks and priests prayed for the souls of their benefactors. In the Catholic Mass the priest alone drank the wine, and he put a piece of wafer into the mouths of the congregation. The Protestants believed that the congregation as well as the priest should drink the wine, and that the bread should not be placed in their mouths by the priest, but that they and the priest should eat it and drink the wine sitting together around a communion table.

Since the days of Pope Gregory VII in the eleventh century the Catholic Church had enforced the rule that priests should not marry but should remain apart from the people as a special celibate caste. As men were unfortunately sinners, the Catholic Church did not object very much if priests lived quite openly with a concubine. The Protestants, finding a text in the Bible that a bishop should be the husband of one wife, believed that all priests should be allowed to marry, but that living with a concubine was a sin.

The Protestants' most serious challenge to the authority of the clergy was their view of the effect of the consecration of the bread and wine by the priest during Mass. The theologians of the Catholic Church, who had been educated in the philosophy of Aristotle and his theory that the 'accidents' of an object – its appearance, feel, taste and smell – were different from its true inner reality, taught that although the consecrated bread and wine had the accidents of bread and wine, they were really the Body and Blood of Christ, because Christ had said at the Last Supper, 'This is my Body'. All the Protestant sects denied this Catholic doctrine of the Real Presence of Christ in the Sacrament, though they differed amongst themselves as to whether his presence there was a Sacramental Presence, a Spiritual Presence or a Figurative Presence, or whether there was no presence at all, and the consecrated bread was only a 'vile cake', as the extreme

Protestant sects called it. They all agreed that anyone who held a lower view of the nature of the Presence than they did was a heretic.

The Catholic Church called those who denied the Real Presence 'sacramentaries', and considered them to be the worst kind of heretics. Nearly all the martyrs of Mary Tudor's reign were 'sacramentaries', and were burned to death for denying the Real Presence, whatever other heresies they might also have committed.

No one was more active in persecuting the Protestants who distributed the English Bible than Sir Thomas More, a brilliant lawyer, writer and intellectual who was a particularly nasty sadomasochistic pervert. He enjoyed being flogged by his favourite daughter as much as flogging heretics, beggars and lunatics in his garden. He humiliated his wife by pointing out to his guests, in her presence, how ugly she was in order to show that he had not married her because he was lusting for a beautiful woman. When he was writing as a propagandist for the Catholic Church, he was a shameless liar. On one occasion he wrote a very favourable review of his own book, pretending that it had been written by a non-existent, eminent, foreign theologian, when in fact he had written it himself.[1]

When he became Lord Chancellor in 1529 he intensified the persecution of heretics. He insisted that anyone who read and distributed Tyndale's English Bible should suffer a 'painful death'. One of his great successes was when they caught the Protestant John Frith, who came from Westerham in Kent and had joined Tyndale in the Netherlands. Frith risked his life by coming to England to organise the illegal distribution of the translated Bible. He had nearly completed his mission and was on his way to board a ship at Milton Shore in Essex when he was stopped by a constable who suspected that he might have stolen goods hidden in his bag. The constable opened the bag and found hidden Bibles, and realised that he had caught a more dangerous criminal than a mere petty thief. Frith was arrested and taken before the Bishop of London's court, and in due course was condemned as a heretic and burned at Smithfield.

Apart from translating the Bible into English, Tyndale's other great contribution to sixteenth-century Protestant doctrine was his book *The Obedience of a Christian Man*, in which he stated that it was the duty of a Christian always to obey the King. In medieval society, the King and the Church were the two dominating authorities. It was therefore to the King that Tyndale turned to break the power of the Church, and he and his Protestant followers believed that they should emphasize the duty of the subject to obey the king. Tyndale wrote that, 'God in all lands hath put Kings, governors and rulers in his stead to rule the world through them. Whosoever therefore resisteth them resisteth God', and shall be damned. To resist a royal official was as wicked as resisting the King himself. Even if the King 'be the greatest tyrant in the world, yet he is unto thee a great benefit of God, and a thing wherefore thou oughtest to thank God highly'. The King 'may at his lust do right and wrong and shall give answer but to God only'.

Tyndale's appeal to the power of the King against the power of the Church was practical politics, because the most Catholic Kings had often quarrelled with the Pope and made war against him. In the eleventh, twelfth and thirteenth centuries Europe was torn by bitter warfare between the Popes and the Holy Roman Emperors, and the King of France had imprisoned the Pope in the fourteenth century. It was therefore not surprising that King Henry VIII, soon after he had been awarded the title of 'Defender of the Faith' by the Pope for his book against Luther, quarrelled with Pope Clement VII when the Pope refused to give him a divorce from his wife Catherine of Aragon. Henry wished to divorce Catherine because he had fallen in love with Anne Boleyn who refused to become his mistress unless he agreed to marry her, and because Catherine had been unable to give birth to a male heir; her only surviving child was her daughter, Princess Mary, who was to become 'Bloody Mary'. History had shown that if a girl, not a boy, inherited the throne, this would lead to civil war.

Before Catherine had married Henry, she had been married to his elder brother Arthur, who had died at the age of sixteen, probably without consummating the marriage. Under the canon law of the Church a Papal dispensation had been necessary to allow Henry to marry his brother's widow. Henry now asked the Pope to declare that that dispensation had been invalid, and that he was therefore not lawfully married to Catherine. Popes had usually been prepared to oblige powerful Kings in such matters, and Clement VII would probably have granted Henry the divorce if he had not been afraid of the Holy Roman Emperor Charles V, who was Catherine's nephew and supported her cause. Charles had recently made war against the Pope, because the Pope had supported Charles's enemy King Francis I of France; and in the course of the war Charles's army had captured Rome and had sacked the city, killing and looting, and raping the women.

The sack of Rome by the troops of the Holy Roman Emperor was difficult for Catholic propagandists to explain and excuse. Some of them, like Sir Thomas More, wrote that the Emperor's troops who committed the atrocity were German Lutherans, or Spanish Muslims who had only pretended to convert to Christianity. But there is no evidence for either of these theories. The Emperor's troops who sacked Rome were not Lutherans or Muslims, but ordinary mercenaries – men who, like other male thugs in other centuries, enjoyed fighting, looting and raping. The Pope was afraid that if he granted Henry his divorce, Charles would allow his mercenaries to sack Rome again.

The argument about the divorce ended with Henry repudiating the Papal supremacy over the Church, and requiring all his subjects – which in practice meant the head of every household –

to swear an oath that they believed that the King, not the 'Bishop of Rome', was the Supreme Head of the Church of England. Those who refused to take the oath were to be hanged, drawn and quartered. Nearly everyone agreed to take the oath, but four Carthusian monks – the priors of the charterhouses of London, of Beaulieu in Nottinghamshire and of the Isle of Axholme in Lincolnshire, and a monk of Sion at Brentford – refused, and a priest. The five men were duly hanged, drawn and quartered at Tyburn on 4 May 1535. In the case of Bishop Fisher and Sir Thomas More, who were executed a few weeks later, the sentence was commuted out of mercy to beheading with the axe.

The sentence of hanging, drawing and quartering meant that the criminal was hanged but cut down while still alive, castrated, disembowelled, and the bowels burned before his eyes while he was still living, before being finally killed by having his head cut off and his body cut into quarters. If the convicted traitor was a woman, she was burned alive.

But Henry continued to burn heretics. More's victim, Frith, was burned as a 'sacramentary' for denying the Real Presence in the summer of 1533 at the very time that Henry was divorcing Catherine of Aragon and preparing for the final break with Rome and the repudiation of Papal supremacy.

In persecuting both the supporters of the Papacy *and* the Protestant heretics, Henry was pursuing a policy which was very popular with the majority of his subjects. New ideas in politics and religion are always embraced first by minorities, and the majority of people are reluctant to break with old traditions. Most of the English people adhered to the Catholic doctrines in which they had been brought up. They were outraged by the actions of the enthusiastic young men who in their Protestant zeal broke into the churches and destroyed the images of the local saint who was traditionally associated with the parish. They were disgusted when these Protestants, quoting passages from the Bible against worshipping images and idols, removed the consecrated Host from the altar, trampled on it, and threw it on to a dunghill. Most English people thought that it was right to burn such troublemakers and all other heretics.

But the English were famous throughout Europe for their hatred of foreigners, unlike the Scots, who travelled all over Europe and welcomed foreign visitors to Scotland. The English hated the Italian Pope and his officials in Rome, and greatly resented the expense and the delays involved when they applied for a divorce or a dispensation or for any other relief in the ecclesiastical courts, and the case was held up for several years while an appeal was referred to the Papal court in Rome. The ordinary Englishman was also very ready to believe the stories that were always circulating about the corruption and immorality of the monks and nuns in the abbeys, monasteries and convents, which in fact were very often true.

As King Henry was now attacking the Pope, he had the support of many of the heretical Protestants, and this raised the possibility of employing them in his service against the Pope's. He considered recruiting Tyndale as a propagandist for the royal authority. When he read Tyndale's *The Obedience of a Christian Man* he is said to have exclaimed: 'This is a book for me and for all Kings to read'. But Henry was too intelligent not to see the dangers of Tyndale's doctrine. For Tyndale made one exception to his rule that the subject must always obey the royal authority. If the King ordered the subject to sin, the subject must disobey, though he must not resist the King and the government and must submit patiently to the punishment inflicted on him for his disobedience.

This exception was seized on by Sir Thomas More in his final denunciation of Tyndale in 1533. More wrote that Tyndale's pretence of supporting royal authority was hypocrisy, because Tyndale seditiously told his followers to disobey the King if they, in their arrogant presumption, decided that the King's order was sinful. More's argument was strengthened when Robert Barnes, a Cambridge theologian who had escaped to the Netherlands after he had been accused of heresy and had recanted and carried his faggot, wrote that if the King ordered a subject to burn the Bible the subject must disobey. More pointed out that the King had given orders that Tyndale's Bible was to be burned; so Tyndale and the Protestants had seditiously urged the people to disobey the laws of King Henry VIII.[2]

Henry was impressed by this argument. In his letter to Luther's protector, the Duke of Saxony, he had emphasized that Luther's doctrines were not only heretical but also seditious, because to challenge the established doctrines of the Church was a defiance of the authority of the ruler who upheld those doctrines. This point was repeatedly emphasized in the orders sent down in the sixteenth century from the authorities to their inferior officers – from the Privy Council to the bishops and the sheriffs, from the bishops to their clergy, from the sheriffs and JPs to the heads of households. Henry sent an agent to Antwerp to have a secret meeting with Tyndale in the fields outside the town where no one could see them talking together; but the King ultimately decided not to invite him to work as a propagandist. Furthermore Tyndale, with his honesty and high principles, had supported Catherine of Aragon in the divorce proceedings; he believed that the claims of Henry's lawyers and propagandists in favour of the divorce were unsound in ecclesiastical law.

Tyndale was eventually denounced as a heretic to Charles V's officers in the Netherlands in May 1535 by an English Catholic who had pretended to be a Protestant, and had infiltrated the English Protestant group in Antwerp. Tyndale was tried before the ecclesiastical court in the Netherlands and condemned. He submitted obediently, but refused to recant. He was sentenced to be strangled and burned. At the beginning of October 1536,[3] he was strangled as he stood bound to the stake, and it was only after he was dead that the faggots were lit. He would not have been shown such mercy in Henry VIII's England.

CHAPTER 2

Henry VIII: The Break with Rome

ALTHOUGH TYNDALE HIMSELF would not support Henry's divorce, many of his followers were prepared to do so, despite the fact that Henry was burning their friends as heretics. The divorce was also supported by men who wished to repudiate the Pope but to preserve the Catholic religion in all other respects. Henry therefore brought into public life many of the men who thirty years later were to play the leading part in the burning of heretics in Queen Mary's reign, both as persecutors and as martyrs.

Thomas Cranmer was the son of a gentleman in Nottinghamshire. He was sent to school, probably at the age of seven, and placed in the charge of a schoolmaster whom he afterwards described as having been 'marvellous severe and cruel'.[1] It was the first of a number of unhappy experiences which were to be the lot of the unfortunate Cranmer. He went to Jesus College, Cambridge; and became a fellow of the college; but while he was there he fell in love with a young woman who worked at an inn in the town called The Dolphin, and married her. As Cranmer had not yet become a priest, there was no reason why he should not have married her; but his relationship with 'Black Joan of the Dolphin' was used to discredit him by his political opponents in later years. When he married he forfeited his fellowship of his college, but, contrary to usual practice, he was readmitted. Soon afterwards he became a priest.

Cranmer has often been criticised as an unprincipled careerist who repeatedly changed his religion in order to curry favour with those in power; but this is an unfair oversimplification. He was a weak man who easily gave way to pressure, who did not like giving offence, and always tended to agree with the person to whom he was speaking. It was perhaps for this reason that people tended to bully him, and that ruthless politicians selected him to be the victim and the scapegoat.

At Cambridge Cranmer developed mildly Protestant opinions. Some years later he was employed on a number of diplomatic missions by Henry VIII. Having suggested to the King that in the divorce case he should go beyond the opinions of the ecclesiastical lawyers, and should consult, not the canonists, but the theologians in the universities of Europe, Cranmer was employed by Henry in securing favourable opinions on the divorce from the Italian universities. He became chaplain to Anne Boleyn's family. He had hitherto kept his Protestant opinions largely to himself.

In 1532 Henry appointed Cranmer as ambassador to Charles V, who was travelling through his territories in Germany. On his way to the Emperor's court Cranmer went to the Protestant city of Nuremberg and met the eminent Lutheran theologian, Osiander. In Nuremberg he married the niece of Osiander's wife. The fact that he was prepared to marry shows that he was already a convinced Protestant.

As the marriage of priests was illegal in England, Cranmer kept his marriage secret, and did this very successfully. Although his Catholic opponents constantly accused him of various acts of impropriety, they did not discover for seventeen years that he had a wife, until he announced the fact after the marriage of priests had been made legal in the reign of Edward VI; but there is no truth in the story that was afterwards told by Catholics that he kept his wife hidden in a chest. The people who noticed that he had a woman in his household probably assumed that she was his mistress, and accepted this as readily as they accepted the fact that many priests had concubines.

While Cranmer was at the Emperor's court, the Archbishop of Canterbury died, and Henry VIII appointed Cranmer archbishop in his place. Henry had separated from Catherine of Aragon, declaring that he could no longer commit the sin of living with his brother's widow, and Anne Boleyn had then agreed to become his mistress. As the Pope was refusing to give judgment in the divorce case in his court in Rome for fear of offending either Henry or the Emperor, and was repeatedly adjourning the proceedings there, Henry decided to prohibit appeals to the Papal court in Rome and to order the case to be tried by the Archbishop of Canterbury in England. He thought that Cranmer was the man who could be relied upon to give judgment in his favour.

Cranmer was unhappy at being appointed archbishop, and having this responsibility placed upon him. When he received news of his appointment while he was at the Emperor's court at Mantua, and was ordered to return to England immediately, he travelled very slowly, making the frozen roads the excuse for covering only fifteen miles a day.

On his arrival in England he was consecrated Archbishop of Canterbury, and sat in a court at Dunstable, where he duly gave judgment that Henry's marriage to Catherine was void and that the King was free to marry Anne Boleyn. Henry had already married her secretly. Cranmer did not even pretend that he was giving an impartial judgment, and wrote to Henry throughout the trial assuring him that he would give judgment in his favour at the earliest moment that was legally possible. Within a week of Cranmer's judgment Anne was crowned as Queen on Whit Sunday, 1 June 1533. Three months later, on 7 September she gave birth to a child. To Henry's great disappointment, it was a girl, not a boy. The child was to become Queen Elizabeth I.

When Henry required all his subjects to swear an oath that they accepted Anne Boleyn's daughter as the lawful heir to the throne and that they recognised the King, and not the Bishop of Rome, as the Supreme Head of the Church of England, he did not force Catherine of Aragon and her daughter the Princess

Mary to take the oaths, or imprison or execute them for refusing to do so; but he held them under house arrest, and refused to allow them to visit each other, even when Catherine was dying. Mary was deprived of her title of Princess; she was to be called 'the King's daughter the Lady Mary'. Henry ordered her to become the lady-in-waiting to the infant Princess Elizabeth. Mary complied with Henry's orders, but deeply resented it, and showed this openly.

Mary was in secret contact with Charles V's ambassador in England, Eustace Chapuys, and was urging him to persuade Charles to invade England, to restore her mother and herself to their former position, and reimpose Papal supremacy. But Charles, though he kept pressurising the Pope to issue Papal censures against Henry, was not prepared to do anything to enforce them. He valued Henry as an ally against France. He also refused to apply economic sanctions and prohibit the trade between his subjects in the Netherlands, and England.

Henry appointed Thomas Cromwell to be his secretary. Cromwell was a lawyer who had been Cardinal Wolsey's secretary, and after Wolsey's fall from power in the autumn of 1529 he entered the King's service. He had Protestant sympathies, not least because Protestantism meant a strengthening of the royal authority. After the repudiation of Papal supremacy, Henry appointed Cromwell to be his vicegerent in ecclesiastical affairs. This meant that Cromwell, though a layman, had supreme power over the Archbishop of Canterbury and all the bishops in questions of religion.

Henry employed the services of another Protestant, Hugh Latimer, who was very different in character from Cranmer and Cromwell. He was born in Leicestershire, and went to Cambridge University, where he came into contact with the Protestants who frequented the White Horse Inn. He was a forceful and brilliant preacher with a rough sense of humour, and had none of Cranmer's hesitation in his adherence to his Protestant opinions; but he was prepared to manoeuvre, if necessary, and did not recklessly provoke persecution. When Cambridge University was asked to express its opinion on Henry's divorce, he was a vigorous advocate of the King's cause.

Latimer became a close friend of Richard Bilney, who was condemned as a heretic for his Protestant opinions but recanted and carried his faggot; and Latimer comforted Bilney when Bilney was deeply ashamed of his weakness in recanting. Bilney was later convicted of heresy for a second time, and burned as a relapsed heretic. Latimer himself was denounced as a heretic, but managed to clear himself of the charge after stating that he believed in the existence of Purgatory, which the Protestants denied. The accusation of heresy did not prevent Henry from appointing Latimer to be a preacher at court.

The Bishop of Worcester had by custom been an Italian cardinal who lived in Rome and represented the King of England's interests at the Papal court. He never visited England, but in return for his services to the King in Rome he was paid the revenues of the bishopric, while the duties of the bishop were performed by a deputy. The same applied to the Bishop of Salisbury, another Italian cardinal who never came to England. After the break with Rome both Italian cardinals were deprived of their English sees. Latimer became Bishop of Worcester, and another ardent Protestant, Nicholas Shaxton, was appointed Bishop of Salisbury. Shaxton had been born in the diocese of Norwich, and went to Gonville Hall, Cambridge, where he became a priest and associated with the Protestants at the White Horse Inn.

But Stephen Gardiner, who also worked in favour of Henry's divorce and the repudiation of Papal supremacy, strongly upheld the Catholic religion in all other respects. He was a native of Suffolk, and went to Cambridge University. He was very intelligent, a skilful diplomat as well as a learned theologian, and a ruthless exponent of power politics. He was a firm believer in authoritarian doctrines, and thought that it was essential to suppress any nonconformity in religion or politics. When he was Chancellor of Cambridge University the eminent Greek scholar there, John Cheke, put forward the view that the accepted pronunciation of Greek was incorrect, and suggested that a different pronunciation should be adopted. Gardiner issued a decree banning the new pronunciation of Greek. Even in this purely academic matter he thought that any innovation by individuals which contradicted the accepted ideas of the authorities should be firmly suppressed.

Edmund Bonner was another energetic advocate of Henry's divorce and the break with Rome. He came from Cheshire, went to Oxford University, and became a priest. Forceful and outspoken, he had an aggressive and bullying manner which aroused great resentment among his opponents. When Henry repudiated Papal supremacy he sent Bonner to tell the Pope. Bonner's manner was so offensive that Clement VII threatened to have him arrested and burned as a heretic. Henry told Bonner that he must do his duty as the envoy of his King, and rely on Henry's power to protect him. Bonner returned safely to England. Henry rewarded him by appointing him Bishop of Hereford, and soon afterwards Bishop of London.

Three years after Henry married Anne Boleyn she had failed to give birth to a son, and Henry had fallen in love with Jane Seymour, one of her ladies-in-waiting. He had Anne beheaded on a charge of adultery with several lovers including her own brother, and of plotting to murder him. Two days before she was beheaded, Cranmer gave judgment that she had never been lawfully married to Henry, reversing the judgment on the validity of their marriage which he had given three years before. Anne's daughter Elizabeth, like Mary, was now officially regarded as a bastard.

Henry immediately married Jane Seymour. Seventeen months later on 12 October 1537 she gave birth, by caesarian delivery, to a son who in due course became King Edward VI. Twelve days after the birth of her baby, on 24 October, Jane Seymour died apparently of septicaemia. Henry gave her a great state funeral.

Shortly before the arrest of Anne Boleyn, Charles V's ambassador Chapuys had a secret meeting with Cromwell, and suggested that as Catherine of Aragon had recently died, relations with the Emperor would be improved if Henry were to get rid of Anne Boleyn and marry a third wife. But Mary's position did not improve after the execution of Anne Boleyn. Henry required her to take an oath acknowledging that she was a bastard, and repudiating Papal supremacy. When she hesitated to comply, he threatened to send her as a prisoner to the Tower of London and proceed against her for high treason. His councillors were shocked, and interceded for her with the King. None of them pleaded for her more ardently than Cranmer, whose mildness and timidity made him shrink from taking so drastic a step against a royal princess, even if she was a bastard.

On Chapuys' advice, Mary submitted and took the oath that was required of her. She was then allowed to come to court. Her resentment at her treatment was stronger than ever, but she kept this strictly to herself.

In the years after the break with Rome, Cromwell and Cranmer succeeded in persuading Henry to approve of certain doctrinal concessions in favour of Protestantism, though they were opposed by Gardiner and his supporters among the bishops. In 1537 Cromwell and Cranmer persuaded Henry to sanction the publication of the Bible in English. The Bible was in fact Tyndale's translation. At the time of his arrest in 1535 Tyndale had translated the New Testament, and the Old Testament as far as the Book of Chronicles. The rest of the Old Testament was translated by John Rogers. After Cambridge, Rogers had been appointed chaplain to the English merchants at

Antwerp, where he met Tyndale, who persuaded him to become an ardent Protestant. Miles Coverdale, a Yorkshireman, who had also graduated from Cambridge, been ordained, and had associated with the Protestants at the White Horse Inn, took refuge in the Netherlands, where he made his own translation of the Bible into English.

Cromwell and Cranmer persuaded Henry to order that a copy of an English translation of the Bible should be placed in every church, and that the people should be allowed to read it. It was named 'Matthew's Bible', but was in fact the Bible translated by Tyndale and Rogers, without Tyndale's controversial marginal notes, in which he had expounded his Protestant doctrines. Coverdale was in touch with Cromwell about the publication, and did all he could to help prepare it.

One of the few people who refused to declare that Henry was the Supreme Head of the Church of England was Friar John Forest, who had been Catherine of Aragon's confessor. Although his refusal to take the oath made him liable to suffer death as a traitor, he was also tried for heresy and convicted because he refused to accept the Protestant interpretation of certain passages in the Bible. In the whole history of the religious persecutions in England in the sixteenth and seventeenth centuries, Forest was the only Roman Catholic who was accused of heresy. All the other Roman Catholic victims were punished as traitors, or fined under the provision of the Acts of Parliament of the reigns of Edward VI and Elizabeth I.

Forest was sentenced to be both hanged for treason and burned as a heretic. He was chained to a gallows which was placed above the fire which burned below him. It was the usual practice for a sermon to be preached at the place of execution immediately before the faggots were lit. Latimer preached the sermon at Forest's execution. His sermon lasted for three hours, which was not unusually long in the sixteenth century, while Forest waited for death. Latimer, in his usual cheerful manner, wrote to Cromwell that he would 'play the fool after my customable manner when Forest shall suffer'.

Forest was hanged in chains above the fire. When the flames reached his feet, he drew them up, then bravely lowered them into the fire, and remained there till he burned to death. The Protestants and most of the English people had no sympathy for him.

The execution of Forest coincided with the campaign against images and superstitious relics. In North Wales there was a wooden image known as David Davelgarthen, who was worshipped as a saint by the local inhabitants. The image was seized by Cromwell's agents, despite the protests and entreaties of the people, and taken to London to be destroyed. There was a legend that Davelgarthen would one day burn a forest, and some official thought that it would be amusing to burn the statue of Davelgarthen as part of the fuel to burn 'a forest' – Friar Forest. This was done, and a verse was fixed to the stake while Forest burned:

> David Davelgarthen,
> As sayeth the Welshmen,
> Fetched outlaws out of Hell.
> Now he is come, with spear and shield,
> In harness to burn in Smithfield,
> For in Wales he may not dwell.
> And Forest the friar,
> That obstinate liar,
> That wilfully shall be dead,
> In his contumacy
> The Gospel doth deny,
> And the King to be Supreme Head.

Despite the treatment meted out to Forest, Henry VIII continued his persecution of Protestants. Six months after the

death of Forest, he presided in person at the trial of John
Lambert, a Protestant who denied the Real Presence. After
Henry had browbeaten and insulted Lambert at the trial,
Lambert was sentenced to be burned as a heretic. For some
reason the executioners took a dislike to him; as he burned, he
was hoisted on a pike and lifted out of the reach of the flames,
and then lowered again into the fire, in order to prolong his
sufferings.

Henry decided to suppress the monasteries, and to seize their
wealth. Commissioners were sent to visit the monasteries all over
England, in order to investigate the charges of immorality which
had been levelled against them. The commissioners knew that
they were expected to find proof of immorality, and in many
monasteries had no difficulty in finding the evidence for which
they were looking. They duly denounced the monasteries in
their report. Latimer stated that 'when their enormities [of
monastries] were first read in the Parliament House, they were
so great and abominable that there was nothing but "Down with
them!"'

Henry then pressurised the monasteries into agreeing to dissolve
themselves voluntarily. He achieved this by bribing the abbots and
priors to agree. The monks who would have to leave the monasteries would receive a pension of about £5 a year (£3,000 in
terms of money today); the abbots and priors would receive a
pension of £100 a year (£60,000 in today's money), and often
were appointed bishops of the new dioceses which Henry created
by carving them out of the old bishoprics so as to be able to reward
the abbots for their compliance. Nearly all the abbots and priors
agreed to surrender their houses voluntarily; but three abbots
refused to agree. They were arrested on far-fetched charges of high
treason, and were hanged, drawn and quartered.

Henry granted the lands of the monasteries to courtiers and
speculators. A few grantees received lands as a reward for their
services. Most of them paid the King for the lands, and then sold

them at a profit to other buyers. This gave many purchasers a vested interest in the lands of the monasteries, and a reason for supporting their suppression.

The greatest sufferers from the suppression of the monastries were the penniless vagrants who had been given hospitality there. They were now ejected from the monasteries, and wandered on the roads until they were arrested and flogged, mutilated and hanged under the severe laws against vagrants which were passed in Henry VIII's reign.

There was one man, a refugee abroad, whom Henry feared in the obsessive way that despots always fear their refugees who criticise them in foreign countries. Reginald Pole was the son of the daughter of the Duke of Clarence, the brother of King Edward IV. Several of his relations had been executed by Henry VII and Henry VIII on trumped-up charges because, as the heirs of the House of York, they might possibly claim the throne of England; but Reginald Pole's mother had been created Countess of Salisbury, and Pole was brought up at Henry's court and educated at Henry's expense.

When Henry began his divorce proceedings against Catherine of Aragon, Pole went to Paris to urge the university there to support the divorce, and acted as Henry's spokesman abroad; but he was shocked when Henry executed Bishop Fisher, Sir Thomas More and the Carthusian monks who had refused to swear the Oath of Supremacy recognising Henry as Supreme Head of the Church of England. Pole wrote a book, *De Unitate Ecclesiastica*, denouncing Henry as a tyrant. He was created a cardinal by the Pope and appointed Papal Legate, though he was not ordained a priest. The Pope sent him to persuade the Emperor Charles V to abandon his war against the Turks and to invade England, or at least to prohibit his subjects in the Netherlands from trading with England.

Pole travelled from Rome to Charles's court in Spain, avoiding the attempts of Henry's agents to assassinate him on his journey. Charles refused Henry's demand that he extradite Pole as a traitor, but told Pole that he was not prepared to take any action against England; he was afraid that Henry would join Francis I of France in a war against him. Francis was equally afraid of antagonising Henry, and refused to receive Pole. Charles V's sister, Mary of Hungary, who ruled the Netherlands as regent for Charles, also refused to receive him. Pole returned to Rome, appalled at the power of the 'Pharoah of England' and the refusal of the Catholic sovereigns to do anything against him.

In England an Act of Parliament was passed convicting Pole in his absence of high treason and condemning him to death. Henry arrested Pole's mother, his brother, and other members of his family, although they had dutifully written to Pole denouncing him for his activities against Henry. They were accused of having said things in the privacy of the family indicating their sympathy with Pole's activities abroad. They were all executed.

As Pole could do nothing against Henry, the Pope appointed him to be governor of the province of Viterbo in Italy. In Viterbo Pole was accused by Jesuits and other Catholics of being too tolerant to heretics. He succeeded in rebutting the charge, but decided that he would not be too soft on heretics in future.

In the spring of 1539 Henry decided to clamp down on the Protestants. He probably thought that this would be popular with the majority of his subjects, at a time when Charles V and Francis I had made peace and there was a danger that they might unite against him. Despite mild protests from Cranmer, he directed Parliament to pass the Act of the Six Articles, going in person to the House of Lords to make sure that the bill was passed. The Six Articles made denial of the Real Presence punishable by burning for the first offence, even if the heretic recanted. Married priests and their wives were to suffer death by hanging. It was made heresy to demand that the wine as well as the bread should be given to the laity at Mass, and to advocate other Protestant doctrines. In the debate on the bill in the House of Lords, Latimer and Shaxton at first abstained, but were later forced to submit and vote in favour of the Six Articles. They were nevertheless made to resign their bisoprics of Worcester and Salisbury, and were placed for a time under arrest in the houses of orthodox bishops.

Next year, after a power struggle at court, Henry had Thomas Cromwell arrested and executed as a traitor. Two days after Cromwell's death, Henry staged a grim event. On 30 July 1540 three Papist supporters were hanged, drawn and quartered, and three Protestant heretics were burned, at the same time and place at Smithfield in London. The traitors and heretics were dragged from their prison to the place of execution tied to a hurdle, with one traitor and one heretic on each hurdle. On the way to Smithfield they denounced each other, each traitor and heretic asserting that though he was about to be unjustly martyred for the true faith, his neighbour on the hurdle would be rightly executed as a traitor or a heretic.

There followed six years of persecution of Protestants. The reading of the English Bible was restricted on the grounds that it made men arrogant and unwilling to accept the teaching of those who should instruct them in religion; no yeoman or labourer was allowed to read the English Bible, and no one was permitted to read it aloud to others. The laws about fasting in Lent were rigidly enforced; in London government agents entered the people's houses at dinner time to see if they were eating the forbidden meat or eggs. Several heretics were sentenced to be burned. Three were burned in Windsor Great Park, but most of them suffered in London, and they were tried before Bonner as Bishop of London.

One of the martyrs was Anne Askew, a young gentlewoman aged twenty-five from Lincolnshire, who had been thrown out of the house by her husband because she was a Protestant. She came to London and distributed Protestant pamphlets there. She was sent to the Tower and tortured on the rack to induce her to reveal the names of her accomplices. She was afterwards tried for heresy before Bonner and other judges and convicted of denying the Real Presence. She was unable to walk after the torture, and had to be carried to the stake at Smithfield in a chair; but they dragged her to her feet and fastened her by a chain to the stake before they burned her, with three other heretics, on 16 July 1546.

A few months after Anne Askew was burned, Henry made another change in policy. He decided to destroy the Howard family – the pro-Catholic Duke of Norfolk and his son, the dashing and irresponsible young poet, the Earl of Surrey. The fact that they had made a coat-of-arms, which they had displayed in the privacy of their house, on which the arms of King Edward the Confessor were quartered with those of the Howard family was supposed to be sufficient proof that they wished Norfolk to become King, and that they were therefore guilty of high treason. Modern historians have assumed that Edward Seymour, Earl of Hertford, the brother of Henry VIII's third wife Jane Seymour, was responsible for the overthrow of Norfolk; but there is no evidence of this, and no contemporary commentator suggested it.

Henry had by this time become so fat and ill that he could hardly walk or stand unaided; but he was still in absolute control of his government and policy. He destroyed the Howards because he thought that they had become too powerful. He also turned against Gardiner, who had been sufficiently confident of Henry's favour that he showed some reluctance to agree to an exchange of lands between his see of Winchester and the King.

After Norfolk and Surrey were arrested, Henry made his Will. He appointed sixteen councillors, including the Earl of Hertford and Cranmer, to form a Regency Council after his death, during the infancy of his son Edward. Gardiner was not appointed a member of the Regency Council. In January 1547

Surrey was convicted of high treason by a London jury, and beheaded. Henry was dying; his doctors knew it, but dared not tell him, because an Act of Parliament had made it high treason to foretell the date of the King's death. An Act of Attainder, condemning Norfolk as a traitor and sentencing him to death, was rushed through Parliament; but Henry was too ill to sign the warrant for his execution.

On the night of 27 January 1547 Henry's favourite, Sir Anthony Denny, ventured to tell him that he would die in a few hours. Henry ordered them to send for Cranmer. It was a freezing night, and the icy roads delayed Cranmer on his journey from Lambeth to Whitehall; but he arrived in time to take Henry's hand and ask him, as he could no longer speak, to indicate by pressing it, that he put his trust in Christ's mercy. Henry died at 2 a.m. on 28 January.

His councillors were stunned by his death. If he had lived, he might have destroyed any of them, as he had destroyed his other favourites, Wolsey, Thomas More, Thomas Cromwell and Norfolk. But they were overcome with grief, as were the members of the Politburo of the Russian Communist Party when Stalin died. Cranmer had seen Henry burn many of the Protestants with whom Cranmer secretly sympathised; but he was so distressed at Henry's death that he never shaved again, and grew a beard. The Protestant John Foxe saw it differently. He afterwards wrote that the Protestants waded 'through dangerous tempests of King Henry's time' and reached 'the mild and halcyon days of King Edward VI'.[2]

CHAPTER 3

Edward VI: The Protestant Reformation

AFTER HENRYS DEATH, Edward Seymour dispensed with the Regency Council, and took office as Lord Protector and Regent for the nine-year-old King Edward VI. He soon created himself Duke of Somerset. The severity of the regime was immediately relaxed. Somerset did not execute Norfolk, though he had only to allow the Act of Attainder to take effect. He spared Norfolk's life, though Norfolk was kept as a prisoner in the Tower for the whole of Edward's reign.

Somerset and Cranmer proceeded slowly to introduce Protestant doctrines into the Church of England. They moved very cautiously; with their emphasis on the duty to obey the King's authority, they forbade the Protestants to introduce any Protestant innovation which had not been sanctioned by the government. Parliament repealed the Act of the Six Articles and the Acts for the Burning of Heretics of 1382, 1401 and 1414. By the beginning of 1549, after Somerset had governed England for two years, an Act of Parliament had been passed allowing priests to marry; Cranmer and his colleagues had drafted the Book of Common Prayer to replace the old service of the Latin Mass with a communion service in English; and the doctrine of the Real Presence had been rejected after a debate between the bishops in the House of Lords.

The Act of Uniformity required everyone to attend the new service laid down in the Book of Common Prayer, and made it illegal to celebrate or attend Mass. Those who broke the law were liable to heavy fines, but they were not treated as heretics and burned.

Gardiner and Bonner opposed these innovations in religion. They had strongly upheld the doctrine of the royal supremacy over the Church in the days of Henry VIII; but they argued that the royal power in religion could not be exercised on behalf of an infant king by his Lord Protector. The religious settlement decreed by Henry VIII must therefore remain in force and unchanged until Edward VI was old enough to rule himself; he might then, if he wished, exercise his royal power over the church and alter his father's orders about religion. Mary adopted the same attitude. She gave no hint that she wished to reunite the realm to Rome and reimpose the authority of the Pope, but demanded that the law on religion should be enforced as it had been laid down by Henry VIII.

In the summer of 1549 a revolt broke out in Cornwall and Devon in protest against Cranmer's English services of the Book of Common Prayer. The people demanded that the old Latin Mass should continue, that the Act of the Six Articles should be enforced, and that heretics should be burned. At the same time another insurrection led by Robert Kett broke out in Norfolk. This was not a pro-Catholic revolt, but a protest against the land enclosures by the local gentlemen which were depriving the people of their rights over common land. Most of the Norfolk rebels were Protestants.

The revolt in the west was suppressed. John Dudley, Earl of Warwick, defeated the rebels in Norfolk and then made a *coup d'état* which overthrew Somerset, for the nobles and gentlemen thought that Somerset had too much sympathy with the grievances of the common people. Mary, Gardiner and Bonner hoped that Warwick, who was now created Duke of Northumberland, would reverse Somerset's Protestant policy and restore the religious laws of Henry VIII. But Northumberland pursued an even more Protestant policy than Somerset had done. Bonner was deprived of his London see after a judicial hearing on the grounds that he had disobeyed the King's commands. He was imprisoned in the Fleet prison in London. Gardiner was similarly deprived of his bishopric of Winchester on the same grounds, and imprisoned in the Tower.

It was probably Nicholas Ridley who persuaded Cranmer to renounce the Real Presence and to adopt the Zwinglian doctrine of a Spiritual Presence, which had been formulated by Ulrich Zwingli – the theologian who dominated the Protestant city of Zurich in Switzerland. Ridley came from a family of gentlemen in Northumberland, in the lawless part of the country near the Scottish Border where the royal authority was ignored. He studied divinity at the college of Pembroke Hall in Cambridge, and became Cranmer's chaplain, the vicar of Herne in Kent, a canon of Canterbury Cathedral, and a royal chaplain. He had come under suspicion of heresy in the last years of Henry's reign, but had kept clear of serious trouble. After the accession of Edward VI he was appointed Bishop of Rochester, and took the leading part in opposing the Real Presence in the disputation in the House of Lords. When Bonner was deprived, Ridley succeeded him as Bishop of London. He was active in suppressing altars, setting the example by removing the altar in St Paul's Cathedral and replacing it with a communion table.

When Ridley became Bishop of London, John Ponet succeeded him as Bishop of Rochester. Ponet was born somewhere in Kent in about 1516,[1] but no one has been able to discover any record of his birthplace. He went to Queen's College, Cambridge, where he associated with a group of brilliant intellectuals who studied the modern sciences, which were developing in the cultural Renaissance in Italy, as well as theology and ancient Greek philosophy. He became a fluent linguist in Latin, Greek, Hebrew, French, German and Italian. He wrote several treatises on mathematics, and designed a clock for Henry VIII, which showed not only the hours of the day but also the days of the month and the movements of the sun and the moon; but despite his scientific interests he decided to become a priest and was ordained in 1536. He was chosen as a fellow of Queen's College, and after serving his term as bursar and dean of the college he was granted his degree of doctor of divinity. Cranmer appointed him to be his chaplain; and although Ponet had developed strong Protestant opinions he kept them to himself during the last years of Henry VIII's reign, when, thanks to Cranmer's influence he was granted several ecclesiastical benefices in London and the rectory of Lavant in Sussex.

Ponet was consecrated as Bihop of Rochester in June 1550, and in June 1551, after Gardiner had been deprived, he succeeded him as Bishop of Winchester. Now, under Edward VI, he made no secret of his Protestant opinions. He translated into English several books by the Italian Protestant Bernardino Ochino, and Ponet himself wrote a book in favour of the marriage of priests. When the Act was passed which permitted priests to marry, he married a woman who was already married to a butcher in Nottingham. This involved Ponet in a scandal soon after he was appointed Bishop of Winchetster. On 27 July 1551 he was divorced from the butcher's wife after a hearing at St Paul's in London in which he was orderd to pay damages to the butcher. Henry Machyn, a merchant tailor of London, wrote in his diary that on 'the 27 day of July the new Bishop of Winchester was divorced from the butcher's wife with shame enough.'[2] Three months later, on 25 October, Ponet married another woman, Mary Hayman, the daughter of a gentleman of Kent who was one of Cranmer's financial officials, at a wedding in Croydon attended by Cranmer and a large congregation.

When Ponet became Bishop of Winchester, John Scory succeeded him as Bishop of Rochester. Scory was born in Norfolk and became a monk in the Dominican monastery in Cambridge. He duly became Prior, and dutifully surrendered his monastery to the King voluntarily, being rewarded with a good pension and promotion to various positions in the Church. He became a Doctor of Divinity at Cambridge, and, like Ridley, was a canon of Canterbury Cathedral and Cranmer's chaplain. He got into serious trouble at Canterbury in the years after the fall of Cromwell in 1540, when he was denounced as a heretic by the Catholic canons there; but Cranmer was able to persuade King Henry to protect him. Under Edward VI, after serving for a year as Bishop of Rochester, Scory was appointed Bishop of Chichester, replacing George Day, who had been deprived for opposing the suppression of altars.

Coverdale, who had returned to England after translating the Bible, was appointed Bishop of Exeter. Latimer did not wish to be a bishop again, but was appointed to preach before the young King at court. In a series of vigorous sermons he dealt, among other things, with the grievances of the common people and their resentment against the enclosure of common lands by the noblemen and gentlemen.

Mary at this time relied on the support of her cousin Charles V. She wished to escape abroad, and go to a country where she could attend Mass without being pestered by heretics as she was in England. She asked Charles V to help her escape. Charles was reluctant to do this, and pointed out to her that if she left England she would be unable to succeed to the throne when Edward died; but he eventually agreed to help when she insisted that her only wish was to live in a country where she could attend Mass in safety.

Charles sent a squadron of eight warships to wait off the east coast of England on the pretext that they were preparing to conduct operations against Scottish pirates, while one of his agents, pretending to be a trader wishing to sell corn in England, sailed to Maldon in Essex within a few miles of the house where Mary was staying. The plan was for Mary to come secretly on board his ship and sail to the protection of the Emperor's squadron. The agent made his way secretly to Mary's house, but found that Mary was not sure that she wished to escape, because the Controller of her household, Robert Rochester, was trying to persuade her to stay in England. Eventually Rochester's arguments prevailed, and Charles's agent and the eight warships sailed away without her. After this, the Emperor refused to make any further efforts to help her escape. If it had not been for Rochester, Mary would probably have escaped abroad, and would have spent the rest of her life in exile; she would never have become Queen of England; the lives of 283 Protestant martyrs would have been spared; she would not be remembered in history as Bloody Mary; and English Roman Catholics might have been spared 400 years of persecution and discrimination.[3]

Charles V, having decided that Mary should stay in England, gave her strong diplomatic support. During Henry VIII's lifetime he had been reluctant to do anything which might offend Henry and endanger his anti-French alliance with him or the trade of his subjects in the Netherlands with England; but he was prepared to adopt a much tougher line with the government of the infant Edward VI. He demanded that Mary be allowed to have Mass celebrated in her household in defiance of the law, and hinted that he would go to war with England if his demand was refused. Northumberland and the Council gave way and allowed Mary to have her Mass.

The young Edward VI, who was a zealous Protestant, was very unhappy about this. Was it not a sin to attend Mass, and would not he himself be committing a sin if he allowed Mary to commit this sin? The Council sent Cranmer and Ridley to tell Edward that although it was a sin to license sin, a sin might be 'winked at' for a time if this was unavoidable.

In August 1551, when Charles V was at war with France and was being hard-pressed in his military campaign against the Protestants in Germany, Northumberland and the government took firmer action against Mary. They arrested Rochester and some of Mary's priests, and sent the Lord Chancellor, Lord Rich, to visit her in her house in Essex, and inform her that the King would no longer permit her to have Mass celebrated in her house. Mary refused to allow Rich to enter the house, but shouted insults at him from the courtyard and from a window. When Rich told her that Rochester and her priests would be punished according to law if they continued to attend and celebrate Mass, she said mockingly that the government's laws against Catholics were so mild that no one would be frightened by them into abandoning his faith.[4] When she became Queen she did not make the mistake of being too mild in her treatment of her Protestant opponents.

Mary was right in thinking that she would get away with it. Rochester and her priests were soon released from prison, and she continued to have Mass secretly celebrated in her house.

But though Northumberland's government, as Mary said, treated the Catholics mildly, they were much more severe with Protestant extremists. These extremists were usually called Anabaptists, or Arians by the Catholics and Protestants who burnt them. The Anabaptists not only objected to infant baptism, but also denied the divinity of Christ or said that he was not born to the Virgin Mary. They advocated a primitive form of Communism, denouncing private property and urging that all goods should be owned by the people in common.

Two of these extremists were burned for heresy in the reign of Edward VI. Joan Bocher, who was sometimes called Joan of Kent, had been a friend of Anne Askew; and after Anne Askew had been burned Joan continued distributing Protestant pamphlets, and expressed the opinion that Christ, the perfect God, had not been born as a man to the Virgin Mary. She was brought to trial before Cranmer, Ridley and other Protestant bishops and theologians, and condemned as a heretic; and all the efforts of Ridley and the others to persuade her to recant were unsuccessful. She was burnt alive at Smithfield on 2 May 1550.

John Rogers, who had returned to England after completing the translation of Tyndale's Bible, was a leading figure in the Protestant movement in London. He took part in the examination of Joan Bocher, and agreed with all the leading Protestants that she must be burned. There was the legal difficulty that the Acts for the Burning of Heretics had been repealed; but the lawyers pointed out that before the Act of 1401 was passed the King had exercised his power, under the common law, to order that heretics who had been condemned by the ecclesiastical courts should be burned.

John Foxe, from Boston in Lincolnshire, after graduating at Magdalen College in Oxford, was ordained as a deacon in London and became an ardent Protestant. He had been horrified at the burning of Protestant heretics by Henry VIII, and was very distressed that Joan Bocher was now to be burned under the Protestant government of Edward VI. He thought that her opinions were wrong and shocking, but that the life of 'this wretched woman' should be spared; she should be imprisoned in some place where she could not propagate her beliefs and where renewed efforts could be made to induce her to recant.

Foxe visited Rogers and pleaded for Joan's life; but Rogers insisted that she must die for her heresy. Foxe said that if her life must be taken away, she should not be burned: 'at least let another kind of death be chosen, answering better to the mildness of the Gospel. What need to borrow from the Papal laws and bring into the Christian arena the torments of this dreadful death?' Rogers said that burning alive was gentler than many other forms of death. Foxe took Rogers' hand and said: 'Well, maybe the day will come when you yourself will have your hands full of the same gentle burning.'[5] Foxe had good reason to realise that Rogers himself would one day be burned as a heretic.

Cranmer, who was in contact with several eminent foreign Protestant theologians, persuaded the government to grant a 'strangers' church' in London to foreign Protestant refugees from the Netherlands and from other Papist countries. They were granted a licence from the King exempting them from the provisions of the Act of Uniformity and allowing them to use their own foreign Protestant church service instead of those laid down in the Book of Common Prayer. They were placed under the supervision of John à Lasco, a Polish nobleman who was a well-known Protestant. Most Englishmen, with their well-known hatred of foreigners, did not like the foreign Protestants in London, and were shocked that England should become 'a harbour for all infidelity'. Even some leading English Protestants, like Bishop Ridley, did not see why the foreign Protestants should be allowed to have their own Church services instead of those of the English Book of Common Prayer.

A Lasco showed that he could be trusted to root out Anabaptists and extremists among his congregation when he denounced George van Parris, a Flemish refugee who had come to England from the Netherlands. Van Parris held opinions which his opponents called 'Arian' because, like the African theologian Arius in the fourth century AD, he did not believe that Jesus was God. He was quite unlearned, knowing nothing about theology, but was a gentle man who had led a blameless life.

A year after the burning of Joan Bocher he was examined by Cranmer and Ridley and other bishops on a charge of heresy. He could not speak English, so Coverdale acted as interpreter at the trial. He was condemned as a heretic. His former employer wrote from Germany asking the English authorities to spare his life; but as he refused to recant he was burned at Smithfield in April 1551. Foxe was one of the few people who thought that it was wrong to burn him.

The Protestant John Hooper was now playing a prominent part in furthering the Reformation in England. He was born in Somerset, went to Oxford University, and was apparently for some time a monk in a Cistercian monastery in Somerset. He was ordained a priest, and became chaplain to a courtier in London. He came under suspicion for holding Protestant opinions, and after he was questioned by Gardiner he went abroad to avoid persecution; but he soon returned to England. He came under renewed suspicion at the time of the Act of the Six Articles, and again escaped abroad, going illegally without a passport and pretending to be a ship's captain. He sailed around the coast of Ireland, and was nearly shipwrecked and drowned on the journey, but at last arrived safely in the Protestant city of Strasbourg. He went on to Zurich, where he became a close friend and collaborator of Henry Bullinger, the leading theologian in this Zwinglian city.

Hooper combined a grim, unsmiling appearance, which some people found frightening and repelling, with an unusually kind and humane attitude. When he heard that Henry VIII's armies were ravaging the south of Scotland, which was welcomed by many Scottish Protestants as a war against the Catholic government of King James V and Cardinal Beaton, Hooper was full of pity for the sufferings of the Scottish people. On questions of religion, he would not compromise. He wrote a number of treatises in which he upheld Zwinglian doctrines against orthodox Catholic teaching, and wrote a powerful criticism of Gardiner's defence of the Mass and the Real Presence. When he returned to England in the reign of Edward VI, he became chaplain first to the Duke of Somerset and then to the Duke of Northumberland.

In 1550 he was appointed Bishop of Gloucester, but refused to dress in episcopal vestments for his consecration, because in the Book of Exodus vestments were the mark of the priesthood of Aaron, which was suppressed. Although Edward VI wished to allow him to be excused from wearing vestments, Cranmer and Ridley stood firm and insisted that he comply with the law. Hooper was placed under house arrest in Cranmer's palace, but as he still remained obdurate he was imprisoned in the Fleet prison where his opponent, Bonner, was also confined. After he had been in the Fleet for a month, Hooper gave way, stated that the bishop's vestments of the Church of England were not Aaronical, and agreed to wear them at his consecration. It was the only time in his life that he made any concession on a religious issue.

Soon afterwards the Bishop of Worcester, Nicholas Heath, was deprived of his bishopric for disobedience to the royal authority by refusing to accept the new ordinal for the ordination of priests. The bishoprics of Gloucester and Worcester were then merged, and Hooper became bishop of both dioceses. He played a leading part in the government of the Church of England in the closing months of Edward VI's reign, when the Second Book of Common Prayer of 1552 was issued. This went much further than the First Book of 1549 in imposing Protestant and Zwinglian doctrines.

But Mary, in her house at Hunsdon in Hertfordshire, was confident now. In the spring of 1553, when Edward VI was dying of consumption at the age of fifteen, she was expecting to become Queen very soon. The succession to the throne had been complicated by the enactment and the repeal of several statutes which regulated it, and by the Acts of Parliament which declared that both Mary and Elizabeth were bastards. Parliament had therefore passed another Act granting Henry VIII the power to settle the succession in his Will, and enacting that it would be high treason to challenge the right of his nominees to succeed to the throne.

In his Will, Henry gave the crown first to his son Edward and his heirs, then to his daughter Mary and her heirs, then to his daughter Elizabeth and her heirs, and then to Lady Jane Grey and her heirs. Jane Grey was the granddaughter of Henry VIII's sister Mary, who had married Henry's favourite, Charles Brandon, Duke of Suffolk. Their daughter, Frances Brandon, married Henry Grey, Marquess of Dorset. After the deaths of Charles Brandon and his infant sons, Grey was granted the title of Duke of Suffolk, and after Frances Brandon died her daughter Jane

Grey was next in line after Henry VIII's children; and neither she nor anyone else in her family had been declared illegitimate.

When Edward VI was dying, Northumberland thought of a way by which he could maintain himself in power. His son, Lord Guilford Dudley, married Jane Grey. Northumberland then proposed that Edward VI should make a Will in which he left the crown to Lady Jane, excluding Mary and Elizabeth on the grounds that they were bastards. Northumberland asked Edward's Privy Councillors to sign a document supporting the Will, and pointed out to the Protestant bishops that this would prevent the Papist Mary from becoming Queen and overthrowing the Protestant religious settlement.

The councillors were very reluctant to support the grant of the crown to Jane Grey. Edward VI, unlike Henry VIII, had not been given power by Act of Parliament to leave the crown by Will, and the Act of Parliament had enacted that it would be high treason to alter the line of succession laid down by Henry VIII. But Northumberland had one ardent ally – the young King himself. The dying boy was determined to prevent his Catholic sister Mary from becoming Queen.

Cranmer was particularly reluctant to support the grant of the crown to Jane Grey. Mary might be a Papist; but was it compatible with the duty of Christian obedience to exclude her from the throne? He told Northumberland that he would not sign the document supporting Edward's will until he had had a private talk with the King. Northumberland could safely agree to this. When Edward VI spoke to Cranmer he insisted that Cranmer should sign, and Cranmer agreed, in obedience to his King. Eventually all the councillors, dignitaries and judges reluctantly signed, except Mr Justice Hales, a stickler for legality. He said that the grant of the crown to Jane Grey was illegal, as it conflicted with the Act of Parliament which gave Henry VIII the right to leave the crown by his Will.

Northumberland kept the plan to grant the crown to Jane

Grey a secret for the time being, until he had got Mary safely in his power. He sent a message to Mary ordering her to visit the King at Greenwich. She set out from her house at Hunsdon on her journey to Greenwich; but when she reached Hoddesdon in Hertfordshire she met Sir Nicholas Throckmorton, a Protestant gentleman at the court, who had ridden to intercept her on her journey. He warned her that Edward VI was dying, and that if she went on to Greenwich she would be arrested. She had to make a fateful and irrevocable decision. After a moment's hesitation, she turned her horse's head and rode north, reaching her house at Kenninghall in Norfolk on 6 July 1553. On the same day, Edward VI died at Greenwich.

CHAPTER 4

Queen Mary

AS SOON AS EDWARD DIED, the Council at Greenwich wrote to Mary telling her that Jane Grey was now Queen and ordering her to come to court in obedience to the orders of Queen Jane. Mary replied informing them that she herself was Queen and ordering them, as loyal subjects, to obey her. Both sides had now committed themselves, and there was no going back, for either Jane's supporters or Mary's would be guilty of high treason.

On 10 July, Jane came to London and was proclaimed Queen. Mary went to Framlingham Castle in Suffolk, where she could withstand a siege and would be only twelve miles from the coast if it became necessary for her to escape abroad. Simon Renard and Charles V's other ambassadors in England urged Mary to submit to Northumberland and accept Jane as Queen, because Charles would not be able to send her any help. But the people rose in Mary's support, regarding her as their lawful Queen. Within a few days the news had spread that she had been joined by 40,000 supporters at Framlingham, though the true number was probably about 15,000.

On 14 July, Northumberland marched against Mary with an army of German and Spanish mercenaries. His men were uneasy. Mercenaries were usually prepared to fight for anyone who paid them; but Northumberland's mercenaries knew that they were being asked to fight for a Protestant heretic against a Catholic Queen who was a great favourite of their ruler, Charles V.

In London and south-east England the people rose everywhere for Mary. When Nicholas Ridley preached a sermon at Paul's Cross – the pulpit in the courtyard of St Paul's Cathedral in London where government spokesmen preached – and said that Mary and Elizabeth were bastards and that Queen Jane was their lawful sovereign, he was shouted down by the people. Slogans in support of Mary appeared on the street walls in London.

After Northumberland left London and marched against Mary, the lords of the Council deserted him, though they had all pledged their loyalty to him five days before. They went to the Lord Mayor of London and urged him to proclaim Mary as Queen in the city. When the people of London heard what was happening, they came out into the streets. As the Lord Mayor walked to the cross in Cheapside to proclaim Mary, the cheering crowds were so dense that he had difficulty in forcing his way through them to reach the cross. The bells rang all night long, and the fountains in the city ran with wine – the traditional way of celebrating a great day of rejoicing. On Wednesday 19 July 1553 the Protestant Reformation in England was overthrown, and Mary was placed on the throne by a spontaneous uprising of the people. The slogan *'Vox populi vox Dei'* appeared on the walls in London.

Cranmer and Jane's father, the Duke of Suffolk, had been the only lords of the Council who had not joined in the move to overthrow Northumberland and proclaim Mary as Queen; but after 19 July they also submitted. Suffolk informed his daughter that she was no longer Queen. When Northumberland heard about the events in London he himself proclaimed Mary as Queen in Cambridge, and went to Framlingham to submit to her and implore her pardon. Ridley also set out for Framlingham to submit to Mary. Both he and Northumberland were arrested by Mary's officers on their way and sent back to the Tower of London as prisoners.

Mary slowly advanced from Suffolk, being joined by her sister Elizabeth, and entered London on 3 August. As she passed the Tower she freed the Duke of Norfolk and Gardiner, who were prisoners there, and immediately appointed Gardiner to be her Lord Chancellor.

Many of the people who had risen in Mary's support were Protestants. The Catholic strongholds in the north and west of England were too far away to help Mary; she had triumphed before the news of events in London and Suffolk had reached them. It was south-east England, where the Protestants were strongest, which made Mary queen. The Protestants afterwards alleged that Mary had issued a proclamation promising the Protestants in Norfolk that she had no intention of overthrowing the Protestant religion; according to the Protestants, the people joined her because of this fraudulent promise. No record of any such proclamation has been preserved, and it seems unlikely that she issued it or made any promise to preserve the Protestant religion. The most likely explanation is that her subordinate officers at Framlingham led the people to believe that the Protestant religion would be preserved, and that Mary took care to say nothing to contradict this impression.

The people of south-east England supported Mary because they hated Northumberland and his corrupt and self-seeking hangers-on; because the Protestants in Norfolk especially hated him for the part that he had played in suppressing their revolt under Kett in 1549; because, even in south-east England, there were many Catholics – probably a majority of Catholics – who regarded Mary not as a supporter of Papal supremacy, but as the upholder of the Catholic religious settlement of Henry VIII against the Protestant reformers who had outraged their conservative love of the old religion; and because, despite all the Acts of Parliament which had been passed and repealed in the last twenty years, granting the crown first to one member of the royal family and then to another, there was a feeling among the people that Mary was the next in line of hereditary succession after Edward VI, and that she was therefore the rightful Queen.

The events of July 1553 gave the Protestant religious leaders
the opportunity to prove their sincere attachment to Tyndale's
doctrine of Christian obedience. They must obey their Prince
and the law of the realm and offer no resistance to the victory of
Popery; but they must rigidly adhere to their religious convic-
tions and refuse to recant, patiently suffering martyrdom if this
was God's will. Of all the leading Protestant theologians only
Ridley actively supported Jane Grey. Cranmer had been more
reluctant than any of the other lords of the Council to support
Edward's grant of the crown to Jane: he had complied only
because his King had ordered him to do so. It was a Protestant
sympathiser, Sir Nicholas Throckmorton, who had ridden to
Hoddesdon to warn Mary not to proceed to Greenwich as there
was a plot to arrest her and exclude her from the throne.

That steadfast Protestant, John Hooper, gave the most
striking proof of his devotion to the doctrine of Christian
obedience. When he heard that Jane Grey had been proclaimed
Queen in London and that Mary was calling on the people to
support her at Framlingham, he took the view that though
Mary was a Papist she was the lawful sovereign. He called on
the people in his two dioceses of Gloucester and Worcester to
rise and fight for Mary, and gave instructions to the sheriffs of
the two counties to requisition horses and send them to help
Mary at Framlingham. The ferocious anti-Catholic pamphleteer and playwright, John Bale, who had been appointed
Bishop of Ossory in Ireland by Edward VI, also called on
his congregation to support Mary.

When Mary reached London she did not immediately give
any indication that she was intending to persecute Protestants.
Her first proclamation on religious affairs prohibited anyone
from accusing their opponents of being 'Papists' or 'heretics'. But
her Catholic supporters, confident that Mary's victory meant the
restoration of the Catholic religion, immediately began to
celebrate Mass, though this was still illegal under the Act of

Uniformity of 1552 which had not yet been repealed. Mary made no attempt to stop them.

Her toleration of these illegal Masses shocked the Protestants. When they themselves first came to power under Somerset after the death of Henry VIII they had forbidden their supporters to introduce any Protestant innovation until this had been sanctioned by law. They thought that Mary's failure to act in the same way by prohibiting the illegal Catholic Mass was not only introducing idolatry but was also defying the principle which they regarded so highly of obedience to authority and the law. But for Mary the law of God was superior to the law of England; she would not punish those who worshipped the true religion merely because to do so was, for the moment, illegal.

Far from punishing the Catholics who broke the law, Mary found pretexts for arresting Protestants. Ten days after she entered London she ordered Dr Bourn, a canon of St Paul's, who was a Catholic supporter, to preach at Paul's Cross. The Lord Mayor presided, and Bonner was also present. In his sermon Bourn denounced the Protestants and praised Bonner, who, he said, had been unjustly imprisoned and deprived of his bishopric by the Protestants. There were ardent Protestants in the audience, and they interrupted Bourn and tried to shout him down. The Lord Mayor ordered them to keep silence and to listen to Bourn, who had been chosen by the Queen to preach to them; but the interruptions became more threatening, and it seemed as if a riot was about to break out. Then someone in the crowd threw a dagger at Bourn, which narrowly missed him.

The Protestant John Rogers was in the crowd, along with another leading Protestant, John Bradford from Manchester, who had become a famous preacher in London and one of Edward VI's chaplains. Rogers and Bradford realised the disastrous consequences that might follow if a riot broke out and Bourn was killed or injured; and they were also conscious that it was a violation of the doctrine of Christian obedience to deny a hearing to a preacher who had been ordered by the sovereign to preach at Paul's Cross. They urged their Protestant supporters to listen to Bourn in silence, and succeeded in preventing any further disorder; despite these entreaties they were both arrested and brought before Gardiner, the Lord Chancellor.

They were charged with inciting the riot. When they protested that, far from inciting it, they had succeeded in preventing it, Gardiner said that the fact that the crowd, who had ignored the orders of the Lord Mayor to keep silence, had obeyed the instructions of Rogers and Bradford to end the riot, proved that Rogers and Bradford were their leaders and were therefore responsible for the riot. Gardiner sentenced Bradford to be imprisoned in the Tower and Rogers to be confined under house arrest.

At the beginning of the succession crisis, Charles V and his ambassadors in England had advised Mary to submit to Jane Grey; but when Charles was informed by the ambassadors that a popular rising had placed Mary in power, he was quick to take advantage of the situation. He hoped that she would remember the friendship that he had always shown her, and would marry his son, Prince Philip of Spain, and thus form a permanent alliance between England and his empire. He and his ambassador Renard urged Mary to be ruthless in punishing traitors and anyone who might be a threat to her authority; but they urged her to be very cautious about reintroducing the Catholic religion and persecuting Protestants. Charles was savagely persecuting Protestants in Spain and the Netherlands; but he did not wish the English to think that his son Philip and his Spaniards would encourage religious persecution in England. He knew how the English hated foreigners and that he must be careful that this hatred, which had hitherto been directed against the foreign Protestants in England, did not turn into a hatred of Spaniards. Mary did not take his advice; with her devotion to the Catholic faith, she was much more eager to punish heretics who sinned against God than traitors who plotted against herself.

In August Northumberland and two of his closest collaborators were tried for high treason and beheaded; on the scaffold, Northumberland declared that he had converted to the Catholic faith. But Mary refused to execute any of the other traitors. Renard strongly urged her at least to have Jane Grey put to death, because her merciful policy would be regarded as weakness; Mary said that she would not execute Jane, who had been the innocent dupe of Northumberland. Renard, knowing that Mary was well read in classical history, reminded her that when Maximus had rebelled against the Roman Emperor Theodosius in the fourth century AD, Theodosius had executed not only Maximus but Maximus's son Victor, although Victor was innocent, because this was necessary in the interests of the State; but Mary refused to proceed against Jane Grey.

Renard advised Mary to arrest her sister Elizabeth, and Gardiner also urged her to do this. Mary hoped that Elizabeth would convert to Catholicism and go to Mass. Elizabeth at first refused, then agreed to do so, but let it be known that she had agreed reluctantly under pressure. The result was that the Protestants began to rest their hopes on Elizabeth. Renard and Gardiner thought that because of this Elizabeth was a threat to Mary's safety. But Mary refused to arrest Elizabeth.

Steps were immediately taken to restore the Catholic bishops who under Edward VI had been deprived of their bishoprics for disobedience, and to eject the Protestant bishops who had replaced them. A judicial hearing was held before Commissioners, many of whom had been on Edward VI's Privy Council and had supported the grant of the crown to Jane Grey. Ridley, Ponet, Coverdale, Scory and Hooper were deprived of their bishoprics of London, Winchester, Exeter, Chichester and Worcester, and Bonner, Gardiner, Veysey, Day and Heath were reinstated in their place. Ridley, who was a prisoner in the Tower, was not permitted to appear at the hearing and argue against his deprivation.

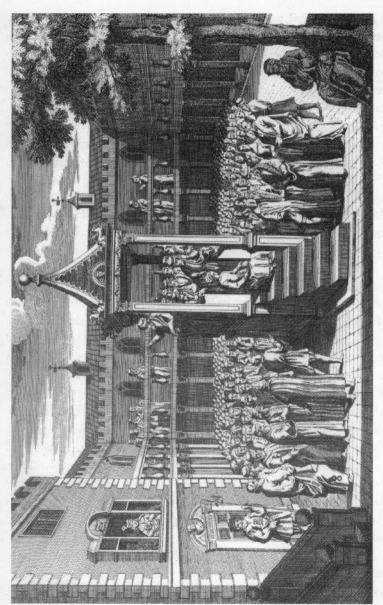

Mr. Latimer preaching before King Edward VI at Westminster

By September 1553 the authorities, though still not officially persecuting the Protestants for their religion, were arresting leading Protestants on even more flimsy pretexts than had been used in the case of Bradford and Rogers. Hooper and Coverdale were proceeded against on the grounds that they owed a debt to the Queen, apparently because they had not paid some dues which had been obsolete for many years.

Latimer, after re-emerging into public life to preach his sermons before Edward VI, had retired to his native village in Leicestershire where he was living quietly; he had reached the age of sixty, which was considered old in the sixteenth century. An officer was sent to arrest him. A man in Coventry found out that the officer was coming, and warned Latimer six hours before the officer arrived; but Latimer made no attempt to escape. He was taken to Westminster to be interrogated by the Privy Council. On his way to Westminster he passed through Smith-field, where the heretics had been burned, and said cheerfully to his escort that 'Smithfield had long groaned for him'. When he appeared before the Privy Council, Gardiner spoke of the need for unity in the church. Latimer said that there must be unity in truth, not in Popery.

The Privy Council decided that 'for his seditious demeanour' Latimer be sent to the Tower, 'where he remain in close prison, having attended upon him one Austey [Bernher] his servant'. The presence of a personal servant with him in his prison could facilitate an escape, because the servant, not being a prisoner, was free to go and re-enter the prison whenever he wished; but it was unthinkable that any gentleman, or a man who had held high rank like Latimer, however great a traitor or heretic he might be, should not have a servant to wait upon him.

Mary expelled all the foreign Protestants in London and those who had gone to Glastonbury in Somerset and elsewhere in the south of England. Among them was the distinguished Zurich scholar, Peter Martyr (Pietro Martire Vermigli); he had been

staying with Cranmer at Lambeth Palace. The foreign Protestants were not allowed to take their property with them. Mary
told Renard when they were coming, so that he could inform
the Emperor who could order the authorities in the Netherlands
to arrest them as they landed and prosecute them there for
heresy; but many of them succeeded in reaching Emden and the
Protestant states of North Germany.

Several English Protestants fled abroad illegally, without being
granted a passport by the government, though it was a criminal
offence to leave the country without one. Ponet, the Scottish
Protestant John Knox, John Foxe and several others left the
realm illegally, in many cases being taken by Protestant fisher-
men from Rye in Sussex. This illegal flight was the only form of
resistance to authority which Hooper considered to be compatible with the doctrine of Christian obedience; although he did
not attempt to flee himself, he urged other Protestants to leave
the country illegally. There was Scriptural authority for this. The
Virgin Mary and her husband Joseph had taken the infant Jesus
into Egypt to escape the massacre of the children which had
been ordered by Herod; and there were the biblical texts urging
the faithful to escape abroad to avoid persecution, and not to run
ahead in search of martyrdom before their time. But Hooper did
not find it easy to persuade his supporters that this was justifiable
and the correct course to pursue, and many rank-and-file
Protestants, despite the exhortations of their leaders, refused
to flee.

Everyone was expecting that Cranmer would be arrested, for
they knew that Mary hated him for the part that he had played in
the divorce of her mother Catherine of Aragon; but he remained
free. In the middle of August he went to Mary's court, but found
that everyone avoided him and would not speak to him. He was,
however, allowed to officiate at the Protestant funeral of Edward
VI. Mary's first intention had been to give Edward a Catholic
funeral, but Charles V persuaded her to allow the Protestant

funeral to take place by pointing out that as Edward had died a
heretic, he was not entitled to a Catholic funeral. Bonner, too,
expected that Cranmer would be arrested. On 6 September he
gloatingly wrote: 'This day is looked that Master Canterbury
must be placed where is meet for him; he is become very
humble, and ready to submit himself in all things, but that will
not serve.' But Cranmer remained free.

The Catholics were celebrating Mass illegally, in defiance of
the law. This shocked Mr Justice Hales. Alone of all the judges
he had refused to agree to the proclamation of Jane Grey as
Queen, because Edward VI's grant of the crown to her was
against the law; and, sitting at Maidstone Assizes, he imposed
fines on Catholics who had illegally celebrated Mass in Kent.
Hales was summoned to appear before Gardiner. The Lord
Chancellor told him that he should obey the Queen's wishes,
not the letter of the law. Hales was imprisoned, and though he
was eventually released, he committed suicide by stabbing
himself.

The rumour spread that Cranmer had approved of the illegal
celebration of the Mass in Canterbury Cathedral. Cranmer
thereupon wrote out a declaration criticising the Mass. Scory
saw the declaration lying on the window-sill in Cranmer's palace
at Lambeth, and asked if he could take a copy of it. Cranmer
agreed, and Scory had it printed and circulated in London.
Cranmer was thereupon summoned before the Privy Council,
and sent to the Tower. Scory saved himself by a recantation, and
was allowed to go abroad.

In October Mary was crowned as Queen. A meeting of
Convocation was held at which Protestant doctrines, especially
their repudiation of the Real Presence, were condemned as
heresy by a large majority of the members. A few Protestants, led
by John Philpot, a canon of Winchester Cathedral, tried to
defend their doctrines, but they were shouted down and
violently denounced. After the decision, the presiding prolo-

cutor, Hugh Weston, the Dean of Westminster, issued the
slogan '*Vicit veritas*' (the truth is victorious). He praised the
Queen in the most lavish terms, hailing her as 'Mary the Virgin'.

The first Parliament of Mary's reign met in October and
passed a statute validating the marriage of Henry VIII and
Catherine of Aragon, and placing all the blame for the divorce,
not on Henry, but on a small group of scheming courtiers and
especially on Cranmer. The Act declared that, 'We, Your
Highness most loving, faithful and obedient subjects' declared
that the marriage 'between the two most excellent Princes of
most worthy memory King Henry VIII and Queen Katherine
his loving, godly and lawful wife and Your Highness lawful
father and mother' had been destroyed when 'Thomas Cranmer,
then newly made Archbishop of Canterbury, most unjustly and
against all laws, equity and conscience' gave his judgment which
caused 'the said most noble King your father and the said noble
Queen your mother' to separate and divorce, because of the
judgment 'given by unlawful and corrupt means and ways by the
said Archbishop of Canterbury'. Parliament now repealed all
Acts which declared that the marriage of Henry VIII and
Catherine of Aragon was unlawful.

In November Jane Grey, the Duke of Suffolk and Cranmer
were tried for high treason for having supported Jane's claim to
the throne. They were sentenced to death, but the sentences
were not carried out. In December an Act of Parliament was
passed repealing the Act of Uniformity and all the Protestant
legislation of Edward's reign and restoring the Mass.

Mary had decided to marry Prince Philip of Spain, the son of
Charles V, who was eleven years younger than she. She reached
the decision with the greatest reluctance.[1] She was disgusted at
the idea of having sex with a man; but the Emperor and his
ambassador were strongly in favour of a marriage which would
unite England with the Emperor's territories in a permanent
alliance. By holding Dover as well as the English enclave around

Calais, Charles and his English ally would control the Channel and the sea-route along which his ships sailed with the gold and silver from his colonies in America to the money market at Antwerp; and he would virtually surround his traditional enemy, France. Mary realised that it was her duty to marry Philip to form this alliance and to produce an heir to the throne of England who would be brought up a Catholic; and after much prayer and soul-searching she agreed to the marriage.

When it was known that Mary was intending to marry Philip, many Englishmen, who had been so pleased when Mary expelled the foreign Protestants, deeply resented her plan to deliver England to the Prince of Spain and his Spaniards. There were hostile demonstrations in London against Philip's envoys when they arrived to negotiate the marriage. King Henry II of France realised that the marriage was a threat to his security. He was persecuting Protestants in France with exceptional cruelty; those who refused to recant were tortured at the stake before being burned alive. But this did not prevent him from inciting the Protestants in England to revolt against Mary to stop her marriage to Philip of Spain.

In January 1554 a gentleman of Kent, Sir Thomas Wyatt, led an insurrection to prevent Mary's marriage to a foreign Prince and the occupation of England by the hated foreigners. He marched on London; but Mary went to the Guildhall in the city and called on the people to support her. Her courage made a deep impression, and again the people flocked to her, as they had done six months earlier. Wyatt was defeated in a battle a mile to the west of the built-up area of Westminster in what is now Hyde Park, and he was taken prisoner.

The Wyatt rebellion persuaded Mary that Renard and Gardiner were right and that she had been too merciful to her rebels. Wyatt and over a hundred of his supporters were executed, and Jane Grey and her father were beheaded under the sentence which had been passed on them in November. The Queen's

sister, Elizabeth, was arrested on Gardiner's advice and imprisoned in the Tower, though there was no evidence that she had
been in contact with Wyatt.

Several of the convicted rebels appealed to Mary for mercy.
She refused in every case to pardon them and commute the
death sentence; but she and the Council decided that she should
give a public demonstration of her merciful nature. Four
hundred of the other rebel prisoners who had not been prosecuted for treason were assembled and marched into the courtyard of the palace at Whitehall, and Mary appeared on the
balcony and pardoned them.

Sir Nicholas Throckmorton, who in July 1553 had inter-
cepted Mary on her journey to Greenwich and warned her of
Northumberland's plan to arrest her, turned against her when he
discovered that she was going to marry Philip of Spain. He
joined Wyatt, and after the defeat of the revolt he was put on
trial at the Guildhall on a charge of high treason. He defended
himself so skilfully that the jury brought in a verdict of 'not
guilty'. Mary ordered that Throckmorton should be detained in
prison, and that the members of the jury who had acquitted him
should be arrested for having given a perverse verdict. All the
Tudor sovereigns used the royal prerogative of imprisoning
without trial anyone who displeased them, which was not
challenged until the seventeenth century; and it was not considered as shocking in 1554 as it would be today to imprison
jurors who gave a verdict that the government did not like. But
Mary's action in imprisoning the jurors who acquitted Throckmorton did not make her popular. She eventually released
Throckmorton from prison and allowed him to go abroad. In
the reign of Elizabeth I he became one of her most able
diplomats.

The authorities arrested Protestants all over south-east England, sometimes for sedition and sometimes for speaking against
the Catholic religion. On 18 January 1554 the Privy Council

ordered the JPs to arrest and imprison in Colchester jail 'a lewd fellow in the parish of Sandon in Essex who nameth himself a priest and speaketh against the Mass'. On 1 March the Council ordered the Bailiff of Hastings to put John London, a fisherman of Hastings, in the pillory, to cut off one of his ears, 'and keep him in prison until he makes a perfect submission'. On 27 May they ordered the arrest of Richard Harman of West Hoathly in Sussex, 'a sacramentary', and imprisoned him in the King's Bench prison 'for his lewd and seditious behaviour in Sussex'. As Harman was described as a sacramentary, he must have preached against the Real Presence; but there is no record that he was burned when the burning of heretics began nine months later. He must either have recanted, or died in prison.

But Cranmer was not executed under the sentence which had been passed on him in November, though he was suspended from exercising his duties as Archbishop of Canterbury, which were entrusted to Nicholas Harpsfield, the Catholic Archdeacon of Canterbury. Instead, Cranmer, Ridley and Latimer were taken from the Tower to Oxford to take part in proceedings which were to be the first step in Mary's policy of burning Protestant heretics. Oxford was chosen because it had always been a stronghold of orthodoxy, and there was strong support in the university there for the Catholic religion.

In April 1554 a disputation was held in Oxford on the Real Presence. For three successive days Cranmer, Ridley and Latimer disputed in turn. Although the traditional form of a disputation was observed, it was not conducted in the usual scholastic atmosphere. The three Protestants faced an audience of nearly a thousand Catholic supporters who interrupted and insulted them. They argued that Christ was present in the Sacrament spiritually, but not corporally. At the end of the disputation the three of them were condemned as heretics.

They were expecting to be burned very soon, but no heretic was burned in England that year. They waited in their prisons in

Oxford while Philip of Spain arrived in England, married Mary in Winchester Cathedral, and made a triumphal entry into London with Mary, bringing great gifts of gold and silver from America. He now had the title of King of England, though thanks to Gardiner's skill in drafting the marriage treaty his powers were strictly limited. Gardiner had at first suggested that Mary should be named before Philip, and that they should be referred to as 'Mary and Philip, Queen and King of England' etc. When the Spaniards said that this would be too humiliating to Philip, Gardiner gave way; he had only put it forward as a bargaining point. They were proclaimed, and referred to in all official documents, as 'Philip and Mary, King and Queen of England, France, Naples, Jerusalem and Ireland, Defenders of the Faith, Princes of Spain and Castile, Archdukes of Austria, Dukes of Milan, Burgundy and Brabant, Counts of Habsburg, Flanders and Tirol.' But Gardiner succeeded in all other matters, and Philip agreed that his Spanish councillors were to exercise no influence in the government of England. Philip's Spanish gentlemen and their retinue were not popular with the English people, and clashes occurred between Spaniards and Englishmen; but any Spaniard who killed or injured an Englishman was severely punished.

Two things delayed the burning of heretics. Parliament was unwilling to re-enact the heresy statutes until the MPs were sure that Mary would not deprive them of the monastic lands which they had been granted by Henry VIII or had bought from his grantees. Mary reluctantly realised that she would have to agree to this; and while she founded a new monastery and granted to it the former monastic lands which were held by the Crown, she agreed not to force the gentlemen and speculators to follow her example and relinquish their profitable gains.

The second reason why the burnings were delayed was because Mary had decided to reunite the realm to Rome, to renounce her royal authority over the Church, and to recognise once again Papal Supremacy over the Church of England. She would wait until the heretics could be burned under the authority of the Pope, and for the heresy of denying Papal Supremacy as well as for repudiating the doctrine of the Real Presence. But meanwhile she would use her royal supremacy to deal with the married clergy.

The Catholic Church drew a distinction between monks and priests who had married. Monks took an oath of celibacy, but priests did not, although their marriage was prohibited by the laws of the Church. So while a monk who had broken his oath of chastity was invariably punished by imprisonment, a married priest could be forgiven and allowed to retain his benefice if he voluntarily agreed to separate from his wife and children. In March 1554 the ecclesiastical authorities conducted an investigation to find out how many priests in England were married. Although the marriage of priests had been permitted only five years before, they found that nearly ten per cent of the clergy were married; in Norfolk the figure was as high as twenty-five per cent.

The priests were told that if they separated from their wives and agreed never to speak to them or to their children again, they could do penance in a public ceremony and continue in their benefices. As the priests had only recently married, many of them were the fathers of babies or very young children; but the priests were ordered to throw their wives with their babies out of their homes and into the street, where they were left to wander without any means of subsistence, unless they could find some friend who dared to shelter them. If the priests refused to separate from their wives, they were to forfeit their benefices, which in most cases also meant leaving their homes. Henry VIII had granted pensions, however small, to the monks who were expelled from the monasteries; but Mary's government paid no pensions or any compensation to the married priests who were deprived of their benefices. Under the strong pressure of the authorities and public opinion, and in the face of the vituperative propaganda against the marriage of the clergy, many priests agreed to put away their wives and families, and retained their benefices.

After negotiations with Mary, the Pope sent Cardinal Pole as Papal Legate to England. In November 1554 Pole landed at Dover, and set foot in his native country for the first time for twenty-three years. While he was travelling in state, by slow stages, from Dover to London, someone noticed that the Act of Parliament of Henry VIII's reign, condemning him as a traitor and sentencing him to death, was still in force; and Parliament hastily passed an Act repealing it.

In a ceremony in Westminster Hall on 30 November 1554 Pole received the submission of King Philip and Queen Mary and the realm of England to the authority of the Pope. He granted England absolution for twenty-one years of separation from Rome, and proclaimed that the anniversary of the cere-mony, 30 November, should be celebrated as a great religious festival, the Feast of the Reconciliation, for all eternity. He also, on behalf of the Pope, confirmed the titles of the grantees and purchasers of the monastic lands.

The lords and MPs were now satisfied that they would be allowed to retain their gains. By January 1555 they had re-enacted the Acts for the Burning of Heretics of 1382, 1401 and 1414. The burning of heretics could now begin.

CHAPTER 5

The First Victims

THEY BEGAN WITH A SELECTION of eminent Protestants. On 22 January 1555 and the following days, Rogers, Hooper, Bradford, Rowland Taylor, Lawrence Saunders, William Barlow, Edward Crome and others were examined by a commission of leading bishops and lawyers. Rowland Taylor was the vicar of Hadleigh in Suffolk; Saunders[1] came from Northamptonshire, and held a position in a college at Fotheringhay. Both of them had been eminent under Edward VI as Protestant preachers in London. Barlow was the former Protestant Bishop of Bath and Wells. Crome was a prominent writer at Cambridge.

Gardiner, the Lord Chancellor, presided at the hearings, which were held in his palace in Southwark, in his diocese of Winchester. The other commissioners included Bonner and several bishops, judges and lawyers; some of them had signed Edward VI's grant of the crown to Jane Grey, and had accepted her as Queen for thirteen days until 19 July 1553. The hearings were held in public before a large crowd of spectators, and many more people stood in the streets to watch the heretics being brought before their judges.

According to Protestant writers, the commissioners interrupted, browbeat and insulted the prisoners; and even if these reports are exaggerated, there is no doubt that the examination was hostile and harsh. When ignorant low-class artisans and labourers were accused of heresy, their judges upbraided them for their presumption in daring to argue theological questions with the learned bishops and theologians who opposed them;

when the heretics were themselves learned bishops and theologians, they were rebuked for misusing the gifts of learning which God had given them by arguing for a wicked cause against God's truth.

Gardiner and his colleagues accused Rogers, Hooper, Bradford, Rowland Taylor and Saunders of heresy in denying the Papal Supremacy over the Church and the Real Presence of Christ in the consecrated bread and wine of the Sacrament, and a long and learned argument took place. The commissioners were particularly severe on those defendants who were married priests. Rogers admitted that he had a wife and eleven children, and Hooper did not deny that he had married a wife in Strasbourg who was now in Germany. Rowland Taylor was also denounced for having married. Their argument that priests were required by the Bible not to refrain from marriage but to live a chaste life was rejected by the commissioners.

John Foxe wrote that Tunstall, who had been deprived of his bishopric of Durham under Edward VI and reinstated by Mary, called Hooper a 'beast'. This has been doubted by some historians, who believe that the commissioners would have behaved with gravity on such an occasion; though the word 'beast' was regularly used by Catholic theologians to describe Protestant priests who had married.

All the Protestants were found guilty of heresy on all charges, but were told that the Queen would grant them a pardon if they would recant and repent. Crome recanted, and was pardoned after doing penance. Bishop Barlow made a more equivocal recantation, but it was enough to save his life. He was ordered to be imprisoned indefinitely in the Tower. He succeeded in escaping from his prison and fled abroad illegally. He returned in the reign of Elizabeth I when England was Protestant again and was made Bishop of Chichester.

The other prisoners refused to recant. Saunders adopted a particularly defiant attitude. He reminded Gardiner that in 1535 he had written his book *De Vera Obedientia*, upholding the royal supremacy over the Church of England, denouncing the Pope, and justifying the execution of Bishop Fisher and Sir Thomas More. Gardiner said that he had sinned in writing that book and in supporting the royal supremacy in Henry VIII's reign, but that he had now repented; and he urged Saunders to follow his example by recanting and accepting the Queen's pardon. Saunders, like Rogers, Hooper and Rowland Taylor, refused to recant.

Rogers told the commissioners that he had only one request to make, and asked that before he was burned he should be permitted to receive one farewell visit from his wife. His request was indignantly refused.

Burnings were carried out in public, usually before large crowds of spectators. Many people came to enjoy the fun of watching a man burn; they often brought their children with them, and fathers lifted the smaller children on to their shoulders to enable them to see. Some of the spectators were Protestant supporters, for they thought it right to show solidarity and give moral support to their friends who were undergoing martyrdom.

The degree of suffering endured by the martyr varied in every case. In some ways the burnings in England were less cruel than in France and the Netherlands, where heretics who refused to recant often had their tongues bored through or cut off as they stood tied to the stake as an additional punishment before the faggots were lit. In England the heretic's friends were allowed to bribe the executioner to allow a bag of gunpowder to be fastened to the heretic's neck or waist, so that when the flames reached the gunpowder it would explode and immediately kill the heretic. But if it had been raining, and the faggots were damp; if the wood was green and fresh, as it often was in the spring; if it was a windy day, and the wind blew the flames away from the heretic and from the gunpowder; or if the gunpowder was sodden, and did not explode; the heretic might live in agony for a long time.

The burning of Master John Rogers, Vicar of St Sepulchre's and Reader of St Pauls in London

A commentator in the twenty-first century might say that how much and for how long the heretic suffered was a matter of luck; to the sixteenth-century Catholic and Protestant, it was not luck but God's will. The Catholics believed that if the heretic took a long time to die, this was because his sins were so great that God had wished to increase his punishment; the Protestants were sure that if God prolonged his sufferings, this was for the greater glory of God and of the martyr, and to expose the cruelty of the Papist persecutors.

On Monday 4 February 1555 Rogers was burned at Smithfield. The Protestants hailed him as the 'protomartyr' – the first martyr to be burned in Mary's reign. On his last night in his prison cell at Newgate he slept so soundly that his jailer had to wake him in the morning and tell him that it was time for him to dress and prepare to leave for the place of execution at Smithfield. He was happy, for he knew that however much he might suffer in the fire, he would go to Heaven. As he walked from Newgate to Smithfield he prayed and recited the *Miserere*.

Near Smithfield he saw his wife and children. She had again been refused permission to have a final meeting with him, but she was standing by the roadside near Smithfield, with ten of her children beside her, while she held the eleventh, who was still a baby, in her arms as she suckled it on her breast. They prayed that they would see Rogers as he passed by, and they did; he exchanged a smile and a few brief words with them before he was ordered to go on, and she was firmly held back from him.

For Rogers, death came quickly. As soon as the faggots were lit, the fire burned fiercely. Very soon it had burned off his legs and reached his shoulders. He held his hands in the fire and went through the motions of washing them, as if the fire had been cold water. Then he withdrew them from the flames, held them aloft in the air, and recited a prayer till he died soon afterwards.

Welcome Life

The burning of Master Laurence Sanders at Coventry

As the fire burned out, a flock of doves flew overhead. Some of the Protestants said that one of the doves was the Holy Ghost who had come to carry Rogers' soul to Heaven.[2]

On the day that Rogers was burned, Hooper, Saunders and Rowland Taylor were degraded from the priesthood by Bonner. The degradation was a ceremony in which the condemned heretic was dressed in a priest's vestments, which were then removed. Priests wore a tonsure, a bald circle on their head surrounded by their hair; in the degradation ceremony, the hair around the tonsure was shaved in order to remove the tonsure. The hands were scraped with a knife to remove the holy oil with which they had been anointed. The scraping could be done either gently or roughly. The Protestants alleged that Bonner did it roughly whenever he took part in a degradation ceremony; but this may have been Protestant propaganda, for Bonner's attitude varied between boisterous and aggressive gloating and a patient attempt to persuade heretics to recant so that their lives could be spared.

When the heretic was a bishop, the degradation ceremony was more prolonged; but Hooper was degraded only from the priesthood, because the authorities did not recognise that he had been lawfully consecrated as a bishop under Edward VI, when the Protestant realm was in schism from the Church of Rome. When it was Rowland Taylor's turn to be degraded, he refused to put on the vestments, which he said were Popish vestments, and he had to be forcibly dressed in them so that they could be removed.

It was decided that Hooper, Saunders and Rowland Taylor should be burned, not at Smithfield but in the districts where they had first officiated. After their degradation on 4 February, Hooper was taken to Gloucester, Saunders to Coventry, and Rowland Taylor to Hadleigh in Suffolk. Saunders was burned in the park at Coventry on 8 February. He was the second martyr to suffer.

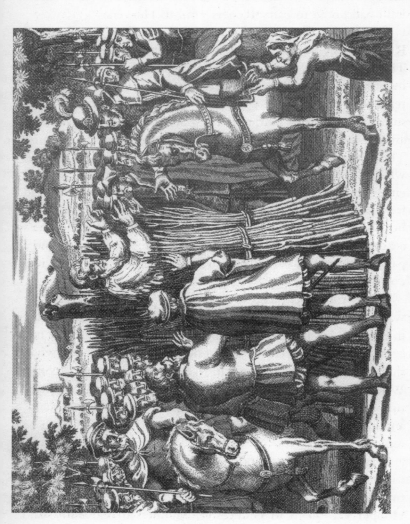

The martyrdom of Dr. Rowland Taylor who was burnt on Aldham Common

Rowland Taylor had a wife and three children. One of them was a grown-up son, who had become a Catholic; another was an adopted daughter, Elizabeth, whose parents had died when she was aged three and was then adopted by Taylor and his wife; in 1555 she was aged thirteen. He had another younger daughter, Mary, his own child. After his condemnation as a heretic, while he was waiting to be taken to Hadleigh, he was imprisoned in the Compter prison in London. The governor of the prison was a kindly man, and he surreptitiously allowed Mrs Taylor to visit her husband in the prison and to have dinner with him.

A few days later, Taylor was to be taken to Hadleigh, setting out from the Compter at 3 a.m. His wife, knowing that he would be leaving early in the morning and would pass through St Botolph's churchyard in the city, waited all night in the churchyard with Elizabeth and Mary. They saw him as he passed, and exchanged some words with him before he was told to move on. She promised him that she would be present to see him burned at Hadleigh.

At Chelmsford he was handed over to the Sheriff of Essex, who brought him to Hadleigh; he was to be burned on Aldham Common, an open space outside the town. He had been very popular in Hadleigh, and the local people turned out in strength, lining both sides of the street to salute him and express their sympathy as he passed. One of the guards, who was named Warwick, was a zealous Catholic. He had no reason to love Protestants, for under Northumberland's rule, in the reign of Edward VI, he had been convicted of writing seditious slogans on walls, and had been sentenced to have an ear cut off as he stood in the pillory. The popular sympathy for Taylor angered Warwick. He was also indignant that Taylor was refusing the Queen's offer of a pardon if he would recant. Mrs Taylor and the children were waiting near the stake, but the guards would not let Taylor say more than a few words to her, though they allowed him to speak for longer to his Catholic son.

Taylor was fastened to the stake, and the Sheriff ordered one of the bystanders, a local butcher, to set light to a faggot. The butcher had known and admired Taylor, and refused to do so, pretending that he was lame and was not strong enough to lift the faggot. The Sheriff threatened to have him arrested, but he still refused. Other bystanders then lit the faggot, which burned well. Warwick was more angry than ever to see the sympathy of the people for Taylor; as the fire began to burn around Taylor, Warwick picked up a burning faggot and threw it in Taylor's face. It was apparently out of rage that soon afterwards he hit Taylor over the head with a halbard, not realising that it was in fact an act of kindness, for it killed Taylor instantly.[3]

Hooper suffered on the same day as Taylor. He left London on 5 February on his three-day journey to Gloucester. On Thursday 7 February, after having dinner at Cirencester at 11 a.m. (the usual time for dinner) he reached Gloucester at 5 p.m. His guards had intended to imprison him in the town jail, but his behaviour was so gentle that they realised that he would not resist or attempt to escape, and they therefore agreed that he should stay for his last two nights on earth in the house of a local gentleman. It is today the New Inn in Gloucester. A blind boy, Thomas Dowry, was brought in to see him. The boy had been born blind, but had become an ardent Protestant, and had been imprisoned for propagating Protestant doctrines. He asked to speak to Hooper, who comforted him, and told him that though God had deprived him of his sight, He had enabled him to see the light of the Gospel.

On Saturday 9 February 1555 Hooper was taken to the place of execution outside the city. A large crowd, estimated at 7,000, turned out to watch the execution. This estimate was perhaps too high, as it was more than the total population of Gloucester, though many people came from the nearby villages. Some were sympathetic, some hostile, and some wished merely to see a rare and memorable event, for it was not every day that the local

The burning of John Hooper at Gloucester

bishop was burned as a heretic. Hooper asked to be allowed to speak to the people, but he was told that he could speak only if he recanted. Like the other martyrs who had been burned that week he was offered a pardon and his life if he recanted; but he refused to recant.

The local authorities had decided to save money and carry out Hooper's execution on the cheap. They brought only as many faggots as could be carried on the backs of two horses; and the wood in the faggots was green. It was a very windy day, and the wind was blowing strongly away from Hooper as he stood fastened to the stake. So the flames, after burning Hooper's legs, did not reach the rest of his body; and soon the flames were almost extinguished. Hooper cried out in agony for the fire to come to him. The Sheriff then sent for more faggots, which were brought, and at last the flames rose to Hooper's hands and the rest of his body. By now both his legs had been burned off, but he stood on their stumps praying, and striking his breast with his hands. Then one of his arms was burned away, but he continued to strike his breast with his other hand as he called on God to receive his soul. He was still alive, and conscious, three-quarters of an hour after the faggots were lit, although he had lost both his legs and arms; but at last he died.[4]

King Philip was worried about Mary's policy of religious persecution. He believed that in Spain and the Netherlands heretics should be burned with every refinement of cruelty, and often went to watch the spectacle, which he apparently enjoyed. But he thought that if Protestants were burned in England, he and his Spaniards, the hated foreigners, would be held responsible, and that this would make the English hate the Spaniards more than ever and sympathise with the heretics. Philip's Spanish biographer, Cabrera de Córdoba, writing twenty years after Philip's death, praised him for the zeal with which he burned heretics when he and Mary were King and Queen of England, and gave him the credit for having inspired the persecution. English Protestants at the time, and some later historians writing in more tolerant centuries, who thought that it was reprehensible, not creditable, to burn Protestants, have followed Cabrera in holding Philip chiefly responsible for the persecution. But all the evidence shows that he did not deserve Cabrera's praise or the censure of the Protestants and the later historians.

Philip's efforts to persuade his wife to abandon her persecuting religious policy was furthered by a sermon preached at court before Philip and Mary by one of Philip's Spanish retinue, the Franciscan friar Alfonso à Castro, on 10 February 1555, just after the burning of Rogers, Saunders and Hooper. Alfonso said that bishops were directed in the Bible to show meekness and kindness to erring heretics, and not sentence them to be burned. His sermon had no effect on Mary and the bishops.

Coverdale, the translator of the Bible into English, which to the Catholics was the source of so much evil, had been held in prison since he was arrested in September 1553. When the burning of the heretics began, he was one of the obvious candidates for the stake. But during his residence abroad he had married Elizabeth Mucheson, the sister of the Scottish Protestant John McAlpine, who had translated the Bible into Danish and was close to Christian III, the Protestant King of Denmark. McAlpine persuaded King Christian to intervene on Coverdale's behalf, and the King wrote to Mary asking her to permit Coverdale to go to Denmark. There was trade between Denmark and England, and Mary did not wish to harm it, any more than she wished to antagonise the grantees of the monastic lands. She agreed to allow Coverdale to go to Denmark with two of his servants. One of these servants was probably his wife, who was secretly living in England.

When Coverdale reached Denmark, Christian III offered him a bishopric, but Coverdale declined to accept it. He returned to England in 1559 after Elizabeth I had become Queen. Here, too, he refused to be reinstated as Bishop of Exeter, or to accept any other bishopric; but he preached important sermons in London, and exercised some influence in the affairs of the Protestant Church until his death in 1568.

Robert Ferrar was the last man who could expect mercy from the authorities. He was a Yorkshireman who in the 1520s studied divinity at Cambridge University, where he came under the influence of the Protestants who frequented the White Horse Inn. He went from Cambridge to Oxford to continue his studies, but did not abandon his Protestant views in the more orthodox university. He remained under the influence of the Protestant preacher Thomas Garret. In 1528 Garret was arrested for being in possession of heretical books, and Ferrar was one of several followers arrested with him. He recanted and carried his faggot, and was accepted back into the Church.

In 1538, after Henry VIII had decided to suppress the monasteries and was pressurising the abbots and priors to surrender their monasteries voluntarily, Ferrar became a monk, and was immediately appointed Prior of the great priory of St Oswald's at Nostell near Pontefract in Yorkshire. Within a few weeks he had voluntarily surrendered the priory to the King, and received a pension of £80 a year. In surrendering his monastery in return for a large pension, Ferrar was acting no differently from most of the other abbots and priors in England; but it was not often that a repentant heretic who had carried his faggot was appointed prior of a monastery immediately after becoming a monk and surrendered his priory within a few weeks of his appointment. It is not surprising that the Catholics believed that Henry VIII and Thomas Cromwell had told Ferrar to become a monk and had appointed him Prior of St Oswald's for the express purpose of surrendering his priory to the King. After the surrender of the priory Ferrar held various ecclesiastical appointments in London. He married a wife, thereby committing what was in Catholic eyes the particularly heinous offence of being a married monk who had broken his oath of celibacy.

When Somerset became Lord Protector after the death of Henry VIII, Ferrar was appointed Bishop of St David's in Wales. He soon came into conflict with his ecclesiastical subordinates there, partly because of personal antipathies and hostility between Welshmen and Englishmen. It was at about this time that Northumberland overthrew Somerset; and Northumberland, perhaps because he considered that Ferrar was too devoted to Somerset, supported Ferrar's critics. Ferrar was ordered to come to London, where he was arrested on a charge of embezzlement of Church money in St David's. He spent the last years of Edward VI's reign in prison, and was still in prison when Mary came to the throne.

Ferrar was duly deprived of his position as Bishop of St David's and replaced by the Catholic Henry Morgan, and in January 1555 he was interrogated by Gardiner and the other commissioners along with Rogers, Hooper and the others. The commissioners dealt with him very harshly as a married monk; but like his fellow-defendants he was offered his life under the Queen's pardon if he recanted, despite the fact that, having carried his faggot in 1528, he was a relapsed heretic; and as this fact was not mentioned in the proceedings against him, perhaps the commissioners had not been informed about his recantation in 1528.

Unlike Hooper, Saunders and Rowland Taylor, Ferrar was not condemned as a heretic and degraded in London before being sent to his locality to be burned; instead, he was taken to Carmarthen in his diocese of St David's to be tried there before Morgan, the new Bishop. The charge against him in the proceedings at Carmarthen was that he had denied the doctrine of the Real Presence. At first he refused to take part in the proceedings because he did not recognise Morgan as Bishop of St David's; but afterwards he stoutly asserted that he believed that Christ was present in the consecrated bread and wine spiritually but not corporally. He was condemned as a heretic and delivered to the Sheriff to be burned.

He was burned in the market place at Carmarthen, on the south side of the market cross, on Saturday 30 March 1555. Shortly before his execution a gentleman came to him and urged him to accept the Queen's pardon and recant; and he asked Ferrar if he realised the extent of the pain that he would suffer when he was burned. Ferrar said that he did, but that he would stand motionless in the fire. He told the gentleman that if he saw him move to try to avoid the flames, he should never believe that Ferrar's religious doctrines were true. When the faggots were lit, Ferrar stood motionless, as he had said that he would do, as the lower part of his legs were burned off. Then one of the guards – did he act out of hatred or out of mercy? – struck Ferrar on the head with his staff, and Ferrar fell into the fire and died.[5]

CHAPTER 6

The Search for Heretics

IN PURSUING THEIR POLICY of burning heretics, and in their choice of victims, Mary, Gardiner and the authorities wished to show the people that everyone would be burned, and no one would escape, however high or low his position in society might be, if he were guilty of the terrible sin of heresy. Having burned two bishops and three other prominent Protestant leaders, they now searched the towns and villages of south-east England to find the most humble and obscure people who had never played a prominent part in religious controversy and whose heretical opinions, and very existence, was known only to their neighbours.

Orders were sent to the bishops by the King and Queen – for Philip's name was always used in official proclamations, even if he personally had had no part in issuing them – and by the Lord Chancellor and the Privy Council to the Sheriffs; and the bishops and sheriffs passed on the orders to their vicars and JPs: Find anyone guilty of heresy and report him to the authorities. So the vicars asked their parishioners if they knew anyone in the parish who was a heretic.

The authorities were duly informed that some old woman or young lad in the parish had been heard to utter heretical opinions, or had gained a reputation in the parish of being a heretic. There were always people who were prepared to send reports about these obscure heretics, either from Catholic zeal, or from fear of the consequences to themselves if they did not report them, or most of all, perhaps, from an ingrained habit of obedience to authority.

The martyrs varied greatly, not only in their class origins and in the extent of their public fame or obscurity, but also in their character. There were learned scholars whose intellectual integrity would not allow them to further their career and save themselves from a dreadful death by accepting arguments that they believed were wrong. There were some with a guilty conscience who tortured themselves with remorse for trivial or imaginary sins and believed that they could atone for them only by suffering martyrdom. There were men who were little better than common criminals who used Protestant doctrines to justify their actions.

Their persecutors were of a more conventional and uniform type. They were in some cases the bishops, but more often the noblemen and gentlemen, who had governed England under Henry VIII and Edward VI and had every intention of continuing to govern the country under Mary. They would burn Protestant heretics under a Roman Catholic sovereign; they would imprison and fine Catholics under a Protestant sovereign; and under an Anglo-Catholic sovereign they would burn Protestant heretics and send Roman Catholic traitors to be hanged, drawn and quartered.

They were not acting solely from selfish careerism and ambition. They had persuaded themselves that it was their duty to obey the sovereign – 'the Prince' – because he alone had the right to decide what religion his subjects should adopt, and he alone would be accountable to God on the Day of Judgment if he had made the wrong decision. No loyal subject would be sent to Hell if he had supported heresy only out of obedience to his Prince. In every century there have been officials who have remained in office under successive régimes by persecuting first one side and then the other; but few of them have found so convincing an excuse for doing this as the noblemen and gentlemen of Tudor England.

In Mary's reign they persecuted energetically and with relish all the heretics whom they detested – the clever intellectual who thought that he was superior to those in authority; the masochistic religious crank whose guilty conscience made him long to be a martyr; the violent thug who used religion as an excuse to justify his thuggery. The noblemen and gentlemen of England hated all these misfits, and thought that they were a danger to society who deserved to be punished.

In February 1555 the authorities arrested Thomas Tomkins, a weaver of Shoreditch. He had a thriving business; women often came to him to ask him to weave their cloth. He was so devout a Protestant that he insisted that these women should join him in a prayer before discussing business. He was denounced to Bonner as a Protestant heretic. Even John Foxe admits that Bonner sometimes treated him kindly; once Bonner set him to work making hay in the fields around his palace in Fulham, and told him that he had worked as hard as if he were a good Catholic. But Foxe says that sometimes Bonner beat him brutally, so that his face was swollen with bruises, which showed up all the more when Bonner forcibly shaved his beard.

Tomkins said that he did not believe in the Real Presence. He wrote out a very short statement in which he stated that the consecrated bread and wine were not the Body and Blood of Christ because Christ's body was in Heaven; and he persisted in adhering to this statement despite all Bonner's efforts to persuade him to save his life by recanting. Foxe states that on one occasion Bonner forcibly held Tomkins' hand in the flame of a candle to make him realise the pain which he would suffer if he were burned as a heretic. Renard told a different version of this story in his report to Charles V; he wrote that Tomkins had called for a candle to be brought to him and had held his hand in the flame to show that he did not fear the pain of the fire. He was burned at Smithfield on 16 March 1555.

William Hunter was a boy of 19, apprenticed to a silk weaver in Coleman Street in the city of London. He had been brought up as a Protestant by his father and mother. When Mary became Queen, William's master told him to attend Mass, but he refused, and said that he would only go to a Protestant Church service. His master threw him out of the house, for he did not wish to be accused of harbouring heretics. William wandered off to Brentwood in Essex, where the vicar ordered him to go to Mass; and when William refused, a local JP denounced him to Bonner as a heretic.

He was convicted of heresy, and sent to Brentwood to be burned. His father, mother and brother, who were not denounced to the authorities, made no attempt to persuade him to recant, and told him how proud they were to see him suffer for God's truth. His brother Robert walked with him to the stake, and William gave Robert his English Psalter just before the faggots were lit. William cried out to the Catholic priest who tried to persuade him to recant: 'Away, away, thou false prophet !' The fire burned well, and he died quickly. Robert was put in the stocks for some hours for showing his support for his brother; but nothing worse happened to him or his parents.

Essex was in the Bishop of London's diocese, and the heretics in the county were therefore dealt with by Bonner. Another active persecutor there was Lord Rich, who in the reign of Henry VIII had been the chief witness against Sir Thomas More, and whose evidence – almost certainly false and perjured – had alone made it possible for More to be sentenced to death. Later, as Lord Chancellor, Rich had been sent by the Council in the unsuccessful attempt to induce Mary to abandon her Mass. He was now living in semi-retirement as a JP in Essex. Having loyally served Henry VIII, Thomas Cromwell, Somerset and Northumberland, he conscientiously carried out his duty of burning heretics in Essex at Mary's orders, and was congratulated by Mary's Privy Council on the way in which he performed this duty.

The victims came from every social class. There was William

Pygot, a butcher from Braintree; Stephen Knight, a barber at Malden; Thomas Haukes, a gentleman in Lord Oxford's household, who was denounced as a heretic by Lord Oxford; two other gentlemen of Essex, Thomas Higbed from Thundersley and Thomas Causden from Horndon-on-the-Hill; Thomas Wats, a linen draper of Billericay; and John Laurence, a priest of Colchester. Another priest, John Taylor – who was also called John Cardmaker – was brought before Bonner. He was a canon in the cathedral at Wells in Somerset, but was sent up to Southwark with Bishop Barlow. John Warne, an upholsterer of Walbrook in London, was also examined by Bonner.

These men were unable to enter into theological arguments with their interrogators; but they were steadfast, and some were defiant. When Bonner told Warne that he should save his life by recanting, Warne replied that he would recant if he were shown a passage in the Bible requiring him to do it. 'I am persuaded that I am of the right opinion,' he said, 'and I see no reason to repent, for all filthiness and idolatry is the Church of Rome.' He was burned, together with Cardmaker, at Smithfield on 30 May 1555.

Wats, the linen draper of Billericay, was examined by Rich and Sir Anthony Browne, who had held high positions at Henry VIII's court. Sir Anthony asked him who had taught him his heretical beliefs. 'Sir, you taught it me,' said Wats, 'and none more than you; for in King Edward's days, in open sessions, you spoke against the religion now used, no preacher more.'

Wats was burned at Chelmsford on 10 June 1555. As he was not a priest, he was allowed to say goodbye to his wife and children before he was taken to be burned. 'Wife and my good children,' he said to them, 'I must now depart from you. Beware ye turn not to this abominable papistry, against which I shall now, by God's grace, give my blood. Let not the murdering of God's saints cause you to relent.' Two of his children who loved their father very much, asked if they could be burned with him;

but they had to stay with their mother when he was taken to the stake. Lord Rich was there to see him burned. Wats called on Rich to repent, 'for you are the cause of my death'.

Stephen Knight was burned at Maldon on 28 March, and Pygot at Braintree on the same day. John Laurence was burned next day at Colchester. In prison he had been shackled with such heavy irons, and kept so short of food, that he could not walk to the stake and had to be carried there and burned sitting on a chair. Some of his supporters had come with their small children, who had been told by their parents that God had promised that those who died as martyrs for the true religion would go to Heaven. The children came close to the fire while Laurence was burning, and chanted: 'Lord, strengthen thy servant and keep thy promise! Lord, strengthen thy servant and keep thy promise !'

Thomas Haukes was burned at Coggeshall on 10 June. He had managed to talk secretly with some of his supporters before he was taken to execution. They asked him to make some sign to them while he was being burned to show the degree of pain that he was suffering. He promised to do so, and said that if the pain was bearable he would raise his hands to Heaven before he died. As they watched him burn, they saw him raise his hands above his head, although his fingers had been burned off, and clap his hands together before he died; and they knew that God had made it possible for him to endure the pain without flinching.

John Simson and John Ardeley, two husbandmen from the parish of Higborough-the-Great, were burned at Rayleigh in Essex in June 1555. They were the first agricultural labourers to suffer martyrdom. Nicholas Chamberlain, a weaver of Coggeshall, was burned at Colchester on 14 June.

Most of the burnings in the early summer of 1555 were in Bonner's diocese in London and Essex, and this helped to establish the idea, from the very beginning, that 'bloody Bonner' was the most cruel of the persecutors. But the policy of burning both the highest and the lowest was also pursued in Wales.

Having sent the Bishop of St David's to be burned at Carmarthen, the persecutors also denounced a very old man, Rawlins White, an English-speaking fisherman in Chepstow, who was always reciting long passages from the English Bible of Tyndale and Rogers to the people whom he met. When he was arrested and interrogated, his judges found, to their surprise, that he was illiterate. Someone had read the English Bible aloud to him, and he had learned large parts of it by heart.

Like most of the low-class heretics, he made no attempt to argue, but simply said that he did not believe that Christ's body was in the sacramental bread and wine, because the Bible said that it was in Heaven. When learned Protestants like Ridley put forward this argument, his judges argued with them, on the basis of quotations from Scripture and the works of Augustine, Origen and Chrysostom, as to whether Christ's body could, or could not, be in several places at the same time; but in the case of Rawlins White, they simply told him that he was ignorant and presumptuous for daring to challenge the opinion of learned doctors. They condemned him as a heretic. On 30 March 1555, the same day on which Ferrar was burned at Carmarthen, Rawlins White was burned at Cardiff.

There was another victim in the north. George Marsh had the misfortune to have to do with a diocesan bishop and a Lord Lieutenant who, like Gardiner and Bonner, had both supported the repudiation of Papal supremacy under Henry VIII, but had opposed the Reformation in Edward VI's reign, and were now eager to prove their devotion to the Catholic religion and the Pope.

Edward Stanley, the third Earl of Derby, was the son-in-law of the Duke of Norfolk. He had been active in suppressing the Catholic revolt of the Pilgrimage of Grace in 1536, when the people of Yorkshire had risen to oppose the suppression of the monasteries. He attached himself to Norfolk's party in the struggle against Cromwell, and had supported the Six Articles and the persecution of Protestants in the last years of Henry VIII. But he was more successful than Norfolk in keeping out of trouble. When Norfolk fell from power and was imprisoned in the Tower as a traitor, Derby remained in the House of Lords and opposed the Acts of Uniformity, the Book of Common Prayer, and the bill legalising the marriage of priests. Yet he continued to hold his great territorial possessions in Lancashire and in the Isle of Man, and was appointed Lord Lieutenant of Lancashire by Northumberland in 1552. Under Mary he supported the re-establishment of Papal Supremacy and the burning of Protestant heretics.

Chester was one of the new dioceses which had been created by Henry VIII after the suppression of the monasteries, chiefly in order to compensate with a bishopric the abbots who had agreed to surrender their monasteries to the King. It was created out of the dioceses of Bangor and St Asaph in Wales and the archiepiscopal diocese of York, and stretched from the southern boundary of the diocese of Carlisle in Cumberland to Flint and Wrexham in North Wales. The first Bishop of Chester was John Bird, who had married and had adopted Protestant doctrines under Edward VI. He was therefore deprived when Mary became Queen, but was pardoned after he had recanted and put away his wife. His recantation was so complete that Bonner appointed him to be vicar of Great Dunmow in Essex.

Bird was replaced as Bishop of Chester by George Cotes, an academic who was not unlearned but had kept clear of religious controversy under Henry VIII and Edward VI. After studying at Magdalen College, Oxford, he became a doctor of divinity in 1537, and was appointed master of the Oxford college of Balliol. He had dutifully repudiated Papal supremacy under Henry VIII, and had uttered no word of criticism of the religious developments under Edward VI. Outside Oxford, no one had heard of him when he was appointed Bishop of Chester by Queen Mary. He was as eager as the Earl of Derby to prove that he was devoted to the Pope and to the reconciliation with Rome.

Their victim, George Marsh, came from the village of Horne near Workington in Cumberland. He was a young farmer who married and had several children; but when his wife died soon after their marriage he placed his children in the care of his mother and went to London. He was ordained as a priest under Edward VI, and sent to be Lawrence Saunders' curate in his parish in Leicestershire. When Saunders was arrested in September 1553, Marsh's friends urged him to escape abroad; but Marsh went first to Lancashire to say goodbye to his children. In Lancashire he preached in his native village of Horne, at Bolton, and in other places, denouncing the Mass and Papal Supremacy. The Earl of Derby issued orders for his arrest. Again Marsh's friends advised him to escape abroad; but instead he informed Derby's officers of where he could be found, and he was arrested and imprisoned, first near Bolton and then in Lancaster Castle.

Derby himself interrogated Marsh, who persisted in denying the Real Presence and Papal Supremacy. When he was imprisoned in Lancaster Castle he prayed so loudly at the top of his voice that he could be heard outside the prison, and the authorities became alarmed that he was propagating his heresies to the people, and ordered him to be silent.

Eventually Derby sent him to Bishop Cotes in Chester, where he was examined at length by the orthodox theologians. He was offered a pardon if he recanted, but he refused. He was condemned as a heretic and sentenced to be burned at Spittle Broughton, just outside the north gate of Chester, on 24 April 1555.

He could not expect much sympathy in the Catholic north, though even here there were secret Protestants who admired and pitied him. They afterwards told their stories, which may or may not be strictly accurate, of how the bishop and his officials, and many members of the public, insulted and humiliated Marsh, and how the Protestants who admired him did not dare to visit him in prison, or make any gesture of support. The vicar of Granpound in Lancashire told him that the Protestant service of the Second Book of Common Prayer, 'was the most develish thing that ever was devised'. An ecclesiastical official warned a man not to stand too close to Marsh, as he would be contaminated by proximity to so wicked a heretic. When Marsh asked Cotes to pray for him, the bishop replied: 'I will no more pray for thee than I would for a dog.' The Catholic priests repeatedly urged him to save his life by accepting the Queen's pardon, which he would be granted if he recanted; but he refused. He told them that he loved life, and wished to live as much as they did, but not at the price of betraying his master Christ.

The jailer at Chester was moved by Marsh's gentleness. As Marsh left the prison to walk to the place of execution, the jailer said to him, 'Farewell, good George'. Marsh was forced to walk to the stake with shackles on his feet. A shoemaker called out to him: 'For shame, man, remember thyself and repent.' Some Catholics in the crowd offered him money for him to give to the priests to pray for his soul, but he refused to concern himself with money at such a time. At the stake he turned to speak to the onlookers, but one of the sheriffs stopped him: 'George Marsh, we must have no sermonizing now.'

After they had fastened him to the stake with a chain around his waist, they placed above his head a little jar shaped like a firkin (a small bottle of beer) filled with tar and pitch, so that when the flames reached it, the jar would fall on his head. The Protestants believed that the authorities had adopted this unusual course in order to increase his sufferings.

The faggots had not been well placed, and were not close enough to him. When they were set alight, the gusty wind blew the flames first towards him and then away from him, and did not reach the firkin above his head for a long time. Marsh stood motionless in the fire as his legs were slowly burned off, and his

Princess Mary, by Master John, 1544.

William Tyndale.

Edward Seymour, 1st Duke of Somerset, by an unknown artist.

Thomas Cranmer, Archbishop of Canterbury, by Gerlach Flicke. The date of the painting usually given is 1546, however, the inscription '*Anno aetate 57, Juli, 20*' shows that it was painted on 20 July 1545 as Cranmer was born on 2 July 1489.

Queen Mary I, by an unknown artist.

Stephen Gardiner, Bishop of
Winchester, 1531-1555.

Hugh Latimer, by an unknown
artist, probably c.1548.

Nicholas Ridley, by an unknown artist,
probably c.1548.

Emperor Charles V, by Titian.

Cardinal Reginald Pole, by an
unknown artist, probably painted
c.1543.

Philip II of Spain, by an unknown artist, c.1580.

Princess Elizabeth aged thirteen, later Queen Elizabeth I, by an unknown artist, c.1546.

John Foxe, by an unknown artist, 1587.

IEAN CNOX, DE GIFFORD
EN ESCOSSE.

John Knox. This portrait, which has often been thought to be a portrait of Tyndale, is almost certainly the only genuine portrait of Knox painted after Knox's death from memory by the Flemish painter Vaensoun; see Borgeaud 'Le "vrai portrait" de John Knox' (in *Bulletin de la Société de l'Histoire du Protestantisme français* lxxxiv pp. 11-36. Paris, 1935).

flesh which surrounded the chain that fastened him to the stake began to drop off. The spectators thought that he must be dead; but suddenly he cried out 'Father of Heaven, have mercy upon me!', and after prolonged suffering he died.

Many people, whatever they may have thought of his religion, were moved by the courage with which he had borne his slow burning at the stake. Bishop Cotes did his best to counter this impression. He preached a sermon in Chester Cathedral in which he said that Marsh was a heretic who had burned like a heretic and was a firebrand in Hell. Cotes died within a year. The Protestants said that this was God's punishment because he had burned Marsh, and that he had died of syphilis. They also said that a footprint in the stone at Spittle Boughton, which survived for many years, was the footprint made by Marsh when he rejected the offer of pardon and refused to recant. Marsh was the only Protestant martyr in Mary's reign to be burned north of the River Trent, in the province of the Archbishop of York.[1]

Sometimes the authorities encountered a heretic who did not subscribe to Tyndale's doctrine of Christian obedience. On Easter Day 1555 the Catholic priest who was assisting at the celebration of Mass in St Margaret's church in Westminster was walking around the church holding up the consecrated bread to be worshipped, when the Protestant zealot, William Flower, rushed in and struck his hand with a knife. The priest's blood sprinkled over the Host that he was carrying. Flower had set out that morning intending to attack the priest celebrating Mass in St Paul's Cathedral. On his way he visited the Protestants imprisoned in the jail at Newgate, and cheerfully told them that he would soon be joining them in their prison. When he arrived at St Paul's he found that he was not permitted to approach the officiating priest; so he went on to St Margaret's in Westminster.

Flower was arrested, and, as he had expected, was imprisoned in Newgate. Here he met another prisoner, Robert Smith, a Protestant who had been appointed as a clerk at Eton College.

He was a painter and a poet. When Mary became Queen, the Privy Council heard about this Protestant at Eton, and Smith was arrested and imprisoned in Newgate. He was worried about Flower's action in striking the priest with a knife; he asked Flower if he had been motivated by personal hatred of the priest, whether he could justify his conduct and if he thought that other Protestants should do what he had done. Flower said that he did not hate the priest, whom he had never met, and had attacked him only because he had been unable to stab the priest at St Paul's; but he was not sure that he had acted rightly, and did not urge other Protestants to imitate him, though he did not regret his action, and had always been prepared to suffer for it.

Flower was sentenced to lose his hand under a statute of Edward VI's reign, and he was also condemned as a heretic. He was taken to the churchyard outside St Margaret's in Westminster where he had committed the outrage on the Host. After he had been fastened to the stake his right hand was cut off before the faggots were lit and he was burned in front of the church.

Robert Smith was condemned as a heretic, and refused to recant. He wrote poems to his Protestant friends urging them in verse to remain true to their Protestant beliefs. He was burned at Uxbridge in Middlesex on 8 August 1555.

The persecution in the south-east had begun in London and Essex, but Kent and Sussex did not lag far behind. The southern part of Kent was in the archiepiscopal diocese of Canterbury. After Cranmer was convicted of high treason he was suspended from exercising his powers in his diocese, which were entrusted to Nicholas Harpsfield, the Archdeacon of Canterbury, and to Richard Thornden, the suffragan Bishop of Dover.

Nicholas Harpsfield, whose brother John was Bonner's secretary, was a learned canon and civil lawyer who had been awarded his degree at Oxford and held various legal appointments in the last years of Henry VIII; but he opposed the Protestant Reformation under Edward VI so strongly that he left

England and resided with the Catholic theologians at Louvain in Charles V's territories in the Netherlands. When he returned to England at the beginning of Mary's reign he was appointed Archdeacon of Canterbury for the purpose of administering Cranmer's diocese. He spent his time directing the persecution of Protestant heretics, and in writing two books, *A treatise on the Pretended Divorce between Henry VIII and Catherine of Aragon* and *The Life and Death of Sir Thomas More, knight, some time Lord High Chancellor of England*, in which he argued that the divorce was illegal and lavishly praised More.

Thornden was a less consistent Catholic. He had been appointed as Cranmer's suffragan Bishop of Dover by Thomas Cromwell, and had distinguished himself by his denunciation of the vices of the monks in Kent at the time of the suppression of the monasteries. His critics called him 'Dick of Dover'. In 1555 he was persecuting Protestants as eagerly as he had vilified the monks in 1536.

John Bland was the vicar of Adisham, five miles south of Canterbury on the road to Dover. After Mary came to the throne Bland told his churchwarden at Adisham that he would walk out of the church into the churchyard while Mass was celebrated because he would not attend Mass. The churchwarden denounced him as a heretic, and also revealed that Bland had married a wife. Bland was summoned to appear at quarter sessions at Cranbrook before Sir John Baker, a lawyer who had loyally served on the Privy Council under Henry VIII and Edward VI. Baker sentenced him to be put in the stocks, and sent him to be examined by Nicholas Harpsfield. As Bland, after long arguments with Harpsfield and Thornden, persisted in denying the Real Presence, he was condemned as a heretic.

Three other heretics were condemned with him. One of these was Nicholas Shetterden, who had been questioned in the reign of Edward VI on suspicion of being a member of an extremist Anabaptist sect. In 1555 his extremist views alarmed the authorities, and he was sent to Southwark to be examined by Lord Chancellor Gardiner. He was condemned as a heretic. John Frankesh, the vicar of Rolvenden near Tenterden, and Humphrey Middleton, a layman from Ashford, were also condemned by Thornden. A man named Thacker was examined by Thornden, but saved his life by recanting and doing penance. The others refused to recant, and steadfastly denounced the Real Presence.

The night before he was burned, Shetterden wrote a farewell letter to his mother. He told her not to believe in the Real Presence and not to worship the consecrated bread as Christ's body: 'O let not that be your God which mice and worms can devour.' He ended his letter: 'Your child, written with his hand and sealed with his blood, Nicholas Shetterden, being appointed to be slain.' Bland, Shetterden, Frankesh and Middleton were burned together in the same fire at Canterbury on 12 July 1555. A priest, William Mings, had died in prison in Maidstone on 2 July before he could be burned as a heretic with them.

The north of Kent was in the diocese of Rochester, where Maurice Griffin was bishop in 1555. He was a Welshman who became a Dominican monk in a monastery in Oxford, and was awarded the degree of doctor of divinity by the university in 1532. He repudiated Papal Supremacy under Henry VIII, and in 1545 was appointed a canon of Rochester cathedral, a position which he held quite happily in the reign of Edward VI, when two leading Protestants, first Nicholas Ridley and then Scory, were appointed Bishop of Rochester. The see became vacant when Scory was appointed Bishop of Chichester in 1552. When Mary became Queen she appointed Griffin Bishop of Rochester. He was determined to show that his association with Ridley and Scory would not prevent him from zealously persecuting Protestants under Mary.

At the beginning of June 1555 Nicholas Hall, a bricklayer of Dartford, and another man of Dartford, Christopher Wade, were arrested and brought to Rochester to be examined by Bishop Maurice Griffin. They were asked if they would be obedient to Mother Church. They replied that the phrase 'Mother Church' does not appear in the Bible. They denied the Real Presence, because the Bible stated that Christ was in Heaven, not in the bread and wine of the Sacrament.

At the same time the authorities arrested Margery Polley, a widow living in Pembury near Tonbridge. When she was examined by Griffin she adopted the same attitude as Christopher Wade; she said that there was no reference to the Roman Catholic Church in the Bible, and that Christ could not be present in the consecrated bread and wine because the Bible stated that He was in Heaven. Griffin condemned her as a heretic.

She was the first woman to be burned in Mary's reign. Two women, Anne Askew and Joan Bocher, had been burned for heresy under Henry VIII and Edward VI; but they were proselytising champions of their cause. Anne Askew had come to London from Lincolnshire to distribute Protestant pamphlets to the ladies at court. Joan Bocher came there from Kent to preach her Anabaptist doctrines in the city. As far as we know, Margery Polley had never left Pembury, except to go to market in Tonbridge, but had told her neighbours there that she would not go to Mass because it was in Latin which she did not understand, that she believed only what she read in the English Bible, and that the Bible said that Christ was in Heaven, not in the bread and wine of the Sacrament.

Wade, Hall and Margery Polley were to be burned at Dartford on 18 July 1555 in a gravel pit called the Brimpt, a quarter of a mile outside the town, where executions usually took place. The local farmers, realising that there would be the usual large crowd of spectators at the burning, came with horseloads of cherries, to sell what remained of their crop very late in the season.★ Wade and Margery Polley were brought to Dartford. From the town they could see the crowds which had

★ 18 July 1555 was 28 July by our modern Gregorian calendar.

gathered at the gravel pit. Margery was kept back in the town while Wade was burned.

The Protestants often referred to their martyrdom as their marriage, in which they were married to Christ; and Wade's wife had given him a white wedding shirt for him to wear when he was burned. He was allowed to go to an inn in Dartford, where he changed from his usual clothes into the wedding shirt. When Margery saw him in his shirt, and looked at the crowds at the gravel pit waiting to see him burned, she called out cheerfully: 'You may rejoice, Wade, to see such a company gathered to celebrate your marriage this day.'

At the stake, Wade called on the people to beware of the whore of Babylon and to stick to the religion of King Edward's time. The Sheriff said to him: 'Be quiet, Wade, and die patiently.' Wade replied: 'I am, thank God, quiet, Master Sheriff, and so trust to die'. When the fire was lit, he held his hands high above his head, calling 'Lord Jesus! receive my soul'. The onlookers who were present afterwards told John Foxe that he still held his hands above his head after he was dead, which is not impossible if *rigor mortis* immediately set in. After he had been burned, they brought Margery Polley to the gravel pit and burned her too. Hall was burned there next day.

In London Bonner had to deal with the case of John Tooley, a poulterer in the city. Like many other Englishmen Tooley hated the Spaniards who came to England with King Philip, and he plotted with some of his acquaintances to rob one of the Spaniards in St James's. He was arrested and convicted of attempted robbery, and sentenced to be hanged, which was the usual punishment in such cases. Foxe commented sourly that Tooley was sentenced to be hanged, 'notwithstanding in this realm there are many more thefts committed than thieves executed'. His statement was true, but the implication that Tooley was only sentenced to be hanged because his victim was a Spaniard was unjustified. The authorities had been equally firm in punishing Philip's Spaniards who committed offences against Englishmen.

Tooley was hanged at Charing Cross. On the scaffold he called on the crowd to reject the Roman Antichrist, citing the words of the Litany of 1544 which Henry VIII had allowed Cranmer to draft: 'From the tyranny of the Bishop of Rome and all his detestable enormities . . . good Lord deliver us.' He then handed to the sergeant in charge of his execution a document headed 'Beware of Antichrist' which he had written in prison.

After Tooley was hanged the sergeant forgot about the document and put it away somewhere; but pious Catholics in the crowd told Bonner what Tooley had said and done before he was hanged. Bonner then went through the accepted process of condemning a dead man for heresy. A summons was displayed at Charing Cross ordering Tooley to appear before Bonner's ecclesiastical court to answer a charge of heresy. When the dead man did not appear, the witnesses gave their evidence about Tooley's words on the scaffold and his handing the document to the sergeant. Tooley was then condemned as a heretic, and his corpse was dug up and burned. The sergeant had to explain why he had not obeyed the recent proclamation of Philip and Mary and handed in to the authorities any heretical book which came into his possession. He was examined by Harpsfield, but escaped with a warning after he had asked pardon for his offence.

CHAPTER 7

The Summer of 1555

IN THE SPRING OF 1555 Queen Mary announced that she was pregnant. Some of her physicians were surprised, and did not believe it; but she insisted that it was true, and said that she had first felt the baby move in her womb at the moment when she saw the Papal Legate, Cardinal Pole, as he arrived to grant absolution to the schismatic realm and reunite England to Rome on the Feast of the Reconciliation on 30 November 1554. If she gave birth to a child it meant that she would have an heir who would be brought up as a Roman Catholic, and that the Catholic counter-reformation would continue and endure. It would mean the ruin of the Protestant hopes that Mary would be succeeded by her half-sister Elizabeth, who had gone to Mass and was pretending to be a Catholic, but who, as everyone knew, was really a secret Protestant.

After the suppression of Wyatt's revolt, when Elizabeth was sent to the Tower, Gardiner had wished to put her to death; but several members of Mary's Privy Council, led by William, Lord Paget, and William Herbert, Earl of Pembroke, strongly opposed the proposal. They knew that Elizabeth was popular with the people, and that many of Mary's subjects would deeply resent it if she were executed. So Mary released Elizabeth from the Tower and confined her under house arrest in her manor of Woodstock in Oxfordshire.

As soon as Philip arrived in England and married Mary, he used his influence in Elizabeth's favour. She never forgot it, and even in later years, when her England and Philip's Spain were engaged first in a cold war and then in a bitterly-fought naval and military war, she remembered how he had helped her in Mary's reign, and she never hated him as so many of her subjects did. At Philip's suggestion, Elizabeth was eventually allowed to come to court. At Hampton Court she was given rooms in the palace next door to Cardinal Pole's rooms; but he never invited her to visit him, or spoke to her when they passed each other on the stairs.

On 30 April 1555 a day of public rejoicing was held for the Queen's pregnancy, and the bells of St Paul's and all the London churches rang to mark the people's joy. Many of the Protestants in prison felt that their duty of Christian obedience required them to pray for the Queen's safe delivery, even though it would be a disastrous blow to their cause. Elizabeth herself, whatever her inner thoughts may have been, is said to have made a layette – which today can be seen in Hever Castle – consisting of a coif, a pair of little shoes, two jackets, two bonnets, some collars and sleeves, in white satin and silk, and a flannel jacket, all of them exquisitely sewn.

Abroad, the rumour spread that Mary's baby had actually been born. The Princess Dowager of Portugal, who was Regent in Spain while Charles V was in the Netherlands, wrote to congratulate Mary on the birth of the child. Mary's physicians did not dare to tell the truth – that Mary had imagined that she was pregnant, but was in fact unlikely ever to have a child.

On 4 June 1555, when Mary, if she was speaking the truth, was in the eighth month, Renard wrote to Charles V, and did not conceal his anxiety.

Sire, everything in this kingdom depends on the Queen's delivery. If God is pleased to grant her a safe delivery, things will take a turn for the better. If not, I foresee disturbance and a change for the worse on so great a scale that the pen can hardly set it down. It is certain that the order of succession to the crown has been so badly arranged that Lady Elizabeth comes next, and that means heresy again, and religion overthrown.

No baby was born, and no official announcement was made explaining what had happened. The forthcoming event which had been officially celebrated on 30 April was not referred to again. But rumour was rife, and everyone was saying that the Queen was not pregnant and never would be, but was a hysterical woman who had imagined that she was about to give birth to a child.

Mary's disappointment was made more bitter by the attentions that Philip was paying to Elizabeth. The story was afterwards told that he had fallen in love with her, and that she played with him for her own ends, never intending to grant him her favours. There is no real evidence of this. No doubt he paid her compliments, and treated her with the courtesy and gallantry that a prince ought to show to a princess; perhaps he was attracted by her lively youthful grace and her red hair, for she was certainly more attractive at the age of twenty-one than her tired, sour, and rapidly fading and ageing sister Mary was at thirty-nine. But for Philip, Elizabeth's greatest attraction was that she stood between Mary, Queen of Scots, and the English throne.[1] Mary, Queen of Scots, who was the daughter of a French mother, Mary of Lorraine, and was the Duke of Guise's niece, was being brought up at the French court. She was only twelve, but it was known that when she was grown up she would marry the Dauphin, the King of France's son, and would one day become Queen of France. King Philip, like his father Charles V, preferred to see a heretic Queen of England than a French Queen of England.

The burnings continued unabated during the summer of 1555. Eight months earlier, in October 1554, Derek Carver, a forty-year-old brewer from the fishing port of Brighthelmstone (Brighton) in Sussex, had invited some of his friends, including John Launder and Thomas Iveson, to meet in his house in Brighton to read the English Bible together and hold a Protestant prayer-meeting. Launder, who was aged twenty-five, was an agricultural labourer, and Iveson, was a young carpenter; they both came from Godstone in Surrey.

Someone sent a report about the prayer-meeting in Carver's house to the High Sheriff of Sussex, Sir John Gage, of Firle near Lewes in Sussex. Gage was an old soldier who had loyally served his King for forty-five years. His first campaign had been in France under the young King Henry VIII in 1513. Since then Gage had fought in many engagements against the Scots. His loyal service included his dutiful submission to the orders of his sovereign in adopting whatever religion he was ordered to adopt from time to time, and in arresting disobedient subjects who refused to obey their sovereign's orders about religion. Under Mary he became a Roman Catholic and rounded up Protestant heretics. He sent officers to raid Carver's house in Brighton, and they arrested Carver, Launder, Iveson and the others, who were sent to London to be examined by Bonner.

Some of the defendants recanted, and were pardoned, but Carver, Launder and Iveson refused to recant. Carver told Bonner: 'Your doctrine is poison and sorcery. If Christ were here you would put him to a worse death than he was put to before.' He denied the Real Presence, and told Bonner: 'You say that you can make a god; you can make a pudding.' Launder, too, denied the Real Presence, and said: 'I will never go from these answers as long as I live.' Iveson told Bonner that he would not forsake his beliefs for all the goods in London.

Carver, Launder and Iveson were condemned as heretics. As their heresy had been committed in Brighton, in the diocese of Chichester, they were all burned in the diocese, but at different places, for the authorities thought that three different towns in Sussex should have the salutary experience of seeing a heretic burned.

Carver was burned at Lewes on 22 July 1555. As he walked through the town on his way to the stake a great crowd gathered around him, as he passed the Star Inn, to express their sympathy for him. The Sheriff's men had brought Carver's English Bible to the stake so that it could be contemptuously thrown into a barrel; but Carver pulled the Bible out of the barrel and threw it into the crowd. One of his Protestant supporters picked it up, but the Sheriff ordered him on pain of death to throw the Bible into the barrel again. The Sheriff told Carver that if he did not believe in the Pope he was damned, and challenged Carver: 'Speak to thy God that he may deliver thee now, or else to strike me down to the example of the people.' Carver replied: 'The Lord forgive you your sayings.' When the faggots were lit he leapt up and down in the fire and cried: 'O Lord have mercy upon me!'; but he died quickly.

Launder was burned next day at Steyning. Before the end of the month Iveson was burned in Chichester.

Bradford was kept in prison for a long time before he was burned. He had been one of the first Protestants to be arrested, having been sent to the Tower after the riot at Paul's Cross in August 1553, only ten days after Mary entered London. He was imprisoned in the Tower in the same cell as Cranmer, Ridley and Latimer; but when his three companions were sent to Oxford to be condemned in the disputation there, he remained in the Tower. Later he was sent to Bonner's palace at Fulham.

Bonner handled him more gently than he usually treated his Protestant prisoners, and was particularly eager to persuade him to recant and save his life; but Bradford refused to recant, and persisted in denying the supremacy of the Pope and the Real Presence. Several prominent theologians argued with him, including King Philip's Spanish friar, Alfonso à Castro, who had preached the sermon at court condemning the persecution of heretics and the bishops who sent them to the stake instead of forgiving them. It was perhaps because Alfonso did not wish heretics to be burned in England that he became so angry when Bradford refused to recant, and shouted at him in a much harsher manner than Bonner did. Eventually Bonner gave up hope of

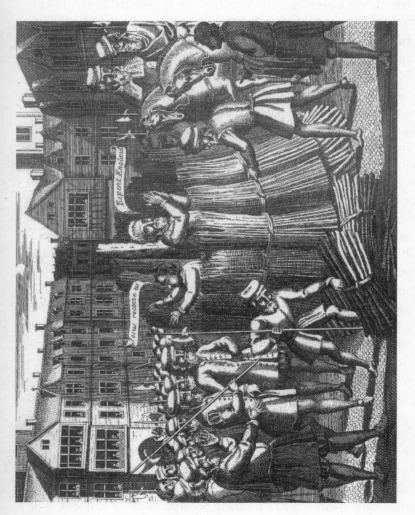

The martyrdom of Mr. John Bradford and John Leaf in Smithfield

persuading Bradford to recant, and reluctantly condemned him as a heretic.

Bradford was taken to the Compter prison in Broad Street in London to await execution. There he met John Leaf, a seventeen-year-old lad who had been born in Yorkshire but had come to London and been apprenticed to a tallow-chandler in the city. Some of the London aldermen discovered that he was a Protestant and ordered him to be arrested and sent to the Compter. He was examined by Bonner and condemned as a heretic, and was in the Compter waiting to be burned. He was very proud to meet Bradford in the prison, for he admired Bradford as one of the foremost Protestant leaders. Bradford spoke to him on several occasions, praising his courage and exhorting him to be constant, to refuse to recant, and to suffer death in the fire for the true religion.

The authorities decided not to send Bradford to his native Manchester to be burned, but to burn him and young Leaf together in the same fire at Smithfield on 1 July. Bradford and Leaf were dragged from the Compter to Smithfield on two hurdles, tied face downwards. When they arrived at Smithfield they were placed, still face downwards, on opposite sides of the stakes and the faggots which had been prepared for them; but they were released from their hurdles so that they could be fastened to the two stakes, and Bradford was able to say a few words of encouragement to Leaf. Bradford asked to be allowed to address the crowd of spectators, and the Sheriff agreed, thinking that he was going to recant; but when Bradford called on the people to remain steadfast and to refuse to bow to idolatry and Antichrist, the Sheriff ordered him to be quiet, and threatened to bind his arms together if he did not keep quiet. 'O Master Sheriff, I am quiet,' said Bradford, 'God forgive you this, Master Sheriff.' One of the Sheriff's men insulted Bradford, and said: 'If you have no better learning than that, you are but a fool, and had best hold your peace.' Bradford did not reply, but called out to Leaf: 'Be of good comfort, brother, for we shall have a merry supper with the Lord this night.' When the faggots were lit, the fire burned fiercely, and they both died quickly.

Edmund Tyrrel, Esquire, Justice of the Peace for the county of Essex, was another gentleman who conscientiously performed his duty to the Queen by arresting heretics. One day in June 1555 he was riding through Essex, having just attended the burning of a heretic, when he happened to meet two men from Maidstone in Kent – John Denley, a gentleman, and John Newman, a pewterer – who were travelling together. They entered into conversation with Tyrrel as they rode along. Something that Denley and Newman said aroused Tyrrel's suspicion; perhaps they seemed to disapprove when he told them that he had just seen a heretic burned. Tyrrel searched them, and found that they had an English Bible and a Protestant tract in their possession. He arrested them and sent them to Bonner, and as they refused to recant Bonner condemned them as heretics, together with Patrick Pachingham, who had also been arrested, condemned as a heretic, and sent to join them.

Denley was burned at Uxbridge in Middlesex on 8 August 1555. Pachingham was burned there on 28 August. Newman was burned at Saffron Walden in Essex on 31 August.

In August another woman was burned. Elizabeth Warne was the wife of John Warne, the upholsterer of Walbrook in London. They were both arrested on 1 January 1555, when the authorities raided a house in the city and found them with other people at a Protestant prayer-meeting. Elizabeth was related to Dr John Story, an eminent civil lawyer and a leading Catholic. At first Story used his influence to obtain her release; but when he found that she was an obstinate heretic who would not recant, he denounced her again to the authorities. 'Do what ye will,' she said, 'for if Christ were in an error then I am in an error.' Her husband was burned with Cardmaker at Smithfield on 30 May 1555, and she at Stratford-at-Bow in Essex in August.

There were several other burnings in August. Richard Hook was burned at Chichester, and a young man, James Abbes, at Bury St Edmunds in Suffolk in the diocese of Norwich. There were more burnings in the diocese of Norwich in September. William Allen, an agricultural labourer, and Thomas Cob, a butcher, were burned in Norfolk, Allen at Walsingham and Cob at Thetford; and a very old man, Richard Coo, was burned at Yoxford in Suffolk.

The burnings continued in the diocese of Canterbury. At the end of August six Protestants were burned in the same fire there, after they had been examined and condemned as heretics by Richard Thornden. One of them, William Stere of Ashford, defied Thornden; he called him 'Dick of Dover' to his face and demanded to be tried by his diocesan bishop, Archbishop Cranmer. On 6 September five more Protestants were burned in one fire in Canterbury – two from Hythe, one from Brenchley, one from Broomfield, and one from the English territory around Calais, which was in the diocese of Canterbury.

Bonner had to deal with an unusual heretic when George Tankerville was arrested and sent to him. Tankerville, a twenty-seven-year-old Yorkshireman, had come to London and became a cook. He had always been a Catholic, and in the reign of Edward VI he had ventured to express his sympathy for the old religion and his disapproval of the Reformation and the Book of Common Prayer. But when the burning of Protestants began in Mary's reign, he was disgusted, and expressed his indignation by reading the English Bible and denying the Real Presence. Bonner dealt kindly with Tankerville, and was very anxious to persuade him to recant and become a Catholic again; but as he refused to do so, Bonner condemned him as a heretic, and he was burned at St Albans in Hertfordshire on 26 August.

*   *   *

Dr Ralph Baines, the Bishop of Coventry and Litchfield, was a more consistent Catholic than many of his fellow-bishops. He came from Yorkshire, and was studying at St John's College, Cambridge, before 1517. He accepted the break with Rome and held the rectory of Hardwick in Cambridgeshire under Henry VIII. But he had always opposed the Reformation, and had gone abroad under Edward VI, becoming Professor of Hebrew at Paris University. He returned to England after Mary's accession, and soon afterwards was appointed Bishop of Coventry and Litchfield after the death of the eminent Richard Sampson, who had been Wolsey's secretary and had adapted himself to every change in religion, from the days when he had actively worked for Henry VIII's divorce from Catherine of Aragon till he loyally supported Mary's measures against Protestant heretics.

Baines was informed about John Glover, the eldest son of a moderately wealthy gentleman of Mancetter in Warwickshire in Baines's diocese. John Glover was a deeply religious Protestant who sold his lands and distributed the proceeds among his poorer Protestant brethren. He was obsessed with a sense of his own guilt, which he believed he could expiate only by suffering martyrdom. John Foxe knew him, and tried unsuccessfully to convince him that his sins were either trivial or wholly imaginary. He found John Glover so convinced that he had sinned against the Holy Ghost that it was difficult to persuade him to eat meat. Foxe reflected that men who have not been guilty of any serious sin are often overcome with unnecessary remorse, while those who really have committed wicked sins have no remorse at all.

Bishop Baines told the Mayor of Coventry to arrest John Glover. But the Mayor, who knew him, thought that he was a harmless crazy crank, and instead of arresting Glover he warned him to make himself scarce. John's friends persuaded him to leave his home and go into hiding in the houses of his friends.

John had a younger brother, Robert Glover, a man of a very different temperament. He was very tall and physically strong, with a confident, tactless and rather aggressive manner. He had studied at Cambridge University, where he was awarded the degree of Master of Arts, before he settled down to live the life of a country gentleman in Warwickshire. Like his brother John, he was sympathetic to the Protestants, but had never been active in propagating their doctrines.

When the Mayor of Coventry reported to Baines that he had been unable to find John Glover, the Bishop sent officers to search the Glovers' house in Mancetter. John Glover was not there, but they found Robert Glover ill in bed. Despite his protests, they arrested him, apparently mistaking him for his brother, and took him, ill though he was, to the common jail in Coventry, where he bitterly complained of the harsh conditions to which he was subjected. He was in due course sent to be examined by Baines.

If Robert Glover had been more tactful, he might have convinced Baines that he had been arrested by mistake for his brother, and released with an apology for the error which had been made; but he strongly denounced the Bishop's men for the way in which he had been treated. Baines then asked him if he believed in Papal supremacy and the Real Presence, and he said defiantly that he did not. As he proceeded to argue rather aggressively, Baines said that Glover, as a layman, should show respect for him because he was a bishop. Glover said that Baines and his colleagues had not shown much respect for bishops when they recently burned two of them. Baines said that that was different, because the bishops who had been burned were heretics. Glover said that if it was possible for a bishop to be a heretic, how could he be sure that Bishop Baines was not a heretic ?

Their conversation ended with Glover again asserting that he did not acknowledge the Pope or believe in the Real Presence,

and with Baines condemning him as a heretic. He was burned at
Coventry on 20 September 1555. Cornelius Bungey, a cap-
maker from Coventry, who had also been condemned as a
heretic, was burned in the same fire with him.

It was some time before Baines and his officers remembered
that they had not arrested John Glover, and they sent officers to
his house in Mancetter to seize him; but the guilt-ridden crank
who had hoped for martyrdom and who was regarded as crazy
by many people, now showed an instinct for self-preservation
and a wiliness in achieving it. When the officers who were
looking for him searched the house, John was in a room with a
door which was opened by a latch inside the room to which a
cord was attached; the cord passed through a small hole in the
door just above the latch and dangled on the door outside the
room. John, inside the room, put his finger above the latch, so
that when the bishop's officer tried to open the door from the
outside by pulling the cord, he could not move the latch, which
was blocked by John's finger. The officer, thinking that the door
was jammed, made no further effort to open it, but entered and
searched the next room; and while he was searching that room,
John opened the door of his room and slipped out of the house
without being noticed by the officer.

John hid in the woods for several weeks, but as a result caught
cold, fell ill, and died. Foxe did not hesitate to include him, as
well as his brother Robert, among the martyrs who had given
their lives for the Protestant cause.[2]

Robert Samuel, the vicar of Bargholt near Ipswich in Suffolk,
had been active as a Protestant preacher under Edward VI, and
had married a wife. When Mary became Queen, and he was
ordered to throw his wife out of his house, he kept her secretly
hidden there. A local JP, Master Foster, who was anxious to
show that he was a zealous Catholic, was told that Mrs Samuel
was in the house. Many of Samuel's parishioners were Protes-

tants who admired him, but others, under the influence of the propaganda against married priests, were indignant that their vicar should keep his wife on the premises. Master Foster feared that if he attempted to carry out a raid on Samuel's house there might be a riot between Samuel's supporters and his opponents; so he waited until after dark, and sent in a raiding party in the middle of the night. They drove Samuel's wife out of the house, and took Samuel to Ipswich jail, where they chained him, standing, to a post, and kept him very short of food. He was then brought before the Bishop of Norwich, John Hopton, who was Queen Mary's chaplain. Hopton condemned him as a heretic, and he was burned at Ipswich on 31 August 1555.

As he was being taken through the town on his way to the stake, a young woman, Rose Nottingham, ran up to him, breaking through the cordon of guards, and kissed him. She was gone before they could arrest her. Orders were immediately given to search for her and seize her, but she did not go to her home, and hid in the houses of her Protestant friends in Ipswich. Two of her friends were Anne Potten and Joan Trunchfield. Joan was the wife of a shoemaker of Ipswich. Rose Nottingham advised both women to leave their homes and escape, but they refused to go. Joan Trunchfield said that she knew that flight from persecution was justifiable, and that Rose had been right to go into hiding; but she herself would not leave her home because she had young children and could not expect her husband to care for them.

Trunchfield had to take care of the children when Joan and Anne Patten were arrested and imprisoned in Ipswich jail. They were condemned as heretics, but it was not until February 1556 that they were both burned in Ipswich.

The authorities never caught Rose Nottingham. She remained in hiding in Ipswich throughout the rest of Mary's reign, and lived to tell the whole story to John Foxe in Elizabeth I's Protestant England.[3]

CHAPTER 8

The Heretics at Oxford

THE TIME HAD COME at last to burn the three arch-heretics in Oxford. Cranmer, Ridley and Latimer had been waiting to be burned ever since they had been condemned as heretics in the disputation in April 1554. They had been separated from each other; Cranmer was imprisoned in the common jail, which was known as Bocardo; Ridley was confined in the house of Master Edward Irish, who was an alderman on the Oxford city council; and Latimer was held prisoner in the house of another city official. They were not allowed to receive visitors, and were deprived of their books, including the Protestant communion service of 1552, and of all writing materials.

Everything possible was done to discourage and humiliate them. On the day after they had been condemned as heretics in the disputation, there was a procession through the streets of Oxford with Weston, who had presided at the disputation, carrying the Host on high for all the people to see, kneel and worship. For Cranmer, Ridley and Latimer this was an act of idolatry which they thought they had abolished and prohibited by the legislation of Edward VI's reign; it marked the victory of their Catholic opponents and the ruin of all their hopes. The authorities decided to force the three heretics to watch it.

The procession passed Bocardo, and Cranmer was taken to the window to see it. When it passed Irish's house Ridley was brought to the door of the house to watch it from there. Latimer was taken to the Carfax to see it pass. Cranmer and Ridley watched in silence, but when Latimer saw it at the Carfax he broke loose from his guards and ran into a shop, shouting that he refused to witness this idolatry.

Ridley, in Irish's house, suffered from the further disadvantage that Mrs Irish was a devout Catholic who, knowing that Catholics were not supposed to have any contact with heretics, did everything she could to show her loathing and contempt for him. Being a gentleman, he could not be deprived of his servant Bernher, who was free to come and go from the house, and could, and did, smuggle in writing materials to Ridley, and smuggle out Ridley's letters to Cranmer, Bradford, and other Protestants in England and abroad. In these letters Ridley urged his fellow-Protestants to stand firm and refuse to recant when they were confronted with the grim choice: 'Turn or Burn.'

A few weeks later the restrictions on the prisoners were tightened. One night a piece of coal fell out of the fireplace in Ridley's room in Irish's house and started a fire which had to be extinguished. The false rumour spread in Oxford that this had been part of a plan for Ridley to escape from prison. After this Bernher was not allowed to leave Irish's house but was himself held there as a virtual prisoner. As Ridley could no longer obtain writing materials he surreptitiously broke off a piece of lead from the leaded lights in the window of his room, and used it to write on the toilet paper that he was allowed to have; and Bernher somehow still succeeded in smuggling Ridley's letters and theological treatises out of the house.

At Michaelmas 1554 Alderman Irish was elected Mayor of Oxford. He continued to enforce all the restrictions on Ridley which had been prescribed by the authorities, but otherwise he did not treat him harshly. Even Mrs Irish thawed towards Ridley after a time. Despite all the regulations of the Church against contact with heretics, she eventually became quite fond of him.

Ridley heard about the controversies which were taking place among the English Protestant refugees in Frankfurt-am-Main in Germany. Richard Cox, who had been the Protestant Dean of Westminster under Edward VI and had escaped abroad illegally when Mary became Queen, came into conflict in Frankfurt with John Knox about the form of service which the refugees should adopt. Cox wished to use the service of the English Second Book of Common Prayer; Knox favoured a more Presbyterian service. Ridley told the refugees in Frankfurt that as the official Protestant service of the Germans in Frankfurt differed only in inessentials from the English Protestant service, the English refugees should obey the authorities there and adopt the Frankfurt service, just as he had thought that John à Lasco's congregation of foreign Protestants in London under Edward VI should have been forced to adopt the English service of the Book of Common Prayer.

If the government had had to deal only with Ridley and Latimer, they might have burned them earlier, for they would probably have handed them over to Gardiner and Bonner to deal with by the usual procedure. But it was another matter in Cranmer's case, for Cranmer had been consecrated as Archbishop of Canterbury in 1533 before the break with Rome, and with the Pope's consent. A special procedure had to be adopted for Cranmer. Pope Paul IV appointed James Brooks, who had succeeded Hooper as Bishop of Gloucester, to act as judge at Cranmer's trial for heresy, which was held in St Mary's Church in Oxford on 12 September 1555. Thomas Martin and Story, who were both doctors of the Roman civil law, appeared as counsel for the prosecution.

Martin subjected Cranmer to a brilliant and merciless cross-examination, asking him about his marriage to 'Black Joan of the Dolphin' in Cambridge forty years before; his second marriage as a priest in Germany; his false oath of obedience to the Pope at his consecration, when he had made a secret protestation that he did not intend to be bound by this oath; the three conflicting opinions which he had held during the last twenty years about the presence of Christ in the sacramental bread and wine, and the part that he had played in the trial of Lambert in 1538, when Lambert was burned for holding the same opinion about the Real Presence which Cranmer himself now held.

Cranmer gave a piteous exhibition; he was utterly broken by his imprisonment, by the humiliations heaped upon him, and by the defeat of all his hopes; and the fundamental weakness in his character, his hesitations and his doubts were clearly displayed. But he steadfastly refused to recant and to acknowledge Papal Supremacy and the Real Presence. He was condemned as a heretic. He was informed that he could appeal to the Pope by appearing in the Papal court in Rome within eighty days, but when he asked to be released from prison so that he could go to Rome, his request was refused.

Ridley and Latimer were tried separately three weeks later. Cardinal Pole, as Papal Legate, issued a commission to John White, Bishop of Lincoln, Bishop Brooks of Gloucester and John Holyman, Bishop of Bristol, to sit in judgment, with White presiding. Ridley was tried first. At 8 a.m. on 30 September he was brought before the commissioners in the Divinity Schools where the disputation of April 1554 had been held; on this occasion too there was a hostile audience there. As Ridley was brought in he raised his cap from his head as a sign of respect for the judge who had been appointed by the King and Queen to try the case, and at the reading of Philip and Mary's commission; but when the name of the Papal Legate, Cardinal Pole, was mentioned, Ridley replaced his cap on his head. White ordered him to remove it. Ridley said that he would willingly pay his respects to Pole as a man because of his learning and royal blood, but would not salute him as Papal Legate. White said that although Pole deserved to be respected for his learning and royal blood, he must be shown even greater respect as Papal

Legate, and again ordered Ridley to remove his cap. Ridley
again refused. White told an usher to pull Ridley's cap off his
head, and it was not returned to him until after the end of the
trial.

After Latimer's trial had opened in the afternoon, Ridley's
trial was resumed next day 1 October, and Latimer's trial
continued that afternoon. White told Ridley that he had been
condemned as a heretic in the disputation in April 1554 for
denying the Real Presence, that there could be no further
argument about this, and that unless Ridley recanted he would
be condemned and burned as a heretic; but he urged Ridley
to acknowledge Papal Supremacy and the Real Presence, and
told him that the Queen would pardon him if he recanted.
Ridley refused to recant, denounced both Papal Supremacy
and the Real Presence, and asked to be allowed to address the
court and justify his attitude. White told him that he must be
brief, but that he would allow him to speak forty words on the
subject. After Ridley had spoken for a few minutes Weston,
who was sitting in the audience, cried out that Ridley had
spoken not forty but four hundred words already, and White
refused to allow Ridley to continue speaking. He then condemned Ridley as a heretic. When it was Latimer's turn, he
was as usual boisterous and defiant, and he too was condemned as a heretic.

On 15 October Ridley and Latimer were degraded from
the priesthood, but not as bishops, because the authorities did
not recognise them as bishops, as they had been consecrated
when the realm was in schism from Rome. After Ridley had
been degraded by Bishop Brooks, he asked to speak to
Brooks, who replied that as Ridley had been condemned
as a heretic he could not speak to him. Ridley persisted, and
asked Brooks to intervene on behalf of his sister Alice and her
husband George Shipside, and his other tenants in London.
When Bonner became Bishop of London again, he treated as

void all the leases granted by Ridley when he was bishop, on the grounds that Ridley's appointment, after Bonner was deprived, was illegal. Ridley pointed out that neither his sister, his brother-in-law, nor any of his other tenants had been responsible for Ridley's religious doctrines, and that it was unjust to eject them from their property in London without any compensation; and he asked Brooks to remind Bonner that when Ridley had replaced Bonner as bishop he had paid £55 (over £15,000 in terms of 2001 prices) to Bonner's creditors in London. Brooks said nothing to encourage Ridley to believe that his request would be granted, and the Shipsides and Ridley's other tenants obtained no redress from Bonner.

Ridley's relations in Northumberland who were Catholics, like most of the inhabitants of the north, interceded with Queen Mary on his behalf. The leading local magnate there, Lord Dacre, who was related to Ridley by marriage, is said to have offered Mary £10,000 if she spared Ridley's life; but she refused to pardon him unless he recanted. Ridley rejected all the efforts of King Philip's Spanish friar, Pedro de Soto, to persuade him to recant. Latimer refused even to see Soto.

On the evening before his execution, Ridley was entertained at an excellent supper in Irish's house which Mrs Irish had prepared. Mr and Mrs Irish and Shipside attended the supper. Ridley was in the best of spirits, and said, like so many other Protestants, that he regarded his martyrdom next day as his marriage. He said that he hoped that both Shipside and Alice would be present at his 'marriage' and Shipside promised that they would be there. Mrs Irish was very moved, and sad that Ridley was to die.

That night he wrote his 'Last Farewell', in which he reviewed the events of his life and saluted many of his acquaintances. He greeted especially his sister Elizabeth, who had married her cousin John Ridley of Walltown in Northumberland and lived with him there. Ridley wrote that he and Elizabeth had always been very close.

He had a good night's sleep, and next morning walked happily to the stake, which had been prepared in the ditch just outside the northern wall of the city near Balliol College. Latimer walked behind him more slowly, because he was old and infirm. Ridley looked back and saw him and called out: 'Oh, be ye there ?' 'Yea,' replied Latimer, 'have after as fast as I can follow.' As they passed Bocardo they looked up, hoping to see Cranmer and wave farewell to him; but Cranmer was busy in conversation with Soto, who was trying to convert him. The authorities had, however, arranged that Cranmer would be brought out on to the parapet of Bocardo to see Ridley and Latimer burned. They thought that this might have a good effect on him and induce him to recant, because they realised that he was not a man who would enjoy watching a burning.

The High Sheriff of Oxfordshire, Lord Williams, was in charge of the execution; he was a typical nobleman who loyally performed his duty under every Protestant or Catholic sovereign. When Ridley reached the stake he handed Lord Williams his petition to the Queen on behalf of Alice, Shipside and his other tenants in London. Shipside was present, but Alice could not bear to come, and Shipside asked Ridley to forgive her for this. Shipside had bribed the executioner to allow Ridley to hang a bag of gunpowder around his neck.

There was the usual sermon before the burning. It was preached by Dr Richard Smith, a learned Oxford theologian who had denounced Papal Supremacy under Henry VIII; but as his attitude to the Reformation under Edward VI had been a little equivocal, he had been deprived of his professorship at Oxford which was given to Peter Martyr. Under Mary he was

The martyrdom of Dr. Ridley and Mr. Latimer at Oxford, Dr. Smith preaching at the time of their suffering.

reinstated, and argued against Cranmer, Ridley and Latimer in the disputation of April 1554.

At the burning of Ridley and Latimer he preached for three hours while the two heretics waited for their dreadful death. Smith said that he hoped that no one would think that, because Ridley and Latimer were prepared to undergo a painful death for their beliefs, they should be praised as martyrs. It was not the manner of death but the justice of the cause for which the victim died that made him a martyr. The Christians who had been burned by the Caesars in ancient Rome had been martyrs because they died for Christ's truth; but Ridley and Latimer would die, not for truth, but for their heresy. Far from deserving praise for this, Ridley and Latimer, who knew that their lives would be spared if they recanted, had in effect, by refusing to recant, committed the sin of suicide.

When Smith had at last finished, Ridley asked if he could reply; but Lord Williams said that he could speak only if he recanted, which he refused to do. He and Latimer were then fastened to the stake. Just before the faggots were lit, Latimer said to him: 'Be of good comfort, Master Ridley, and play the man; we shall this day, by God's grace, light such a candle in England as I trust shall never be put out.'

When the fire was lit, it burned fiercely around Latimer. He held his hands in the flames, and stroked his face with his burning hands; but the flames rose quickly and soon engulfed him. He was almost immediately suffocated by the smoke; he lost consciousness, and died soon afterwards. But on Ridley's side the fire burned slowly. They had surrounded Ridley with gorse, and on top of the gorse they had laid faggots; but though the gorse burned well, the faggots had been piled so thick above the gorse that the flames could not burn through them. Soon Ridley's legs were burning, but the flames did not rise higher to the rest of his body and to the gunpowder around his neck. Ridley screamed in pain, 'I cannot burn', and then called loudly on God to sustain him in his agony.

Shipside rushed forward to try to end his torments. He seized faggot after faggot and threw them around Ridley's face and head, as he wildly added fuel to make the fire burn faster. But the faggots which Shipside piled on only deadened the fire still more; the flames could not rise, while the burning gorse set fire to the bottom of the faggots and burned off Ridley's legs. Ridley was moving under the faggots which covered him, and he cried out: 'For God's sake, let the fire come unto me!' As he turned and writhed in pain, the spectators could see that he was not burning at all above the waist, and that even his shirt was untouched. He was still quite conscious, and called out 'I cannot burn', and then found relief in his faith, and cried 'Lord have mercy upon me'. But still he could not die, and with the lower part of his body burned away, he swayed over the chain around his waist, which fastened him to the stake, and seemed about to fall into the flames right over on Latimer's side. Then one of Lord Williams' men-at-arms hauled some of the faggots away with his bill, and the flames leaped upwards. Ridley could see what was happening, and he knew what to do. He swung what was left of him towards the rising flames, and the fire reached the bag around his neck. It touched the gunpowder, which exploded, and he died, and his body fell at Latimer's feet.

Cranmer had watched it from Bocardo, and was overcome with horror. When he was asked what he thought of it, he merely murmured that Ridley's burning had been badly bungled. But the Catholics insisted that it was all Shipside's fault. God had punished Ridley for his great heresies not only by prolonging his agony but by making his own brother-in-law the instrument of his suffering.[1]

A few days after Latimer and Ridley were burned in

Oxford, a Protestant who was much less famous, but just as brave and steadfast, suffered less than twenty-five miles away. Soon after 16 October 1555, William Dighel was burned at Banbury.

The martyrdom of Mr. John Philpot, Archdeacon of Winchster

CHAPTER 9

More Burnings in London

JOHN PHILPOT, the son of a knight of Compton in Hampshire, studied at Oxford and abroad. He became a leading Protestant in the reign of Edward VI, and was appointed Archdeacon of Winchester. He was arrested on suspicion of heresy after he had been one of the few spokesmen who had dared to defend the Protestant position in the disputation in Convocation in October 1553. He was imprisoned in the King's Bench prison in London.

Under Edward VI, Philpot had played an active part in denouncing the Anabaptists Joan Bocher and George van Parris and in justifying their execution. He had no hesitation in burning 'Arians' who questioned the divinity of Christ, or denied that Christ, the Son of God, had been born as a man to the Virgin Mary. When the burning of heretics under Mary began in 1555, the authorities arrested another Arian heretic and imprisoned him in the King's Bench prison where Philpot was also a prisoner. When Philpot met the Arian in the prison, he spat in his face.

Some of the other Protestant prisoners did not approve of what Philpot had done. They did not think that this was the right way to behave towards a fellow prisoner who was also accused of heresy. So Philpot wrote a book in his prison, *An Apology of John Philpot written for spitting upon an Arian, with an invective against the Arians, the very natural children of Antichrist*. In the sixteenth century the word 'apology' did not have the meaning it has today, but meant 'justification'; and Philpot, far from apologising, justified his action.

What faithful servant can be content to hear his master
blasphemed? and cannot you, good Christian brethren and
sisters, bear with me when, for the just zeal of the glory of
my God and Christ, being blasphemed by an arrogant,
ignorant and obstinately blinded Arian . . . did spit on
him?

He hoped all Christians would do the same, and would spit not
only on Arians but also on all other heretics.

Our God is a jealous God, and requireth us to be zealous in
his cause . . . Canst then be angered with thy brother, being
lawfully called to be a minister in Christ's Church and to be
a teacher in the same, for spitting at an obstinate adversary
of Christ, refusing to obey the truth? . . . Thus have I
touched to give you warning, how to behave yourselves
with the Arians and other adversaries and heretics.

He went on to comment that he was sure that the authorities
would treat heretics like the Arian much more leniently, 'than
the poor faithful afflicted flock of Christ'. But he need not have
worried about this. A few weeks later the Arian was burned at
Smithfield. Philpot himself was burned there on 18 December
1555.[1]

On 12 November 1555 Gardiner died in the Queen's palace of
Whitehall, at the age of 58, from the dropsy from which he had
suffered from time to time. He had shown great courage and
resilience in resisting the disease during his last days. He was
given a great state funeral. There was a requiem Mass in St Paul's
Cathedral, where Bonner officiated, which was attended by the
bishops, lords and MPs; dirges were sung in every parish church
in London; and Gardiner's body lay in state for two days in his
church of St Mary Overy in Southwark. In February, when the

floods had subsided sufficiently to make it possible to travel, the body was taken to Winchester and buried in a splendid tomb in the cathedral.

Gardiner was succeeded as Bishop of Winchester by White, the Bishop of Lincoln, and as Lord Chancellor by Heath, the Archbishop of York. Heath was a far less forceful character than Gardiner; but Gardiner's death did not lead to any relaxation of the campaign to suppress heresy, which was carried on as energetically as ever by Bonner and above all by the Queen.

During the winter, seven Protestants were arrested in London. Thomas Whittle was a priest in Essex; John Tudson of Ipswich and John Went of Langham in Essex were both skilled craftsmen who had come to London to work; Thomas Brown of Histon near Cambridge lived in the parish of St Bride's off Fleet Street in London; Isabel Foster also lived in the parish of St Bride's. She was a woman aged fifty-five who had been born at Greystock in Cumberland but had come to London to marry a cutler. Joan Lushford was a young woman, the daughter of Elizabeth Warne by her first marriage; Joan's mother and stepfather, Elizabeth and John Warne, had both been recently burned for heresy. Bartlet Green was a gentleman and a barrister of the Temple. He had come under suspicion because he had been in contact with Christopher Goodman, who had gone abroad illegally without a passport and was playing a leading part among the Protestant refugees in Geneva, though he had not yet written the book which made him one of Mary's greatest enemies.

These seven heretics were all burned together in one fire at Smithfield on 22 January 1556.

Soon afterwards, four women and one man were burned in Canterbury. John Lomas, a young man from Tenterden, refused to go to confession and denied the Real Presence. Agnes Smith, a widow of Smarden, also refused to confess to a priest; she said that in the communion service she received the Sacrament as Christ and his apostles did, not in the manner in which it was now received in the Church in England. Joan Sole of Monks Horton denied the Real Presence; so did Joan Catmer of Hythe, a widow whose husband had recently been burned as a heretic. Anne Albright was particularly defiant; when her interrogators asked her why she refused to go to confession, she replied: 'You priests are the children of perdition, and can do no good by your confession'. The five were burned in Canterbury on 31 January 1556. They all sang psalms together as they were burning in the fire.

CHAPTER 10

The Great Miscalculation

MARY AND HER GOVERNMENT and the Spanish friars in Oxford had forced Cranmer to watch the burning of Ridley and Latimer because they thought that it would bring home to him what it meant to be burned alive, and would make him more likely to recant in order to avoid a similar fate. But they had miscalculated. Soto had been encouraged by his talks with Cranmer; he felt that, unlike Ridley and Latimer, there was some hope that Cranmer might recant. But when he spoke again with Cranmer after the burning of Ridley and Latimer he found that Cranmer was more determined to resist and to suffer as his two colleagues had done. Soto reported to Pole that Cranmer was an obdurate heretic who would never be persuaded to recant.

This was probably not unwelcome news for Queen Mary and Pole. They knew that it was their religious duty, as good Catholics, to persuade Cranmer to recant and thereby save his soul from Hell; but in the sixteenth century, as in earlier and later times, religious duty often gave way to the cold calculations of power politics. A recantation from Cranmer might have some propaganda value; but it would be much better to burn him. What a splendid gesture it would be to burn the Protestant Archbishop of Canterbury for heresy! How it would bring home to the people the wickedness of the leaders of the Protestant Reformation, and that Protestants who had been elevated to the highest positions in the Church were nothing better than the lowest and most contemptible criminals and would be treated as such.

If we study the events of the winter of 1555-6 and the actions of Mary and Pole and the government in Cranmer's case, it is difficult to avoid the conclusion that they wanted to burn Cranmer; and it would be much easier to burn him if he did not recant. Although there was nothing in law to prevent the government from burning a heretic who had recanted, it had become the established practice that any heretic, apart from a relapsed heretic who had already once been condemned and pardoned, could save his life by a recantation. But though Mary and Pole would really have preferred it if Cranmer did not recant, they could not admit this even to themselves, and certainly not to their subordinates; so the officials and the Spanish friars in Oxford continued to make every effort to persuade Cranmer to recant.

The authorities now proceeded to treat Cranmer in a manner worthy of expert interrogators in the secret police of a modern totalitarian state. They combined the most harsh and subtle physical and psychological cruelty with kindness and better treatment; while one interrogator was brutal, another was apparently kind and understanding.

We know all about it from a contemporary manuscript which is headed *Bishop Cranmer's Recantacyons*, and was obviously written by a Catholic who was in close contact with Cranmer in his Oxford prison. The author was probably Alan Cope, who was sent to Oxford by the government in order to deal with Cranmer. He was violently hostile to Cranmer, whom he damned in his book in the most violent language, and his explanation conflicts with the traditional and over-simplified explanations given both by Foxe and the Catholic writers; but there is no reason to doubt that what he wrote was the truth. Not only is it very plausible – more plausible than the usual Protestant and Catholic propaganda versions – but it shows, without intending to do so, that the authorities pursued a policy of calculated cruelty towards a lonely and broken old man whom they hurt in every way they could.

Cranmer, as a devoted servant of his sovereign and believer in the duty of Christian obedience, wrote a respectful letter to Mary, urging her to assert and defend her royal supremacy over the Church of England and not to submit to the domination of the Bishop of Rome. When Mary received the letter she said that she considered it a sin to read, or even to receive, a letter from a heretic, and handed the letter to Pole for him to reply to Cranmer. Pole had once been a brilliant polemicist who had denounced the tyranny of Henry VIII; but now, in his letter to Cranmer in November 1555, he wrote nothing but vulgar abuse, insulting his aged and defeated opponent as a hardened sinner who would obviously never repent. There could have been nothing more painful for Cranmer, after he had appealed to his Queen to assert her royal supremacy against the foreign Pope, than to receive a reply from the Bishop of Rome's Legate informing him that the Queen had asked him to reply to Cranmer's letter to her.

Although Soto had given up, Cranmer was targeted by a brilliant young Spanish friar, Brother Juan de Villa Garcina, who had come to England with King Philip and had been appointed Regius Professor of Divinity at Oxford before he was aged 30. Garcina made every effort to induce Cranmer to recant, not realising that Mary did not wish him to do so. Even if Garcina had known this, it might not have deterred him, for he was a man of some independence of mind; a few years later, after he returned to Spain, he was denounced as a heretic to the Inquisition.

The experts in psychological pressure now decided to substitute kindness for harshness. Cranmer was released from his prison in Bocardo, and sent to the house of the Dean of Christ Church. Here he was well fed, and was allowed to associate with the fellows of the college and play bowls on the college green. Garcina visited him in Christ Church, and felt that he was continuing to make progress with him. Meanwhile the Pope confirmed the sentence condemning Cranmer as a heretic, and Cranmer's effigy was burned in Rome. It was perhaps because the appeal to the Pope had been dismissed, and he had now been irrevocably condemned as a heretic, with whom Christians were not supposed to associate, that he was removed from the Dean of Christ Church's house and sent back to Bocardo. Or was it a calculated step by experts in psychological warfare?

The change from the kind treatment at Christ Church to prison life in Bocardo had a depressing effect on Cranmer; but the governor of Bocardo, Woodson, was a kind man, and in his rough, layman's way did his best to persuade Cranmer to recant. Alone in his prison, with no contact with the outside world, Cranmer made the mistake – which political prisoners today know is a fatal one – of making a friend of his jailer. He came to depend completely on Woodson's friendship.

On the evening of 28 January 1556 Woodson lost patience. He told Cranmer that as he was clearly an obstinate heretic he would not speak with him any more. Cranmer was shattered. In the middle of the night Woodson heard him weeping and groaning in his bed. When he went to see what had happened, Cranmer said that he wished to recant, and in the middle of the night wrote out his first recantation. He stated that he would accept the supremacy of the Pope because the King and Queen had ordered him to do so, and that he would always obey the orders of his sovereigns.

In the eyes of the Catholics, this recantation was insufficient, as it accepted Papal supremacy for the wrong reasons. So Garcina asked him for more, and better, recantations, and pressed him harder than ever; and Cranmer, having once given way, proceeded quickly to yield on every point. He asked permission to carry a candle at Candlemas on 2 February, and signed three more recantations, each more abject than the last.

But in January 1556 there was an ominous development. It had hitherto been the invariable practice, after a heretic had been condemned by the ecclesiastical court, that no preparations were made for burning him until the case had been referred to the Queen, who might wish to pardon him. A royal proclamation now stated that after a heretic had been condemned, he could be burned immediately without referring the matter to the Queen. The proclamation did not go so far as to say that a heretic should be burned even if he recanted; but it was a move in this direction.

Despite Cranmer's recantation, the next step was taken, and as a heretic he was degraded from all his ecclesiastical offices, including that of an archishop consecrated with Papal consent. The degradation ceremony was performed by Bonner and Thomas Thirlby, the Bishop of Ely; they had travelled from London to Oxford for the purpose. Bonner had never concealed his hatred for Cranmer; Thirlby had been Cranmer's friend and protégé, and thanks to Cranmer's influence had been appointed Bishop of Westminster by Henry VIII; and when his bishopric was abolished under Edward VI, Cranmer saw to it that he became Bishop of Norwich. After Mary became Queen he was appointed Bishop of Ely.

Foxe and other Protestant writers stated that Bonner behaved brutally to Cranmer at the degradation proceedings, deliberately cutting his fingers when he scraped them to remove the consecrating oil, and gloating over Cranmer's downfall; but even if these stories are exaggerated or untrue, nothing could have been more wounding for Cranmer than to have the degradation carried out by his bitterest enemy and his ungrateful friend.

Early in March Cranmer, who was completely cowed, signed his fifth recantation. It was as complete as any Catholic could have wished, and Garcina, delighted, arranged for it to be printed and given the widest publicity. The Protestants immediately denounced it as a forgery.

To Garcina's surprise, the Privy Council summoned the printer of the recantation to appear before them and ordered him to destroy all copies of the recantation and not to circulate it. No official reason for this order was given, but the French ambassador reported, and the rumour spread, that it was because the recantation had been witnessed by a Spaniard, Garcina, and that the government feared that this would make the people doubt its authenticity and hold the hated Spanish foreigners responsible for the persecution of heretics. No contemporary commentator suggested the reason, which was first put forward by historians in the nineteenth century and is generally accepted today, that it was because the publication infringed the copyright of the official printer; and this is very unlikely. It was probably because Mary and Pole did not want it to be known that Cranmer had recanted, which would make it more difficult to burn him.

But once the news of the recantation had spread and the Protestants had denounced it as a forgery, the government was forced to change its policy. They decided to take the unprecedented step of publicizing the fact that Cranmer had recanted but to burn him just the same. On 17 or 18 March Dr Henry Cole arrived in Oxford; he had been chosen to preach the sermon when Cranmer was burned. He had held various important ecclesiastical appointments in London and Oxford under Henry VIII and Edward VI, when he had supported the break with Rome and even the earliest stages of the Reformation under Edward VI. Under Mary he was equally ardent in supporting Papal Supremacy and the Real Presence and in denouncing heretics, and as a result had been appointed Archdeacon of Ely and Provost of Eton College.

Foxe and the other Protestant propagandists wrote that Cranmer was not told that he was going to be burned until 20 March, the day before his execution, and that when he signed a sixth, and even more abject, recantation on 18 March, it was because he had been promised that his life would be spared if he recanted; but according to the author of *Bishop Cranmer's*

Recantacyons, Cole told him when he arrived in Oxford on 17 or 18 March that he would be burned, and Cranmer knew this when he signed the sixth recantation. This is strong evidence, because it would have suited this author very well if he could have claimed that Cranmer only signed the sixth recantation in the hope of saving his life, which was the line that Mary's government afterwards put forward.

Cranmer was in an agony of indecision. He could not decide whether he would go to Heaven or to Hell if he remained a Protestant or recanted and became a Catholic. After he had signed the fifth recantation he had a dream in which he saw two kings wrestling together for his soul; one of the kings was Jesus and the other was Henry VIII. It had at last occurred to Cranmer, at least in his sleep, that service to Henry VIII had not always been compatible with service to Christ.

Cranmer told Cole that he had one request to make. His wife Margaret had escaped illegally from England, and was living safely in the Protestant states of Germany; but he was worried about his son, for after Cranmer's conviction for high treason all his property had been forfeited to the crown, and he feared that his son would be left penniless. He asked Cole to intercede with the Queen to allow his son to retain part of his property. This favour was often shown to the sons of convicted traitors; but Cranmer should not have expected that it would be granted to the son of a married priest. Cole told him sternly to forget about the son of his sinful marriage and to concentrate on saving his soul by recanting.

Cranmer had a sister, Alice, who was a good Catholic. She became a nun, and in 1534, thanks probably to Cranmer's influence, she was made prioress of a convent in the Isle of Sheppey, which was suppressed a year later. She received a pension of only £14 a year because she had been prioress for such a short time. She came to visit Cranmer in Bocardo, and tried unsuccessfully to intercede for him with Pole, and apparently lost her pension because of this.

Some of the Protestant exiles wrote to Mary from abroad reminding her how Cranmer had interceded for her with Henry VIII in 1536, when Henry had wished to send her to the Tower because of her refusal to admit that she was a bastard. 'I doubt not but that Your Grace knoweth of it', wrote the author of *A Supplicacyon to the Quenes Maiestie*, 'and therefore I trust Your Grace will requite him with mercy, and not suffer that wicked Bishop of Winchester to work his wicked will and purpose of him.' But Mary, as usual, refused to read any letter from a heretic.

The authorities had decided that Cranmer should read out a statement at the stake before he was burned; it would be published, with his six recantations, as his Seventh Recantation. He discussed the wording with Cole, Garcina, and Roscius, another Spanish theologian who had arrived in Oxford. In this 'Seventh Recantation' he declared that he believed in all the doctrines of the Catholic Church, and stated that there was one thing that most troubled his conscience,

> more than any other thing that ever I did, and that is, the setting abroad untrue books and writings, contrary to the truth of God's word, which now I renounce and condemn, and refute them utterly as erroneous and for none of mine. But you must know also what books they were, that you may beware of them . . . for they be the books which I wrote against the Sacrament of the Altar since the death of King Henry VIII.

He ended by stating that he believed in the Real Presence.

Cole and the Spanish friars left this copy of his final speech with Cranmer as he prepared for his last night on earth. But it was now that something happened which his persecutors could not explain, and which no historian for 450 years has been able to explain. During the night, four hours before he was due to be taken from Bocardo to the stake, a messenger called at Bocardo and brought Cranmer a message from his sister. The author of *Bishop Cranmer's Recantacyons* wrote that it was not the Catholic sister, but another one (Cranmer in fact had several sisters), and added that the sister's messenger 'brought him a ring, but I do not know with what instructions. This ring seemed to be the first sign of evil.'

Who sent the ring? What was its significance? Did it remind him of some childhood experience which only he and his sister knew about? Only two people knew, and they both died before the end of the sixteenth century, and their secret has died with them. But that ring changed Cranmer's mind, and it changed the course of history. During the next three hours Cranmer wrote out another and very different version of the statement that he was to make at the stake, and hid this new statement in his bosom.

It was raining on the morning of Saturday 21 March 1556, as it had so often rained during that wet spring. It had therefore been decided that the sermon which preceded the burning, which would normally have been delivered at the stake, would take place in the shelter of St Mary's Church. It might also mean that the 150 faggots of wood and furze which had been brought for the execution would be wet, and burn slowly, so that Cranmer would suffer the slow and dreadful death that Hooper and Ridley had endured.

Cranmer walked through the rain from Bocardo to the church with Garcina and Roscius, the two Spaniards, on either side of him. In the church, he was made to stand on a raised daïs. Lord Williams again did his duty by presiding at the ceremony; he had been ordered to bring an unusually large number of men-at-arms with him in case the Protestants tried to make any kind of demonstration at the burning.

Dr Cole's sermon was even more vicious than his audience expected, for he had to try to explain the unprecedented action

of burning a heretic who had recanted. He said that Cranmer
had repented of his heresies and died reconciled to the Church,
and therefore Masses would be held in every church in Oxford
with prayers for his soul; but he explained that Cranmer's
heresies were so wicked that even though he had recanted he
would have to be burned. Then Cole made an extraordinary
statement. He said that the deaths of those two blessed martyrs
Sir Thomas More and Cardinal Fisher of Rochester had to be
atoned for; the death of the layman More had been atoned for by
the death of the layman Northumberland, but the death of the
cleric Fisher would have to be atoned for by the cleric Cranmer.
This is the version given by the author of *Bishop Cranmer's
Recantacyons*. Foxe's version makes Cole's statement even worse.
According to Foxe, Cole said that the death of Sir Thomas More
had been atoned for by the death of Northumberland, but that
the execution of so worthy a man as Fisher was not sufficiently
atoned for by the death of the three bishops Hooper, Ferrar and
Ridley, so Cranmer must be added to even the balance. Let us
judge Cole on the report of his Catholic supporter and not of his
Protestant enemy, and assume that he demanded only an eye for
an eye and not four eyes for an eye; the fact remains that the
burning of Cranmer, after he had recanted, was justified by Cole
the official government spokesman, in his sermon, as an act of
vengeance.

It was now Cranmer's turn to make his statement which
would be published as the Seventh Recantation. He began as the
friars and his audience expected, with a declaration of his belief
in Jesus Christ and his repentance for his sins; but then he
concluded:

And now I come to the great thing which so much
troubleth my conscience, more than anything that ever I
did or said in my whole life. And that is setting abroad of a
writing contrary to the truth, which now here I renounce

and refuse as things written with my hand contrary to the truth which I thought in my heart and written for fear of death, and to save my life if it might be. And that is all such bills and papers which I have written or signed with my hand since my degradation, wherein I have written many things untrue. And forasmuch as my hand offended, writing contrary to my heart, my hand shall first be punished therefor, for, may I come to the fire, it shall be first burned. And as for the Pope, I refuse him as Christ's enemy and Antichrist, with all his false doctrine. And as for the Sacrament, I believe as I have taught in my book against the Bishop of Winchester, the which my book teacheth so true a doctrine of the Sacrament that it shall stand at the last day before the judgment seat of God, where the Papistical doctrine contrary thereto shall be ashamed to show her face.

He was not allowed to complete his statement. When he reached the point where he said that the Pope was Antichrist, uproar broke out in the church, and he was forcibly dragged from the stage. They took him to the place of execution and fastened him to the stake. He took the text of the statement which he had made in the church, and which he had hidden in his bosom, and threw it into the crowd. A man whose initials were J. A. picked it up and made a copy of it, for although J.A. was a Catholic, he was impressed by Cranmer's courage, and wished to preserve a copy of his speech, though he knew that it was illegal and dangerous to do so; and thanks to J.A. it was possible for Foxe to see it and publish it, and for future generations to know exactly what Cranmer said.

When the faggots were lit, Cranmer held his hand steadily in the flames. Once he withdrew it to wipe his face – or was it because of the pain? – but he immediately replaced it in the fire and he did not move it again. He cried out: 'I see Heaven open

The martyrdom of Dr. Thomas Cranmer at Oxford.

and Jesus on the right hand of God.' The Catholics were shocked that he could tell such a lie, when in fact he was on the way to Hell. They found something in the ashes which they thought was Cranmer's heart, and said that it could not burn because it was so wicked.

As a propaganda exercise, Cranmer's death was a disaster for Mary. Two days later, the official government printer published *All the Submissions and Recantations of Thomas Cranmer*, including the Seventh Recantation – Cranmer's statement at the stake – in the form in which it was not delivered. But an event which has been witnessed by hundreds of people cannot be kept secret and the news quickly spread that Cranmer had repudiated his recantations before he died. The government then changed their line; they admitted that Cranmer had retracted his recantations, and argued that this showed that his recantations were insincere, that he had recanted only to save his life, and that they had been justified in burning him despite his recantations. The Protestants then circulated the story of Cranmer's statement at the stake in an improved form; they spread the rumour that Cranmer had denied at the stake that he had ever signed any recantations, and that the alleged recantations had all been forged by King Philip's Spanish friars.

The events of 21 March 1556 shook the government. Three days later, the Venetian ambassador reported that the effect of all the contradictory stories had been to discredit the Queen and to make everyone believe that the authorities could not be trusted, as they obviously did not speak the truth. He told the Doge that there had been demonstrations against the government in some of the churches.

Perhaps if Cranmer had lived longer he would have changed his mind again. But he died a Protestant, and by his weakness, his hesitation and his indecision he in fact did more harm to Mary's régime than if he had suffered with the constancy of his fellow-martyrs. Foxe, who had strongly condemned Cranmer for the part that he had played in burning Protestants under Henry VIII, summed up the Protestant view in his *Book of Martyrs*:

> Lest he should have lived longer with shame and reproof, it pleased God rather to take him away, to the glory of His name and profit of His Church. So good was the Lord both to His Church, in fortifying the same with the testimony and blood of such a martyr, and so good also to the man, with this cross of tribulation to purge his offences in this world, not only of his recantation, but also of his standing against John Lambert and Master Allen, or if there were any other, with whose burning and blood his hands had been before anything polluted. But especially he had to rejoice, that dying in such a cause, he was to be numbered amongst Christ's martyrs, much more worthy the name of St Thomas of Canterbury than he whom the Pope falsely before did canonize [Thomas Beckett].[1]

CHAPTER 11

The Unpopular Queen

MARY HAD DECIDED to appoint Cardinal Pole to succeed Cranmer as Archbishop of Canterbury. But Pole, though he had been a cardinal for nineteen years, had never been ordained as a priest. On 20 March, the day before Cranmer was burned, Pole became a priest, and three days later Archbishop of Canterbury.

Pole was not a ferocious persecutor. He offended the Protestants by ordering that three foreign Protestants, who had died during the reign of Edward VI, should be posthumously tried and condemned as heretics, their bodies disinterred and burned, and their ashes thrown on to a dunghill.[1] But even Foxe admitted that Pole preferred burning dead than living heretics.

Pole had undoubtedly wished to burn Cranmer and, after Mary herself, was chiefly responsible for the unprecedented decision to burn a heretic who had recanted; but this was a case where he allowed the necessities of power politics to prevail over his more humanitarian instincts. He had, after all, been accused of being too soft towards heretics when he was governor of Viterbo, and could not afford to be accused of this again.

Nearly everyone in England in 1556 accepted the fact that heretics would be burned. The burning of heretics had been going on throughout their lifetime and their fathers' and grandfathers' lifetimes, for the last 150 years. But the scale of the persecution was something new. Mary was burning far more victims than any earlier sovereign. Sixteen heretics had been burned in 39 years under Henry IV, Henry V and Henry VI. Henry VII burned 12 heretics in 24 years. Henry VIII burned 90 in 37 years. Two Anabaptists were burned for heresy by Northumberland's government during Edward VI's six-year reign. But in the year that had passed since the first burning of Rogers the protomartyr, Mary had burned 88 heretics − 16 at Smithfield, 16 in Essex, 3 in Middlesex, 3 in Hertfordshire and 1 in Westminster, a total of 39 in Bonner's diocese of London; 26 in Kent, of which 23 were in the diocese of Canterbury; 4 in Sussex; 3 in Oxfordshire, Cambridge-shire and Warwickshire; 2 in Staffordshire, Suffolk, Norfolk and South Wales; and 1 in Gloucestershire and Cheshire.

The burnings went on. John Maundrel was the son of a farmer of Rawle in Wiltshire, but he moved to the village of Buchampton (today Bulkington) in the parish of Keevil near Trowbridge, where he married and farmed his smallholding. He was an independent-minded and rather truculent local firebrand who was prepared to stand up for what he thought was right and would not knuckle under to anyone. He could not read or write, but when he heard that Tyndale had translated the Bible into English he bought a copy and carried it around with him; and when he met someone who was literate he asked him to read passages aloud. After a while he had learned large parts of the Bible by heart.

He had got into trouble nearly twenty years before, when he had criticised holy bread and holy water, and had been ordered to walk through Devizes on market day dressed in a white penitent's garb carrying a candle; but in 1556 he was as troublesome as ever. He became friendly with two other Protestants. John Coberley was a tailor, and John Spicer was a skilled mason; Foxe called him a freemason. This was before the time when gentlemen who believed in religious toleration and in a simple all-embracing deism had taken over the lodges of the working masons. When people in 1556 called Spicer a freemason they meant that he was an operative freestone-mason who worked in the soft freestone which was used for work on the face of the churches and cathedrals. The freestone-masons were the most highly skilled workers of the building trade.

Maundrel, Spicer and Coberley met in Bulkington for secret

Protestant prayer-meetings; but when they heard that the Catholic vicar of Keevil had organised a procession in the town the following Sunday and that a statue of a local saint would be carried through the street to the church followed by the people worshipping it, they decided to make a public protest. They went up to Master Robert Berksdale, a prosperous tradesman who was the most important man in Keevil, and demanded that he order the people to abandon this idolatrous worship of the saint, to halt the procession, and to worship again the living God as they had done under Edward VI; but Berksdale paid no attention to them, and ordered the procession to continue.

After the procession had reached the church and the people had assembled there, the vicar arrived and began the service with prayers for souls in Purgatory; but Maundrel, Coberley and Spicer marched into the church. When the vicar mentioned Purgatory, Maundrel interrupted him, shouting out that Purgatory was the Pope's pinfold (the pound in country districts where stray cattle were rounded up and confined). Spicer and Coberley joined in, loudly repeating that Purgatory was the Pope's pinfold. The vicar ordered them to be arrested and placed in the stocks, where they remained till the church service was finished. They were then brought before the local JP, who next day sent them to Salisbury to be examined by the Bishop.

The Bishop of Salisbury was the very aged John Capon, who was sometimes called Salcott, because he was a native of Salcott near Colchester in Essex. He was nearly ninety – a very great age in the sixteenth century – and was already a monk in the Benedictine monastery in Colchester in 1488. In due course he became a doctor of divinity at Cambridge, and as his brother was Cardinal Wolsey's secretary he was soon appointed to important positions. He strongly supported Henry's divorce from Catherine of Aragon and the break with Rome, and, thanks to Cranmer's influence, became Bishop of Bangor. When the Act of the Six Articles was passed, and the Protestant Shaxton resigned as Bishop of Salisbury, Capon succeeded him, denouncing both the Pope and Protestant heretics during the last years of Henry VIII, but accepting the Protestant Reformation and continuing in office under Edward VI.

Under Mary he became a firm supporter of Papal supremacy. He was excused from attending her coronation because of his great age, but he felt young enough to take his place among the judges who tried and condemned Hooper for heresy, and he was young enough now, with the assistance of his Chancellor, to examine Maundrel, Coberley and Spicer, the farmer, the tailor and the mason who would not accept the authority of the Church. When he asked them what they believed, they said that they believed in the Bible from the Book of Genesis to the Apocalypse. Capon told them that this was not what was required, but that they should believe that the Pope was the head of the Church and should also believe in the Real Presence. Maundrel said that the Pope had usurped the power of Emperors and Kings, and that the Queen was the Head of the Church of England, though Capon denied that a woman could be the Head of the Church; and Maundrel said that he believed in a spiritual, not a corporal, Presence. He volunteered the statement that a wooden image of a saint was good enough for roasting a leg of mutton but should not be worshipped as an idol. As Coberley and Spicer supported his attitude, all three were condemned as heretics.

When the men-at-arms came to arrest Coberley, his wife declared that she, too, was a Protestant, and she was taken with him to the county jail in Salisbury. The jailer's wife was a good Catholic and felt bitter about the three Protestants who had brawled so disgracefully in the church during the service in Keevil. She was eager to teach Mrs Coberley a lesson. She heated a key in the fire, and placed it on the lawn in front of the jail, and told Mrs Coberley to fetch it. When Mrs Coberley picked up the key, it burned her hand, and she cried out in pain. 'You drab,' said the jailer's wife, 'you cannot bear the pain of a burned hand; how do you suppose you will be able to stand the pain when your whole body is burned at the stake?' Mrs Coberley was shaken by the experience and by the arguments of the jailer's wife, and after she had been subjected to repeated pressure she agreed to recant.

Her husband was more steadfast. On 24 March 1556 – three days after Cranmer was burned – he was taken with Maundrel and Spicer to a place outside Salisbury on the road to Wilton where the stake had been prepared. The three men were fastened to two stakes and told that they would be pardoned if they recanted. They all refused. Maundrel, as usual, was particularly defiant; when asked if he would recant, he replied, 'Not for the whole of Salisbury.'

Maundrel and Spicer both died quite quickly in the fire, but Coberley's death was prolonged and horrible; because of the wind, the fire did not reach his body, but only his left arm. After a while the arm was burned off, and he leaned over the fire, holding his right arm in the flames, hoping that they would reach his body. The blood then began to pour out of his mouth and nose, and he fell into the fire. Everyone thought that he was dead, but he was still alive. After a while he rose and stood upright in the fire to the amazement and horror of the spectators. Then he died.[2]

The burnings went on. People were beginning to say that they should stop. Some of them said this too loudly and too openly for the government's liking; in London there were sometimes protests from the spectators when a heretic was burned. In January 1556 the Privy Council sent instructions to the Lord Mayor and Sheriffs of London that, 'when any obdurate man condemned by order of the laws shall be delivered to be punished for heresy, that there be a good number of officers and others who are appointed to be at the execution'; and they were to arrest and imprison those people who 'shall misuse themselves either by comforting, aiding or praising the offenders or otherwise use themselves to the ill example of others'.[3]

More heretics were burned in April 1556. Six men of Essex, in Bonner's diocese, were arrested on suspicion of heresy. Most of them were tracked down by Rich, though Edmund Tyrrel also played his part. The six victims as usual varied in their rank and occupations. Robert Drakes had been a Protestant vicar under Edward VI; he was learned enough to be able to quote Latin texts when he was examined by Bonner. He said to Bonner: 'As for your Church of Rome I utterly defy and deny it, with all the works thereof, even as I deny the Devil and all his works.'

William Tyms was the curate of Hockley. He was questioned first of all by Tyrrel. 'Why, sir,' he said to Tyrrel, 'in King Edward's days you did affirm the truth that I do now.' Tyrrel said that in his heart he never believed the Protestant doctrine. 'Well then,' said Tyms, 'I pray you, Master Tyrrel, bear with me, for I have been a traitor but a while, but you have been a traitor six years.' Tyrrel sent him to Bonner, who urged him to believe in the Real Presence, which was supported by the authority of the Catholic Church. 'No,' said Tyms, 'you have the Popish Church of Rome for you, for which you be perjured and foresworn. And the see of Rome be the see of Antichrist.'

Richard Spurge was a shearman; John Cavel was a weaver; Thomas Spurge and George Ambrose were fullers who shrunk and thickened cloth. Ambrose was sufficiently educated and daring to tell Bonner that he repudiated Papal Supremacy because he had read Gardiner's *De Vera Obedientia*. All six were condemned as heretics, and were burned together in one fire at Smithfield on 6 April 1556.

Later in April six more martyrs suffered. Christopher Lyster was an agricultural labourer at Dagenham; Steven Joyce was a sawyer who sawed wood; John Mace was an apothecary; John Spencer and Richard Nichols were both weavers; John Hamond was a tanner who turned hides into leather. Mace, Spencer, Nichols and Hamond all came from Colchester. All six were burned together at Colchester.

In the diocese of Rochester another woman was burned. Joan Beech, a widow of Tonbridge, and John Harpole of Rochester were burned together at Rochester on 1 April. John Hullier, who had been educated at Eton and at King's College, Cambridge, was burned for heresy at Cambridge on Maundy Thursday, 2 April.

In May Hugh Laverock of Barking, a lame old man of sixty-eight, and John Aprice, a blind man, were arrested and sent to be examined by Bonner on a charge of heresy. They were both condemned, and burned together in one fire at Stratford-at-Bow on 15 May. After they had been fastened to the stake, just before the faggots were lit, Laverock called out to Aprice to take comfort from the thought that Bonner had been a good physician to them both, for he would shortly put an end to Aprice's blindness and Laverock's lameness.

In Gloucester the blind boy, Thomas Drowry, who had been imprisoned as a heretic and had been comforted by Hooper before Hooper was burned, was still in prison, and was kept there for more than a year after Hooper suffered. But he did not escape the fire, and was burned in Gloucester in the same fire as a bricklayer, Thomas Croker, on 15 May 1556.

There were more burnings in the diocese of Norwich. Thomas Spicer, a boy of nineteen, was an agricultural labourer employed by his master, a farmer, and living in his master's house at Winston in Suffolk. He was a convinced Protestant, and refused to go to church because he would not be present at Mass. Some JPs denounced him, and men-at-arms were sent to arrest him in his master's house. They broke in at dawn while Spicer was still in bed. He was taken with two other Protestants, John Denny and Edmund Poole, to Beccles in Suffolk to be examined by the Bishop of Norwich's Chancellor. They all denied the

Real Presence and refused to recant. Poole said that they
believed in the Catholic Church, but not in the Popish Church.
They were burned together in the same fire at Beccles on 21
May.

In Essex Edmund Tyrrel and another JP arrested four women
and sent them to Bonner. Katherine Hut of Bocking was an
elderly widow; Joan Horns and Margaret Ellis of Billericay, and
Elizabeth Thackvil of Great Burstead, were young unmarried
women. Old Katherine Hut told Bonner that she did not believe
that the bread and wine of the Sacrament were Christ's body. 'I
deny it to be God, because it be a dumb God and made with
men's hands.' Young Joan Horns was just as forthright. 'If you
can make your God to shed blood, or to show any condition of a
true living body, then will I believe you; but it is but bread and
that which you call heresy I trust to serve my Lord God in.'
Bonner condemned them all as heretics. Margaret Ellis died in
prison, but the other three survived to be burned together in one
fire at Smithfield on 16 May.

On 6 June thirteen martyrs were burned together at Stratford-
at-Bow, after they had all been condemned as heretics by
Bonner; it was the largest number that had ever been burned
in one fire during Mary's reign. They all came from various parts
of Essex. Eleven were men – a weaver, a smith, a serving man, a
tailor, a sawyer, and several agricultural labourers. Two of them
were young married women, Elizabeth Pepper, the wife of a
weaver of Colchester, and Agnes George, the wife of an
agricultural labourer of Great Barefield. Eighteen women had
now been burned.

At a time when people were becoming increasingly angry that
so many heretics were being burned, Miles Huggarde set out to
destroy any sympathy they might have for the Protestants.
Huggarde had originally been a shoemaker of Pudding Lane
in London, but by 1556 he was well known as a Catholic
pamphleteer, and he had no difficulty in obtaining a licence from

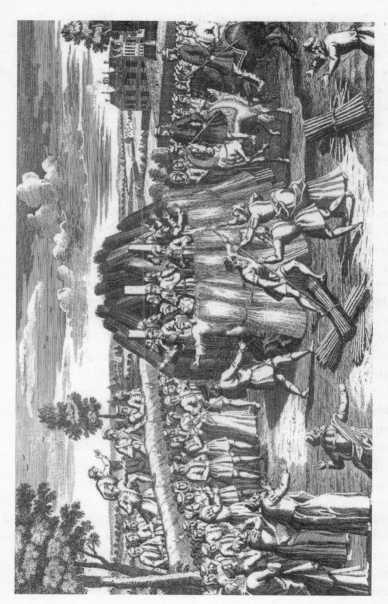

The burning of thirteen martyrs at Stratford-at-Bow.

the Privy Council to publish his book, *The Displaying of the Protestants*, which he dedicated to Queen Mary. Huggarde denounced the hypocrisy of the Protestants in weeping over the sufferings of their martyrs when they themselves, in the reign of Edward VI, had without compunction burned Joan Bocher and George van Parris as Anabaptists and Arians; and he ridiculed those Protestants who had claimed, absurdly and blasphemously, that one of the pigeons which had flown over the fire in which their protomartyr Rogers had been burned was the Holy Ghost who had come to carry Rogers' soul to Heaven.

But Huggarde's chief target was Protestant women. Several women had been burned as martyrs for obstinately asserting their Protestant beliefs; but what business had women to argue with bishops and learned Catholic doctors on theological matters? The wives of the married Protestant priests were their harlots; but it was not only the wives of the priests, but all Protestant women who were harlots. It was thanks to the Protestant women that so many Protestant men refused to recant when they were offered the Queen's pardon if they did; they chose instead to die in the fire because their wives exhorted them to remain steadfast to their beliefs and suffer martyrdom; and the wives did this because they wanted their husbands to be burned so that they could get rid of them and elope with a new lover.[4] But many people did not believe Huggarde's propaganda, and did not believe the proclamations and official statements of Mary and her government.

There were several burnings in the diocese of Chichester in the summer of 1556. Bishop George Day, who had been deprived of his bishopric under Edward VI for opposing the removal of altars, and reinstated by Mary, was vigorously dealing with heretics during the last weeks of his life. In June four heretics suffered at Lewes. Thomas Harland was a carpenter of Woodmancote near Henfield. John Oswald, who also came from Woodmancote, was an agricultural labourer. Thomas Avington of Ardingly was a turner who operated a lathe used for cutting wood. The fourth man was Thomas Read. They had all been arrested by the JPs some time before they were burned; they had been sent up to London to be examined by Bonner, and stoutly denied the Real Presence.

Read decided to recant and go to hear Mass in a Catholic church; but then one night he had a dream, in which he saw a group of young men dressed in spotless white. In his dream he wished to join them, but could not do so because his white clothes were soiled with dirty black spots. He realised that this was because, in his dream, he had attended a Catholic church where Mass was being celebrated. When he awoke from his dream he decided that he would not recant.

Bonner sent the four heretics to Bishop Day in Chichester, who sent them to Lewes, where they were burned together in the same fire on 6 June. Later in June Thomas Athoth, a Protestant priest, and Thomas Milles were also burned in Lewes.

Soon afterwards the authorities arrested three Protestants in East Grinstead, Thomas Dungate, John Foreman, and an old woman, Anne Tree. When Anne Tree was examined by Day's Chancellor in Chichester, she said that she believed in the doctrines taught by Thomas Athoth, and that she would not go to Mass or to confession. Her interrogators reminded her that Thomas Athoth had already been burned for heresy, and that if she shared his beliefs she too was a heretic. They were shocked by her fearless and aggressive manner, which had attracted the attention of her neighbours and which she continued to show towards the theologians and lawyers who questioned her in Chichester. She was condemned as a heretic and sent back to East Grinstead, and burned there in the same fire with Foreman and Dungate on 18 July.

In September four more heretics were burned in the diocese of Chichester. John Hart, a shoemaker of Withyham, and Thomas Ravensdale of Rye, a currier who dressed tanned leather, were burned with two other martyrs whose names

Foxe did not know, but were probably John Milles of Hellingly and John Ashton of Rotherfield. They were burned together in one fire at Mayfield in Sussex on 25 September.

There were other burnings in the summer and autumn of 1556. In June, an agricultural labourer aged twenty-four and a merchant's servant were burned in Leicester, and three men were burned at Bury St Edmunds. In September a man aged sixty-nine was burned in Bristol, and a man and a woman were burned together in one fire at Wootton-under-Edge in Gloucestershire; in October, a shoemaker was burned in Northampton.

An unusual type of martyr suffered in July 1556. Julins Palmer was the son of a former mayor of Coventry. He went to Magdalen College at Oxford and was a student there in the reign of Edward VI. He took a dislike to the Protestants who were being given offices in the university, and became known in Oxford as a Catholic critic of the Protestant Establishment. He denounced and mocked them, accused them of being unprincipled careerists, and said that none of them would be prepared to suffer death for their beliefs if the Catholics came to power again.

Then someone distributed in the college a poem criticising the Protestant President of the college. Many people, knowing that Julins Palmer was a poet, thought that he was responsible for the poem, though he denied it. But they did not believe him, and for this, and for his defiant attitude, he was expelled from the college.

When Mary became Queen, he was reinstated and praised as a Catholic who had opposed the Protestant Reformation under Edward VI; but when she began to burn Protestants, Palmer did not like it. He heard about the courage of the Protestant martyrs at the stake, and felt that he had done them an injustice when he had said that they would not be willing to suffer for their beliefs. He was shocked when he heard reports of Hooper's slow and agonising death, and he sent a man to Gloucester to find out if these reports were true. The man returned to Oxford and told Palmer that he had spoken to several people in Gloucester who had been present when Hooper was burned, and they all confirmed the stories of his prolonged suffering in the fire.

When Palmer, in Oxford, heard that Ridley and Latimer were to be burned in the city, he went to watch, so that he could see for himself what really happened when heretics were burned. He witnessed Ridley's dreadful torments in the fire, and how the well-intentioned efforts of Ridley's brother-in-law Shipside had only made things worse. He was horrified, and called out in indignation: 'O raging cruelty! O tyranny tragical and more than barbarous!'

The authorities at Oxford were not pleased when they heard how Palmer was criticising the burning of heretics. He had a talk with Alan Cope, who had come to Oxford to deal with Cranmer, and Cope advised him to leave Oxford and take employment as a schoolmaster in Reading. His disgust with the persecution led him to repudiate the Pope and accept Protestant doctrines. When he visited his mother and told her that he had become a Protestant, she drove him out of the house; but as he sadly walked away without reproaching her, she relented and threw a coin after him and wished him well.

Palmer's statements about religion in Reading aroused the suspicions of the authorities, and he was sent to Newbury to be examined by the Bishop of Salisbury's officials. He told them that he had repudiated the Pope and the Real Presence, and he was eventually condemned as a heretic. He was taken to be burned at the end of July at a place called the Sandpits just outside Newbury, in the same fire as two other heretics. After they were fastened to the stake, one of the Sheriff's men-at-arms, who hated heretics, picked up an unlit faggot and threw it violently in Palmer's face. It cut open his face, and the blood gushed out of his nose and ears. The Sheriff was indignant at the action of the man-at-arms, and struck him on the head with his staff, so that he, too, was bleeding from the head. When the faggots were lit, the fire raged around the three heretics, and they fell down under the burning faggots. All the spectators thought that they were dead; but then Palmer arose, lifting his burning body up from underneath the faggots. He could hardly speak, but he was seen moving his lips, and appeared to speak the word 'Jesus' before he died.[5]

The Channel Islands were in Mary's realm, and in the summer of 1556 a case arose in Guernsey which had repercussions which continued after Mary's death in the reign of Elizabeth I. A woman named Katherine Cowchen lived in St Peter's Port with her two daughters, Perotine and Guillemine. Perotine became involved with a woman, Vincent Gosset, who stole a gold goblet and tried to sell it to Perotine; but Perotine informed the authorities, and Vincent Gosset was arrested and flogged. In revenge she denounced Katherine Cowchen and her two daughters as heretics, and the three women were convicted of heresy and sentenced to be burned. Perotine did not tell the judges at her trial that she was pregnant.

When the faggots were lit, the heat of the fire caused Perotine to give birth to her baby son, who fell on to the faggots while the flames burned around him. One of the spectators rushed forward to save the baby, and pulled him out of the fire, and laid him on the grass. A man-at-arms picked him up, and he was handed from one official to another till he was given to the Sheriff in charge of the execution. The Sheriff ordered his men to throw the baby back into the fire, and he was burned with his mother, his grandmother and his aunt.

After Elizabeth I became Queen, the Protestants prosecuted the Sheriff for murdering the baby. The Sheriff said that he had thought that as the baby had been in the mother's womb when she was sentenced to be burned as a heretic, the baby had also been sentenced to death; but he now admitted that he had acted wrongly. He was convicted of murder, but granted a pardon.

The case involved John Foxe in a controversy with Thomas Harding, who had supported the Protestant Reformation under Edward VI, but became a Roman Catholic under Mary, and

continued to be a Catholic under Elizabeth I, when he emi-
grated to the Netherlands and joined the Catholic propagandists
at Louvain. Harding wrote that Perotine was a whore, and that
her baby was illegitimate. If she had told the judges at her trial
that she was pregnant, they would not have burned her until
after her baby was born; but she did not tell them because she did
not wish to compromise her reputation and the reputation of
Protestant women. Foxe wrote that this was a wicked libel on
Perotine, who was a married woman; he stated that he had met
her husband, a man called Massey, the father of the baby who
had been murdered by the Sheriff.[6]

Apart from the heretics who were burned, many of them died in
prison. The Protestants often accused the authorities of deliberately starving them to death, or of having killed them by brutal ill-
treatment; but even if some of these stories were exaggerated, the
number who died in the jails show that their treatment was harsh,
and that conditions in the prisons were severe.

One of the most prominent of these victims was John
Careless, a weaver of Coventry, who was arrested on a charge
of heresy and sent to the King's Bench prison in London.
Despite his lack of education and his humble occupation, he
held his own very skilfully in his arguments with the learned
theologians who interrogated him; and he wrote many letters to
Protestants, including some of their famous leaders, in which he
comforted them and urged them to be steadfast. The fact that he
died in prison before he could be burned did not prevent Foxe
and the Protestants from praising him as a martyr.

Public opinion turned against Mary in 1556. By a strange
coincidence, the length of her reign, just over five years, was
about the same as the maximum term for which a government is
elected in a general election in the United Kingdom at the
beginning of the twenty-first century. Mary came to power in
July 1553 on a wave of popular enthusiasm. Six months later,
some of her supporters became disillusioned when she decided

to marry Philip of Spain, and they tried to overthrow her by an insurrection; but the people again rose in her support, and approved when she crushed the rebellion and executed the defeated rebels. When she began burning Protestants, the victims and their friends indignantly protested, but most of the people still supported Mary, and thought that the heretics who were burned got what they deserved. The people could admire a Queen who was so strong and dominating that she was prepared to force the dissident minority to obey her, however much they howled. Why were these Protestants so arrogant and opinionated that they chose to be burned when they could have saved their lives by recanting? Why did they not do as the ordinary Englishman did, and change their religion when they were ordered to do so by the government?

Then things began to go wrong. First there was the fiasco of Mary's pregnancy. The church bells had rung in London, and the whole country celebrated, when it was announced that she was pregnant, and everyone assumed that there would be even greater celebrations when the child was born. But there were no celebrations, only rumours. Why was there no official explanation of what had happened? Were the Protestants right, after all, when they whispered that the Queen was a hysterical woman who had imagined that she was pregnant when in fact she could never have a child?

But the Protestants were troublemakers, and the ordinary Englishman was still prepared to give Mary the benefit of the doubt. They would support her against the whining minority, and did not seriously object to the burning of heretics in the summer of 1555. But Mary's policy of burning both the highest and the lowest, both the most eminent and the most obscure, had drawbacks; and the decision to burn Cranmer despite his recantation, and the even greater fiasco of the official attitude to the events at Oxford on 21 March 1556, caused a very sharp fall in the Queen's popularity as she approached the third anniversary of her coming to power. If an Archbishop of Canterbury could be burned, although he had recanted, because he had once been a heretic, would even the most powerful lord and gentleman be safe if he had supported the break with Rome and the Reformation under Henry VIII and Edward VI?

And the search for heretics in the villages all over England went on and on. Was it really necessary to burn quite so many troublesome young louts and so many silly old women? These burnings were not being carried out by a great English King like Henry VIII, who had shown the French and the Scots that the English were the masters, but by a foreign King and his doting wife, by Spanish friars and by a Queen who wanted to bring England under the rule of an Italian Pope. Whatever the truth may have been about Cranmer's recantation, it was clear that the government had lied; and if they had lied about the burning of Cranmer, why should people believe anything they said?

In August 1556 a heretic was burned in Derby whose fate aroused great sympathy and indignation among increasing numbers of people. Joan Waste, who was a twin, was born blind. Her father was a barber in Derby who supplemented his income by making ropes. He loved his blind daughter very much, and was determined to do all he could to enable her to live a happy and normal life. He taught her to knit and sew, and to make ropes by feel. She became a very skilled ropemaker; people said that she made the best ropes in Derby. Her father told her little brother Roger to look after her, and lead her by the hand when she wished to move about the town. After her father and mother died, Joan and Roger lived together, and he continued to lead her by the hand.

During the reign of Edward VI they went regularly to church to attend the Protestant church service. Joan wished to learn the text of the Bible. Being blind she could not, of course, read herself, but she saved up the money which she made from her ropemaking and bought a copy of Tyndale's New Testament.

An old man of seventy was in prison in Derby for debt, and Joan visited him in the jail and asked him to read the Bible aloud to her, which he did. She also found other people who were prepared to read the Bible to her; in some cases she paid them to do so. She learned long passages from it by heart.

When Mary became Queen, Joan continued to recite passages from the Bible to her acquaintances, and she was denounced to Baines, the Bishop of Coventry and Litchfield, and examined by him, his Chancellor Dr Draycot, and other officials. She said that she did not believe that the consecrated bread in the Sacrament was the body of Christ. They asked her why she did not realise that as Christ had been able to change water into wine and raise Lazarus from the dead, he could also turn the sacramental bread into his body. She replied that being a poor, uneducated, blind woman she could not argue with them, but as Dr Rowland Taylor had been prepared to die for his beliefs, she was ready to do the same. At one point it seemed as if Baines might persuade her to recant; but then Draycot intervened, and persuaded Baines that she was an obstinate heretic who must be condemned.

Before she was burned on 1 August 1556, Draycot preached the execution sermon in a church in Derby. He said that she was not only blind in her body but blind in her soul, and would burn not only at the stake but eternally in Hell. Her brother Roger was allowed to take her by the hand and lead her to the stake in the Windmill-pit outside the town of Derby, just as he had always led her everywhere. As she could not see him, he stood beside the fire calling out to her while she was burning, so that she should know that he was there.

Many people were disgusted by Draycot's conduct, and by his sermon. The story spread that while Joan was being burned, Draycot went to a local inn, got drunk, and slept soundly on the lawn in front of the inn. In the fire Joan called on Jesus to help her, and her lips were seen to move and repeat the word 'Jesus' until she died.[7]

CHAPTER 12

The Continuing Persecution

EVERYONE KNEW THAT THE CARDINALS in Rome received a 'pension' – another word for it might be a bribe – from the great European rulers for protecting their interests at the Papal court. For many years before Henry VIII broke with Rome the Bishops of Salisbury and Worcester were Italian cardinals who never visited their English dioceses, which were administered for them by subordinates, while the bishops received the revenues of their sees in return for representing the King of England in Rome. Several cardinals received pensions from the Emperor Charles V; but Cardinal Giovanni Caraffa, Archbishop of Naples, received a pension from the King of France.

In March 1555 Pope Julius III died. Charles V was not pleased when Cardinal Marcello Cervini was elected as Pope Marcellus II on 9 April, because when Cervini was President of the Council of Trent[1] he had advocated the supremacy of the Pope over temporal rulers with such vigour that he seemed to be challenging the Emperor's authority; but Marcellus II died on 30 April, twenty-one days after he was elected. It was the shortest pontificate in the history of the Papacy, and was not equalled even in 1978, when Pope John Paul I died thirty-three days after his election. In the election of Marcellus's successor, Charles V, Philip and Mary used their influence to try to get Pole elected as Pope, and he was apparently only two votes short of the number required to obtain the Papacy; but the cardinals elected Cardinal Caraffa, who became Pope Paul IV.

Caraffa was aged seventy-nine when he was elected Pope. He came from a noble Neapolitan family, and his uncle had been a prominent cardinal. He had an enormous appetite for food which made it easy for his enemies to accuse him of gluttony; and he had a violent temper, sometimes indulging in outbursts of rage. He was a particularly savage persecutor of heretics. Charles V, Philip and Mary did not object to him on these grounds, but they strongly objected to a Pope who received pensions from the King of France. Nearly forty years earlier, Caraffa had been Papal Nuncio in both England and Spain, but afterwards he decided to support French interests in Rome. People thought that, as a Neapolitan, he resented the fact that the Kingdom of Naples was ruled by the King of Spain; and this, and his French pension, made Charles V regard him as quite unacceptable. Charles announced that he would veto Caraffa's election; but however unwise it might be to antagonise Charles, no law of the Church required the Emperor's consent to the cardinals' choice of Pope.

Pole was very distressed at the split that was dividing Catholic Europe. In May 1555 he presided at a meeting held at Marcq in the English territory around Calais where he tried to persuade the envoys of the Emperor and the King of France to make peace and end their quarrels. But he failed completely in his attempts to bring about a reconciliation between France and the Empire. He commented sadly that this was a situation from which only the heretics could benefit.

In October 1555 Charles V abdicated the government of his territories in the Netherlands and in Naples in Philip's favour, and in January 1556 he also granted his kingdom of Spain to Philip. He gave the Empire and his possessions in Austria and Germany to his brother, the Emperor Ferdinand I.

Philip's relations with Paul IV became very bad. When Philip discovered that the Pope had made a secret treaty with Henry II of France by which they agreed to make war against Philip and conquer Naples, he ordered the Duke of Alba, his commander-in-chief in Naples, to invade the Papal States. Henry II then sent a French army under Francis of Lorraine, Duke of Guise, across the Alps to support the Pope. Alba had overrun the Papal States before Guise arrived, but on Philip's orders he did not enter the city of Rome.

Philip insisted that he was a devoted son of the Church. He said that if a dutiful son saw his father go mad and brandish a knife he would rush forward to snatch the knife from his insane father's hand; so he, seeing the Holy Father go mad and make an alliance with France, had sent Alba's army to prevent this act of insanity. In the summer of 1557 Philip came to England again in order to persuade Mary to declare war on France. Pole strongly urged her not to do so.

Then Henry II allowed Thomas Stafford, who was related to Pole, to sail from Dieppe with a small number of followers to liberate England from Spanish domination. Stafford landed in Yorkshire and captured Scarborough Castle; but he was quickly taken prisoner, sent to London, convicted of high treason, and hanged, drawn and quartered. This decided Mary; she declared war on France, and Philip returned to the Netherlands.

Paul IV, thinking that Pole was too sympathetic to Philip and Mary, deprived him of his position as Papal Legate in England. In his place he appointed William Peto. Thirty years before, Peto had been Mary's confessor when she was a child. In 1532 he preached against Henry VIII's divorce from Catherine of Aragon in a sermon at Greenwich, and went abroad, where he stayed for twenty years, denouncing Henry for repudiating Papal supremacy. In his absence he was sentenced to death in England as a traitor by an Act of Parliament. When Mary became Queen he returned to England, and Mary appointed him Prior of his old monastery in Greenwich, which was one of the few monasteries which she restored, granting it the monastic lands which were still held by the crown.

In June 1557 Paul IV created Peto a cardinal, and sent an envoy to take the cardinal's hat to him. Mary announced that if the Papal envoy landed in England the envoy would be arrested.

Mary and her government hoped that they could win popular support, and arouse English nationalist feeling and hatred of the French, by portraying King Philip as a second Henry V invading France, where he would be the great victor in another Battle of Agincourt. For a brief moment they thought that they had succeeded. When Mary and Philip rode through the streets of London together after the declaration of war against France on their way to Greenwich, where he said goodbye to her before leaving England for the Netherlands, the people cheered them. The campaign began successfully. Philip's army under his general Emmanuel Philibert, Duke of Savoy, invaded France from the Netherlands, and Mary sent a small force under the Earl of Pembroke to march from Calais to their assistance.

Emmanuel Philibert's army besieged St Quentin in north-eastern France, which was defended by Admiral Gaspard de Coligny, who had not yet openly declared his support for the French Protestants. Henry II sent an army under his famous general Anne, Duke of Montmorency, to relieve St Quentin. On St Lawrence's Day, 10 August 1557, a very bloody battle was fought in the intense summer heat outside the walls of St Quentin. The French were defeated, and Montmorency was taken prisoner. The sufferings of the wounded, as they lay pleading for water under the burning sun, were terrible. Philip joined Emmanuel Philibert's army a few days after the battle, and was present when his army captured St Quentin by storm on 27 August; Coligny was wounded, and, like Montmorency, was taken prisoner. Mary organised great celebrations in England; a *Te Deum* service was held in St Paul's, and all the church bells in London were rung to celebrate the victory. But the English people did not acclaim St Quentin as another Agincourt; they obstinately refused to hail Philip as a second Henry V and a great English King.

Meanwhile the burning of heretics continued throughout 1557. In the diocese of Canterbury, Harpsfield and Bishop

Thornden ('Dick of Dover') were as zealous as ever. During the winter of 1556 they arrested fifteen more Protestant heretics, all of them men. Five of them died of starvation and ill-treatment in prison, and ten were burned in January 1557. Four of them came from Tenterden, two from Biddenden, one from Cranbrook, one from Sellinge, one from Norgate, and one from Hythe. Six of them were burned in Canterbury, two at Wye, and two at Ashford. They were all accused of refusing to accept the supremacy of the Pope, with refusing to attend the Latin Mass, and sometimes with other heresies. In April 1557 three men and two women, who had all been arrested by Rich, were burned together in the same fire in Smithfield; and three men were burned in St George's Fields in Southwark in May.

As the summer went on, the burnings increased. Edmund Allin was a miller at Frittenden in Kent. He sold his corn at half the price which other millers charged, in order to help the poorer inhabitants of the village. But he was denounced by John Tailor, the ardent Catholic vicar of Frittenden, and by the vicar of Staplehurst. He was brought before Sir John Baker, who was still sentencing heretics for believing what he himself had believed under Edward VI. Allin escaped, and fled to Calais, where he met John Webbe, another Protestant from Frittenden, who had also escaped to Calais to avoid Tailor's persecution. After a few weeks in Calais, Allin told Webbe that he was returning to England, 'for God had something to do for him in England'.

Tailor soon heard that Allin had returned to Frittenden, and noticed that Mr and Mrs Allin did not come to Mass in his church. He denounced them to the authorities, and they were taken to Maidstone jail. They were both burned at Maidstone on 18 June 1557 in the same fire with a married couple from Maidstone, a widow from Staplehurst whose husband had been burned in January, another married woman from Maidstone, and a young unmarried woman who was blind.

Next day three men and four women were burned together in Canterbury. One of them was Alice Benden, the wife of a man from Staplehurst. She had two small children, named Patience and Charity. Bishop Thornden came to see the heretics burned. Alice Benden asked him if he would take care of the two children; but Dick of Dover was too cautious to do anything which might make people think that he was a friend of heretics. 'Nay', he said, 'by the faith of my body, I will meddle with neither of them both.'

One of the most remarkable of the Sussex martyrs was Richard Woodman, an ironmaster from Warbleton near Heath-field, who could hold his own in a theological argument as ably as any doctor of divinity. Fairbanks, the vicar of Warbleton, had been an ardent Protestant in the reign of Edward VI, when he had married a wife, and in his sermons had urged his congregation never to abandon the doctrines of the Book of Common Prayer; but that was exactly what he did when Mary became Queen. Fairbanks drove his wife out of the house, recanted, and continued as vicar of Warbleton, officiating at the Catholic Mass.

One day in June 1554 Woodman stood up in the church at Warbleton and denounced Fairbanks for betraying the true religion. Fairbanks now had a good opportunity to prove the sincerity of his conversion; he reported Woodman to the local JPs. They arrested Woodman and sent him to London, where he was imprisoned in the King's Bench prison. After he had been imprisoned there for nearly eighteen months, he was examined by Story, who sent him to Bonner's coalhouse at his palace in Fulham, where he was imprisoned for another month.

This was not the only occasion on which Bonner showed the more patient and less brutal side of his character. After he had examined Woodman on several occasions, he told him that he could go home. Woodman noted that it was on 18 December 1555 and that it was the day on which Philpot was burned. The Catholics afterwards said that Woodman had recanted; and though Woodman strongly denied this, it is difficult to see why Bonner should have released him if he had not made some submission or recantation.

Woodman returned to Sussex, and continued to make Protestant propaganda in Warbleton and the neighbourhood. Reports of his activities were sent to Sir John Gage, the High Sheriff of Sussex, who sent constables to arrest him. Woodman asked the constables if they had a warrant authorising them to arrest him; and when their leader told him that he had left the warrant at his home, Woodman demanded that they fetch the warrant and show it to him. Surprisingly, they went off to fetch the warrant; they were probably overawed by Woodman's personality, his self-confidence, and his superior education. When they returned with the warrant they found that Woodman had gone.

The authorities believed that he was trying to escape abroad, and searched all along the coast between Portsmouth and Dover; but Woodman was hiding in the woods only a few hundred yards from his house in Warbleton. He had his Bible, pen and ink with him in the woods, and stayed there quite happily for six or seven weeks. Then he thought that the search for him had cooled off; he ventured out of his hiding place, reached the coast, and crossed the Channel. He contacted other English refugees abroad, but longed to return to England; he wrote that while he was in France and Flanders, 'I thought every day seven years.'

He returned to England and went to his house at Warbleton. The authorities had searched the house so often without finding him that he did not think that they would search it again, and; he also had a secret hiding place in the house which the constables had never found when they searched it. But Sir John Cage heard that he had returned to England. He sent constables to search the house again. They hid in the bushes near the house so that they would be able to raid it without warning; and they captured two of Woodman's children, and held them, so that that they could not go and warn their father. They then suddenly approached the house. Woodman's little daughter, who was in the house, saw them and called out to her mother that they were coming. Woodman just had time to reach his hiding place; but he had not put on his shoes, though otherwise he was dressed.

Woodman's father, brother and brother-in-law were Catholics, and did not approve of his Protestant proselytising. They had threatened several times to denounce him to the authorities; but his father and his brother-in-law always refrained from doing so. Eventually it was his brother who betrayed him. When the constables were searching the house, the brother showed them Woodman's secret hiding place. As they broke down the entrance, Woodman jumped out and ran out of the house with the constables in hot pursuit. Woodman was a fast runner and if he had had his shoes he would probably have outrun them and escaped; but he found it difficult to run without shoes along the garden path with its sharp cinders, which wounded his feet and slowed him down; so the constables caught him.

They took him to be examined by John Christopherson, who had become Bishop of Chichester after Day died. Christopherson and other learned doctors examined Woodman repeatedly; but he had answers to all their arguments, and they could not shake him. In the end he was condemned as a heretic. He was taken to Lewes and burned there on 22 June 1557, together in the same fire with five other men and four women, some of whom had been arrested only a few days before.[2]

Simon Miller of King's Lynn in Norfolk must have been a simple soul. One day in the spring of 1557 he travelled forty-five miles to Norwich, and stood in front of a church as the people were coming out of the church after Mass. In a loud voice he asked where he could find a place where he could attend the communion service of the Book of Common Prayer. Most of the people just stared at him, aghast at his boldness; but an ardent Catholic, who heard his words, came up to him and said that he would show him the way to a place where he could attend the communion service. He took Miller to the Bishop of Norwich's prison, and told the keeper of the prison that Miller was a heretic who should be examined by the Bishop or his Chancellor. Then they noticed that there was a piece of paper sticking out of Miller's shoe. They pulled it out and read it, and found that Miller had written on the paper that he rejected the Papist Mass. The man who had brought Miller to the keeper of the prison went off, telling the keeper to be sure to take proceedings against Miller for heresy.

But the keeper of the prison must have been either a secret Protestant sympathiser or an easy-going man who thought that Miller was a poor lunatic who should not be treated too harshly. He told Miller to go back to King's Lynn and to behave more sensibly in future. Miller returned to King's Lynn, but a few weeks later he came to Norwich again, and again stood in front of the church as the people were leaving after Mass, and declared his devotion to the communion service of the Book of Common Prayer. He was arrested, and this time he was brought before Hopton, the Bishop of Norwich, who examined him several times. Miller persisted in saying that he rejected the Mass and the doctrine of the Real Presence, and was eventually condemned as a heretic.

He was burned in Norwich on 13 July 1557 in the same fire as Elizabeth Cooper, the wife of a pewterer of Norwich. She had been suspected of being a Protestant heretic, but when she was examined by the authorities she recanted. She blamed herself for having recanted, and one day she walked into a church in Norwich while Mass was being celebrated there. She called out to the people that she retracted her recantation, and denounced the Papist Mass. She was examined by Hopton and condemned as a heretic.

When she stood beside Miller in the fire she was frightened, and cried out as the flames began to burn them both. Miller managed to free one of his arms from the fetters that bound it to the stake, and put it around Elizabeth. He told her not to be afraid, as they were both going to their wedding and would soon be in Heaven. They both died happily in the fire.

Cicely Ormes, a woman aged thirty-two, was the daughter of a tailor of East Dereham, and had married a weaver who lived in Norwich. She went to watch the burning of Simon Miller and Elizabeth Cooper. After they had been burned she called out in a loud voice that she held the same religious beliefs as they did. She was arrested and taken before the Bishop's chancellor. She recanted out of fear, but was then ashamed of having done so, and told the chancellor that she repudiated her recantation. When he asked her what the consecrated bread of the Sacrament was, she said it was only bread, and if anyone pretended that it was something more than this he made it less than bread. She was burned in Norwich on 23 September 1557 at the same place, and fastened to the same stake, where Simon Miller and Elizabeth Cooper had been burned two months before. In the fire she called out, 'My soul doth magnify the Lord and my spirit rejoiceth in God my saviour', and stood motionless in the flames with her hands folded on her breast. She died quickly.

The burnings continued. In September 1556 the authorities suddenly swooped on twenty-three Protestants in Colchester and the neighbourhood who were suspected of heresy. Among them were William Mount, a man aged sixty-one of Much Bentley (today Great Bentley); his wife Alice Mount, aged forty-one; and Alice's daughter by a previous marriage, Rose Allin, an unmarried young woman of twenty. They were rounded up and told that they would be taken to London to be examined by Bonner. One of the twenty-three ran off and escaped, but the other twenty-two – fourteen men and eight women – were tied together and made to walk from Colchester to London. They attracted a good deal of attention in the towns and villages through which they passed, walking two and two hand in hand

and fastened together with ropes; many of the spectators who saw them pass expressed their sympathy for them. When they reached London they were imprisoned near Aldgate.

Soon afterwards all the twenty-two prisoners were released, and told to go home. They owed their release to Cardinal Pole. In the summer of 1556 Pole told Bonner and the other bishops to treat heretics more leniently. It was on Pole's orders that Bonner freed the twenty-two prisoners who had been brought to London from Colchester.

But the authorities continued to keep them under observation. William Mount and his wife Alice, and Alice's daughter Rose Allin, were carefully watched. On the evening of 7 March 1557 Alice asked Rose to fetch her some water from a nearby well, and Rose set out, carrying an iron pot for the water in one hand and a candle in the other. Edmund Tyrrel, who was the local JP, was watching the house with some of his constables. He stopped Rose Allin as she walked to the well. He told her that she should advise her father and mother to abandon their heretical doctrines and become good Catholics. She replied that her father and mother had received better religious instruction than she had, and she was sure that the Holy Ghost would not allow them to err. 'Thou naughty housewife,' said Tyrrel, 'it is time to look upon such heretics indeed.' Rose replied that what he called heresy she regarded as God's truth. 'Then I perceive you will burn, gossip, for company's sake', said Tyrrel. 'No sir', said Rose, 'not for company's sake, but for my Christ's sake.' Tyrrel then turned to his constables and said: 'Sirs, this gossip will burn, do you not think it?' One of the constables said, 'Marry, sir, prove her, and you shall see what she will do by and by.'

This gave Tyrrel the idea of testing her. Seizing the candle that she was carrying, he put her hand in the flame of the candle. A man who lived in Great Bentley happened to walk past, and saw what was happening. Tyrrel held her hand in the flame of the candle for so long that her flesh was burned away as far as the bone; but she did

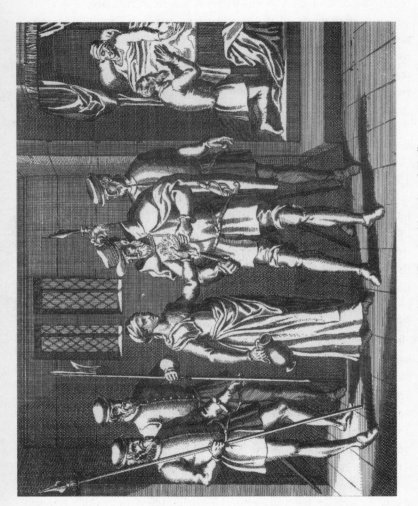

The burning of Rose Allin's hand by Edmund Tyrill.

not cry out. Her silence and courage infuriated Tyrrel. 'Why, whore', he shouted, 'wilt thou not cry? Thou young whore!' She said that she thought that he had more reason to weep than she had. At last he released her hand. She asked him: 'Sir, have ye done what ye will do?' 'Yea,' he replied, 'and if thou think it not well, then mend it.' 'Mend it!', said Rose, 'nay, the Lord mend you and give you repentance, if it be his will. And now, if you think it good, begin at the feet and burn to the head also, for he that set you a work shall pay you your wages one day, I warrant you.'

He let her go, and she carried the water to her mother. Rose afterwards told a friend, who was with her in prison, that at first the pain had been great, but the longer her hand burned the less she felt the pain, and at the end she hardly felt it at all. She also said that all the time that Tyrrel was burning her hand, she held the iron pot in her other hand, and might have struck him in the face with it, for neither he nor any of his constables had made any effort to restrain her hand that held the pot. 'But I thank God', she said, 'with all my heart, I did it not.'

Foxe quotes the evidence of three witnesses to prove the truth of this story: the man from Great Bentley who was passing by and saw it; a woman to whom Rose told the story immediately afterwards and who put ointment on her burned hand; and another woman to whom Rose later told the story in prison. A twentieth-century Roman Catholic historian, after claiming that the story, if true, shows the cruelty of Tyrrel, not the cruelty of the Catholic Church, states that he does not believe it and thinks that Foxe and his three witnesses were all lying. His reason for not believing it is that it resembles other stories about Catholic officials burning the hands of heretics.[3] But there is plenty of evidence to show that, just as Sir Thomas More thirty years earlier, and Bonner, sometimes flogged heretics in the hope that the pain would deter them from continuing to be heretics and would therefore save them from being burned, so several officials burned the hands of heretics to bring home to them the pain that they would suffer at the stake, thinking that this would induce them to recant.

If Tyrrel thought that by burning Rose Allin's hand he had frightened her into submission, he did not know the young woman whom he had tortured. A few months later she was arrested with William Mount and her mother Alice. When the authorities examined her, she was defiant. They asked her what she thought of confession, of going to Mass, and of the seven sacraments. Rose said that they stank in the face of God, and that she would have nothing to do with them. She said that she was not a member of their Church, for they were the members of Antichrist, and that if they did not repent they would have the reward of Antichrist. When they asked her if she would submit to the authority of the see of Rome, she said that she would not obey the Bishop of Rome. 'As for his see,' she said, 'it is for crows, kites, owls and ravens to swim in, such as you be; for by the grace of God I shall not swim in that see while I live, neither will I have anything to do therewith.'

She was burned just outside the walls of Colchester on 2 August 1557. Three men and three women had been burned there at half-past-six that morning. Rose Allin, William and Alice Mount, and another man were burned there the same day in the afternoon. They died peacefully and quickly in the fire.[4]

CHAPTER 13

The Revolutionaries

BY 1556 MARY AND HER GOVERNMENT were dealing with a different class of Protestant from the heretics whom they had so happily persecuted and burned in 1554 and 1555. Their first victims had believed in the doctrine of Christian obedience, and had patiently suffered without resistance, alone or with a few fellow-martyrs, all the taunts and the humiliations inflicted on them, and they had faced their last agony in the fire, confident that they were going to their wedding and would soon be with Christ in Heaven. Two years later the authorities were confronted with heretics who were members of a secret revolutionary organisation dedicated to overthrowing their evil Queen and her government.

The early martyrs did not seek revenge; they forgave their enemies, as Christ had directed them to do, confident that God would punish their persecutors. 'Vengeance is mine, saith the Lord, I will repay.' This was emphasized in the books and pamphlets published by the English Protestants in exile. One of the earliest of them, John Knox's *Letter to the Faithful in London, Newcastle and Berwick*, was published in Dieppe in the spring of 1554. It contained on the front page a poem, *The Persecuted Speaketh*, which was almost certainly written by William Kethe.

> I fear nor for death, nor pass out for bands;
> Only in God I put my whole trust,
> For God will require my blood at your hands;
> And this I know, that once die I must.
> Only for Christ my life if I give;
> Death is no death, but a mean for to live.

This poem became famous among Protestants after February 1555, when Hooper, on the night before he was burned, wrote it with a coal on the wall of his prison, which is today the New Inn in Gloucester. But Hooper, like most English Protestants in February 1555, believed that it was in the next world that God would require the Catholic persecutors to atone for the blood of the martyrs. Only a few Protestants, including Knox, were beginning to wonder whether they themselves should punish their persecutors in this world for the blood of the martyrs that they had shed.

Knox went from Dieppe to Geneva and met Calvin. He asked Calvin to answer these questions: Whether an infant, or a woman, could exercise the sovereign powers of a King; whether powerful nobles, who had armed followers and fortresses, were lawfully entitled to resist an idolatrous King; and what Christians should do if they lived in a country where Christian nobles rose in revolt against an idolatrous King. This was a situation which had arisen in Germany when the Lutheran Princes went to war against Charles V in 1547, and might soon arise again in France, where the King and Queen of Navarre, with their large possessions in south-west France, were likely to go to war against their sovereign, the Catholic King of France, and against their powerful rivals, the Catholic Guises in eastern France.

Calvin told Knox that infant Kings were referred to in the Bible, and that in the Book of Judges God had chosen a woman, Deborah, to lead the people of Israel. He said, very firmly, that under no circumstances were Protestants justified in resisting a Catholic sovereign by armed force. So Knox went to Zurich to see Bullinger, and asked him to reply to the same questions. Bullinger's answers were more ambiguous than Calvin's had been, but he said nothing to encourage Knox to believe that it was justifiable to resist a Catholic sovereign by force.

Knox went ahead without support from Calvin or Bullinger. In July 1554 he published a pamphlet, *A Faithful Admonition unto the Professors of God's Truth in England*, which was probably

printed in Dieppe, but was smuggled into England and circulated there illegally. In it he violently attacked 'bloody Bonner',
'dreaming Durham' (Tunstall), and 'wily Winchester', the 'Devil's Gardener', for inciting Queen Mary to persecute the Protestants. These attacks were commonplace in Protestant
propaganda, but Knox shocked many of his readers, including
the Protestants, by doing what none of the other Protestant
propagandists had done: he attacked the Queen herself. He
wrote that if, in the reign of Edward VI, the Protestant government had put Gardiner, Bonner and Tunstall to death for
idolatry, they would not now be burning Protestants. He was
more cautious in his comments about Mary herself; but he
hinted, though he did not expressly say, that the same applied to
her. If the government of Edward VI had put 'mischievous
Mary' to death for illegally celebrating her idolatrous Mass,
everyone would have said that this poor princess had been
unjustly persecuted; but God had ordered Jehu to put Jezebel
to death, and Jezebel had killed fewer of God's chosen people
than Mary had burned in London alone. Knox also denounced
Charles V for burning Protestants in the Netherlands, and wrote
that the Emperor was worse than Nero.

During the winter of 1554–5, Knox played the leading part in
the controversy among the English Protestant refugees in Frankfurt. The controversy ended when Cox and Knox's opponents
showed the authorities in Frankfurt a copy of Knox's *Admonition
to England*, to use the short title which Knox himself adopted.
The authorities were shocked to see that Knox had written that
Charles V was worse than Nero. They expelled him from
Frankfurt, for they feared that the Emperor would invade the
territory of the free city if they allowed Knox to remain there.

Knox moved to Switzerland, followed by a substantial minority of the English Protestants in Frankfurt, including Christopher Goodman, William Whittingham, John Foxe and Kethe.
Both Goodman and Whittingham were born in Chester, Good-

man in about 1520 and Whittingham in 1524. They both went
to Brasenose College, Oxford, and were granted their degree as
Master of Arts; and both were senior scholars at Christchurch.
Under Edward VI Whittingham was elected a fellow of All
Souls; and Goodman served as University Proctor, and became
Lady Margaret Professor of Divinity. Whittingham was granted
leave of absence to visit foreign universities, and studied at Paris,
Lyons and Geneva before returning to England shortly before
Edward VI died. Kethe was a Scotsman, and like Knox, Good-
man, Whittingham and Foxe became a radical Protestant. He
wrote poems, based on texts from the Psalms and other books of
the Bible, and set them to music to be sung as hymns.

Cox and his supporters, both in England and in exile, strongly
repudiated Knox's attacks on Mary. They accused him of
violating the duty of Christian obedience, and with having
incited Protestants to murder Mary. They went so far as to
say that Mary, who for the first eighteen months of her reign had
refrained from persecuting Protestants, only began burning them
because she had been enraged by Knox's book. This was
palpably untrue, as there were other reasons why she had
delayed burning Protestants until February 1555, and it was
clear that she would in any case have burned heretics who
denied the Real Presence and Papal supremacy.

It was perhaps not surprising that these revolutionary ideas
should have been advocated by a Scotsman. Respect for royal
authority and law and order had always been much weaker in
Scotland than in England. When the Privy Council in London
ordered a man to appear before them to answer some accusation,
he nearly always came obediently, without waiting for constables or men-at-arms to be sent to arrest him; but in Scotland
the accused man often took refuge in the territory of some
powerful lord or chief. The fugitive was then 'put to the horn',
which meant that a herald, after blowing on his horn, proclaimed him an outlaw who could be seized or put to death;

though the outlaw was safe in the territory of the nobleman who sheltered him. Henry VIII, in the last year of his life, had paid a band of Scottish Protestant gentlemen to assassinate Cardinal Beaton, the anti-English Chancellor of Scotland, in St Andrews Castle; and Knox, though he had no part in the assassination, had afterwards joined the murderers in the castle. When the French sent a fleet to capture the castle, Knox and his colleagues were taken prisoner. Knox was forced to work as a galley-slave in the French galleys until he was exchanged for a French prisoner-of-war and allowed to go to England in the reign of Edward VI.

But Knox did not now urge English Protestants to assassinate Mary; on the contrary, he expressly told them not to do so. 'God shows himself so offended with idolaters that He commands all such to be slain without mercy. But now, shall some demand, what then? Shall we go and slay all idolators? That were the office, dear brethren, of every civil magistrate within his realm. But of you is required only to avoid participation and company of their abominations.' This did not prevent many Protestants, as well as Mary, her government and her supporters, from denouncing Knox as an instigator of regicide.

Meanwhile Ponet, who had been a Professor of Greek at Cambridge University, not a Scottish revolutionary like Knox, was living in the Protestant city of Strasbourg with Peter Martyr and a group of English refugees, including some of his academic Cambridge friends. He wrote several books in Strasbourg; but in one of them, *A Short Treatise of Politic Power*, he considered the relationship of a ruler and his subjects. It had none of the polemical vigour and the savage humour and irony of Knox's works, but was an academic dissertation by a Cambridge classical scholar.

Ponet argued that God had appointed rulers to govern His people because this was necessary in order to preserve law and order. The system of government might be either monarchical, aristocratic or democratic, the rule of a king, of the nobility, or of the elected representatives of the people. In all these cases the government must ordinarily be obeyed; but those who believed that an absolute monarch should always be obeyed, even if he was a tyrant, committed as gross an error as did the Anabaptists who rejected the need for any kind of government. God appointed kings to rule justly, not unjustly. They must not violate the natural law which gives fundamental rights to the people: 'Neither Pope, Emperor nor King may do anything to the hurt of his people without their consent.' It was particularly important that the King should not seize and confiscate his subjects' property.

How far should subjects obey their King? And were they entitled to depose and kill a tyrant? In dealing with the first part of this question, Ponet became more academic than ever. It was necessary for a man's health that he should stretch his sinews, but they must neither be stretched too far, nor be too tightly constricted. Similarly there must be neither too much nor too little government, 'Too much maketh the governments to forget their vocation and to usurp upon their subjects'; but 'too little breedeth a licentious liberty and maketh the people to forget their duty.' Ponet, unlike the religious zealots on both the Catholic and the Protestant side during his lifetime, believed in limited constitutional monarchy, in the middle way, the compromise between absolute monarchy and anarchy, favoured by the men who made the English Revolution of 1688 and the American Revolution of 1775.

Ponet had no doubt that though the King must be obeyed if he ordered a subject to do good, he should not be obeyed if he ordered them, 'to dishonour God, to commit idolatry, to kill an innocent, to fight against their country'. In such cases the subject should 'leave it undone, for it is evil'. All the paper in England 'would not serve to sort out the mischiefs' that follow from the doctrine that 'princes' evil commandments should be obeyed and fulfilled'.

But was the subject entitled to go further and resist a King who was a tyrant? Yes, said Ponet, because as God appointed kings to rule justly, if the King became a tyrant he ceases to be a King, and so could be resisted, and if necessary killed. The oppressed subject's first remedy was to appeal to the nobles to restrain their tyrannical King, as the barons in Parliament were authorised to do by Magna Carta. But if the nobles in Parliament refused to act against the tyrant – as Mary's Parliament had done when it voted for the laws which allowed her to burn heretics – then the people were entitled to act. There were many examples in the Old Testament and in English history when the people had risen and overthrown a tyrant, and God had approved their action.

Ponet, like Foxe, Bale and the other Protestant propagandists, cited several recent examples of monstrous births, like the Siamese twins in Oxfordshire and the child born without legs or arms in Coventry to prove that God was displeased with the actions of Mary and her government; but he also used arguments which are more familiar to people in the twenty-first century. He referred to the economic inflation which had occurred in England during the previous ten years. It began when Henry VIII debased the currency in 1545 to pay for his war with France, and was increased by the arrival of gold and silver from the Spanish colonies in America at the international money market in Antwerp. Inflation had caused prices to double. Ponet asked his readers:

When were ever things as dear in England as in this time of the Popish Mass and other idolatry restored? Whoever heard or read before that a pound of beef was at fourpence? A sheep 20 shillings? A pound of candles at fourpence. A pound of butter at fourpence. A pound of cheese at fourpence. Two eggs a penny. A quarter of wheat 64 shillings. A quarter of malt at 50 shillings or above. The people driven of hunger to grind acorns for bread meal, and to drink water instead of ale?[1]

Soon after he had finished writing his book, Ponet's house in Strasbourg was burned, apparently in a fire which was started accidentally, and he lost most of his money. He was negotiating with the authorities in Strasbourg about the possibility of obtaining compensation when he died of some disease, though he was only forty years old.

The English Protestants were anxious to preserve and record the names of the martyrs who were being burned in England. A leading part in this work was performed by John Foxe. In the reign of Edward VI, when the persecution of Protestants had stopped, he wrote a book about the martyrs who had been burned in England and other European countries during the previous 145 years from William Sawtrey in 1401 to Anne Askew and her fellow-sufferers in 1546.[2] He had just finished writing the book when Mary became Queen. He escaped abroad, taking his manuscript with him. He translated it into Latin for the benefit of the continental Protestants, and it was published under the title *Rerum in Ecclesia gestarum* in Strasbourg in August 1554. He afterwards wrote an account of the persecution of the early Christians by the Roman Caesars beginning with the first martyr, St Stephen, who suffered a few years after the crucifixion of Christ;[3] This was in order to portray the Protestant martyrs of the sixteenth century as the successors of the early Christian martyrs. These new passages were incorporated into the second Latin edition of Foxe's book which was published in Basle in 1559.

Within six months of the publication of the first edition of 1554, Foxe had heard that a new persecution was beginning in England which would provide many more martyrs than those who had suffered under previous sovereigns. He collected information which he obtained from England, intending to write another edition of his book which would include these victims who were suffering under Mary. Other Protestants in England and abroad were also compiling a list of their comrades who were suffering martyrdom. One of these lists was compiled by a person whose identity is unknown, but who sent his list to

William Cecil for Cecil to use as anti-Catholic propaganda when he was Secretary of State in the reign of Elizabeth I. This list contained some names which Foxe missed. Another list was sent to Knox in Geneva. The compilation of these lists certainly indicates that there was a well organised secret Protestant group which could arrange for news to be collected from all parts of England and sent to Geneva.

One list was compiled by Thomas Bryce. We know nothing about him except that he was a clergyman, and no records have been discovered which show in what part of England he lived. Like many other English Protestants, Bryce placed his hopes on the Queen's sister Elizabeth, and longed for the day when, on Mary's death, Elizabeth would become Queen.

Elizabeth had returned to court; she had become a Catholic, and went to Mass. But both her friends and her enemies believed that she was a secret Protestant. Mary thought so too, and was very suspicious of her; but King Philip would not let Mary harm Elizabeth, for Elizabeth was the alternative to Mary, Queen of Scots, who was engaged to marry the King of France's son. Philip wanted Elizabeth to marry Emmanuel Philibert of Savoy – a marriage which would bind England to his ally Savoy after Mary's death. Elizabeth did not wish to marry Emmanuel Philibert, for she wished to remain free of all binding political alliances; Mary did not favour the marriage to Emmauel Philibert which she thought would increase Elizabeth's influence. So Elizabeth had to manoeuvre, and play a very difficult game, and by a mixture of skill and luck she managed to play it very successfully.

Bryce compiled his list of martyrs, and expressed the Protestants' hope in Elizabeth, in a poem which he called *The Register*. He could not publish it, or show it to anyone, until after Mary died; but he was obviously compiling his list of martyrs, month by month, and may even have begun writing the poem at this time. He missed the earliest of the martyrs, as he did not begin the register until June 1555; and for some reason he omitted the martyrs during several

months. He missed out some of Foxe's most famous martyrs, and
included others whom Foxe did not name. In all, in sixty-five
verses, he gave the names of 248 martyrs.

He began, in June 1555:

> When worthy Watts with constant cry
> Continued in the flaming fire;
> When Simson, Hawkes and John Ardite
> Did taste the tyrant's raging ire;
> When Chamberlain was put to death
> We wished for our Elizabeth.
>
> When blessed Butler and Osmonde
> With force of fire to death were brent;
> When Shittenden, Sir Franke and Bland
> And Humfrey Middleton of Kent;
> When Minge in Maidstone took his death
> We wished for our Elizabeth.
>
> July
> When Bradford, beautified with bliss;
> When young John Leaf in Smithfield died;
> When they like brethren both did kiss,
> And in the fire were truly tried;
> When tears were shed for Bradford's death
> We wished for our Elizabeth.

After another nineteen verses Bryce came to March 1556:

> When constant Cranmer lost his life
> And held his hand unto the fire;
> When streams of tears for him were rife
> And yet did miss their just desire;
> When Popish power put him to death
> We wished for our Elizabeth.

And on to May 1556:

> When Margaret Eliot, being a maid,
> After condemning in prison died;
> When lame Laverock the fire assayed
> And blind Aprice with him was tried;
> When these two impotents were put to death
> We wished for our Elizabeth.
> When Katherine Hut did spend her blood
> With two maids, Elizabeth and Joan;
> When they embraced both rede and wood,
> Trusting in Christ His death alone;
> When men unnatural drew them to death
> We wished for our Elizabeth.

In July 1556:

> When John Foreman and Mother Tree
> At Grinstead cruelly were slain;
> When Thomas Dungate, to make up three,
> With them did pass from woe and pain;
> When these with other were put to death
> We wished for our Elizabeth.

In June 1557:

> When Jame Bradbridge and a blind maid,
> Appleby, Allen and both their wives,
> When Manning's wife was not afraid,
> But all those seven did lose their lives;
> When these at Maidstone were put to death
> We wished for our Elizabeth.
> . . . .

> When William Mainard, his maid and man,
> Margery Morris and her son,
> Dents, Burgess, Stevens and Woodman,
> Glove's wife and Ashdon's to death were done;
> When one fire at Lewes brought to their death
> We wished for our Elizabeth.[4]

Knox continued to write his books and pamphlets, and to go further in developing his revolutionary doctrines. In 1557 he wrote a book *The First Blast of the Trumpet against the Monstrous Regiment of Women*. 'The Monstrous Regiment of Women' should be translated into twenty-first-century English, as 'the unnatural government of women'. It established Knox's reputation during his lifetime as a revolutionary firebrand, and after his death as a woman-hater. Knox was not, in fact, a woman-hater; nor was his book written, in the first place, against Mary, Queen of Scots. It was written as an attack on Mary of Lorraine, the Regent of Scotland; on Charles V's sister, Mary of Hungary, who was Regent of the Netherlands; and above all on Mary Tudor, Queen of England.

Knox wrote the book out of pure political opportunism. He was closely associated with many women who were among his most devoted followers; and he knew very well – if he had ever forgotten it, Calvin had recently reminded him – that God had chosen a woman, Deborah, to lead the people of Israel. But he could not resist the temptation of pandering to popular masculine prejudice. Henry VIII had several times complained about women who thought that they could teach and lecture him; and when Mary Tudor's herald had gone to Henry II of France to declare war, Henry had burst out laughing, and had said: 'Consider how I stand when a woman challenges me to war!'

Knox began his book with a denunciation of women. They were 'weak, frail, impotent, feeble and foolish, and experience hath declared them to be inconsistent, variable, cruel and lacking the spirit of counsel and regiment'. It would be interesting to know what Knox's devoted women followers thought of this violent denunciation of their sex. They probably accepted it as happily as the modern Marxist of middle-class origin accepts the denunciation of the bourgeoisie as a class; for Knox made it clear that there were exceptions to the rule. 'I except such as God, by singular privilege and for certain causes known only to Himself, hath excepted from the common rank of women', as in the case of Deborah; and it was clear, from all Knox's other writings and actions, that the only way of becoming one of these exceptional Deborahs was to belong to Knox's religious organisation, which was becoming every day more like a political party than a Church.

Nearly all the passages in Knox's book in which he denounced the wickedness and inferiority of women were quotations from the early Christian fathers of the Church between the second and the fifth centuries after Christ. He had no difficulty in finding quotations from Tertullian, St John Chrysostom, St Ambrose and St Augustine proclaiming that evil had entered the world through the woman, Eve, and that the sin of Eve would be visited on the daughters of Eve who would be punished for it by being kept for ever in subjection to man. This was accepted Christian theology.

But there was an exception to this rule. Everyone agreed that it was a disaster if a king did not have a male heir, but only daughters; but if God had decided to punish the realm by giving it a female sovereign, this must be accepted; and the female sovereign had all the powers of a male king. Knox pointed out the inconsistencies of a society, which was to continue for another 350 years after his time, in which women could not hold any position of authority in the family, in national or local government, in the professions or in the universities, except that of head of state. In attacking this position, Knox was attacking the crown and the whole mystique of monarchy. His book was rightly regarded, not as an attack on women, but as an attack on the monarchy. The theologians who taught that though women must obey men in all other fields, men must obey a queen as they would obey a male sovereign, believed that the divinely ordained power of the prince was strong enough to prevail over the divinely ordained superiority of men over women. Knox's book, because it directly challenged this, was seditious.

But Knox committed a grave political blunder by writing his *First Blast of the Trumpet*. He completely overlooked Elizabeth. This was a mistake which only a refugee could have made. If he thought about Elizabeth at all, he doubtless thought that she had weakly recanted and become a Catholic while the exceptional Deborahs were bravely dying at the stake. He did not realise that the Protestants in England 'wished for our Elizabeth'. His book caused him difficulties after Elizabeth became Queen. She was indignant with Knox. He tried to appease her by telling her that he was prepared to recognise her as an exceptional Deborah; but this only enraged her more. She thought that her subjects should obey her, not because some religious fanatic thought that she was a Deborah, but because she was a queen. It needed all the political genius of Cecil to persuade her that it was in her interests, and in the national interests of England, to support Knox's Protestant revolution in Scotland.

As Knox had expected, his book caused an outcry when it was published early in 1558 giving a fictitious place of publication; it had in fact been secretly printed in Geneva without the knowledge of Calvin and the city authorities. It was violently denounced, not only by Mary's government in England, but by most of the English refugees abroad and by Calvin and other eminent continental Protestants. Meanwhile Christopher Goodman had also written a book, *How Superior Powers ought to be Obeyed*, which caused as much indignation as Knox's book. It was published in Geneva on 1 January 1558. Goodman stated in the book that he did not wish to encourage rebellion; but it is not surprising that Mary and most other people did not believe him. The full title of the book was enough to anger Mary: *How superior powers ought to be obeyed of their subjects; and wherein they may lawfully by God's word be disobeyed and resisted. Wherein also is declared the cause of all the present misery in England and the only way to remedy the same.*

After stating that Papists were more wicked and more blasphemous than the Jews, and 'deny Christ as well as the Jews do', he denounced Queen Mary as a bastard born of an incestuous relationship between her father and her mother; and he argued, like Knox, that a woman could not lawfully reign in a kingdom. She was 'a tormentor of the saints of God'.

Christ had forbidden Peter to draw the sword in his defence for the same reason that He had forgiven the woman taken in adultery: He wished to show that He had not come to exercise temporal power. David had not raised his hand against Saul when Saul was at his mercy, because as Saul hated David because he knew that David would succeed him as king, David's quarrel with Saul was a private and personal one. It would therefore have been wrong for David to take revenge on Saul. But 'if the superior power be an idolator or a cruel tyrant suppressing the religion and murdering the saints of God (as Jezebel of England doth with all her rabble of papistical bishops and shavelings) who is so ignorant of God, or destitute of all humanity or natural judgement that will not acknowledge such a one to be unworthy the society of the good and honest; much less to have the authority and rule over great nations and whole kingdoms?'

It was not only the magistrates and nobles, but also the common people, who had a duty to force the Queen to abandon idolatry. It was their duty to God to overthrow 'this ungodly serpent Mary, the chief instrument of all this present misery in England'. If they supported Mary and obeyed her, 'Well, the day of the Lord will come, when you shall feel what it is to fight for your Mass and to betray the Gospel.' They would sin in the eyes of God if they did not rise in revolt against 'the usurped power of ungodly Jezebel and her merciless Papists, the soldiers of Antichrist'.

Kethe contributed a poem which was published in Goodman's book.

> Rebellion is ill, to resist is not so
> When right through resisting is done to that foe . . .
> A brute beast untamed, a misbegot then,
> More meet to be ruled than reign over men.

The principle which Knox and Goodman had put forward of
the difference between private wrongs and wrongs against God
played an important part in their philosophy. A good Christian
must forgive his enemies, but he must not forgive God's
enemies. This principle was emphasized in the Geneva Bible
which Knox and Whittingham, with the help of some of their
colleagues, were compiling between 1556 and 1559. It became
very popular, at least in extremist Protestant circles, in the second
half of the sixteenth century. As in Tyndale's translation, there
were marginal notes – in some chapters they were longer than
the biblical text – in which Knox and his colleagues put forward
their own interpretation of the passages in the Bible. The ideas
put forward in the marginal notes to the Geneva Bible were very
different from those which Tyndale had expressed in his translation. Knox and his collaborators advocated, not Christian obedience, but revolution.

Tyndale had placed great emphasis on the passage in the First
Book of Samuel where David, finding his enemy Saul asleep,
does not kill or harm him because Saul is a king; and David said:
'Destroy him not; for who can stretch forth his hand against the
Lord's anointed and be guiltless?' Knox's comment in the
marginal notes was: 'To wit, in his own private cause; but Jehu
slew two kings at God's appointment.' In the passage in the
Book of Kings where Jehu kills Jezebel, the Bible text states that
when Jehu came to her, Jezebel called out to him: 'Had Zimri
peace who slew his master?' Knox's notes commented: 'As

though she would say, Can any traitor, or any that rises against his sovereign, have good success?' But Jehu threw her down, and her blood sprinkled on the wall, and he trod her underfoot. Knox wrote in the notes: 'This he did by the motion of the Spirit of God, that her blood should be shed that had shed the blood of innocents, to be a spectacle and example of God's judgments to all tyrants.'

In Dieppe Knox wrote and published open letters to the rulers of Scotland. He began with a letter to Mary of Lorraine, the Regent of Scotland during the infancy and absence in France of her daughter Mary, Queen of Scots. In his letter Knox urged Mary of Lorraine to abandon her policy of supporting Popish idolatry. He cannot have been surprised when she paid no attention to his exhortation. He followed this with a letter to the Scottish nobility. He told them that as their ruler was not suppressing idolatry, the duty of doing this had passed to them, for they were subsidiary rulers, under their Queen, in their districts.

By 1558 Knox was writing an appeal to the common people of Scotland. If neither the Queen nor the nobility would act to suppress idolatry and uphold the true religion, then they, the people, must do it themselves. In his *Letter to the Commonalty of Scotland*, Knox took the final step and denounced the doctrine of Christian obedience as sinful. If the people obeyed idolatrous rulers and did nothing to stop them, they were conniving at idolatry and in effect were in revolt against God.

He cited passages from the Old Testament where God had called on subjects to revolt against their evil rulers. He referred to the drowning of Pharoah's soldiers in the Red Sea, and asked the question: Why did God drown the soldiers? It was not the soldiers, but Pharoah, who had sinned against the people of Israel; so why were the innocent soldiers drowned as well as the guilty Pharoah? Knox's answer to this question shocked six-teenth-century Europe: God had punished Pharoah's soldiers

because they were not innocent; they, too, were guilty. They
had sinned in obeying Pharoah's wicked orders, when they
ought to have mutinied and made a revolution against Pharoah.

The *Letter to the Commonalty of Scotland* was dated 14 July
1558. It was printed and published soon afterwards together with
Knox's *Appellation to the Nobility and Estates of Scotland*. To
Calvin's great annoyance and embarrassment, the place of
publication was given as Geneva, though Knox was careful
not to give the printer's name. Apart from Knox's two treatises
the volume contained a revolutionary poem by Kethe based on
the 94th Psalm, *Who now will up and rise with me against this wicked
band?*, and Anthony Gilby's, *An Admonition to England and
Scotland to call them to Repentance*. Gilby came from Leicestershire.
He was a Master of Arts of Christ's College, Cambridge, and had
written a number of Protestant pamphlets before emigrating
under Mary; but he was not widely known, and many readers of
his *Admonition to England and Scotland* thought that it had been
written by Knox under a pseudonym.

Gilby called on the people to revolt against Mary Tudor and
Mary of Lorraine. He was also the first English Protestant writer
to attack Henry VIII. Foxe, in his account in his *Book of Martyrs*
of the burning of Protestants in Henry's reign, had referred to
Henry's brutality at Lambert's trial and to his persecution of
Protestants; but he had criticised him more in sorrow than in
anger, as a good King who had been deceived by the wicked
machinations of Gardiner. Gilby did not hesitate to attack the
great King who had so successfully won the support of the
English nationalists by his triumphs over the French, the Scots
and the Italian Pope; Henry, the father of Queen Mary, the
father of the Protestant heroine Elizabeth, a King whose royal
authority should not be questioned. Gilby denounced Henry
VIII as a persecutor of God's saints, the Protestants. 'Thus was
there no Reformation but a deformation in the time of that
tyrant and lecherous monster.'[5]

CHAPTER 14

The Secret Congregations

IN THE AUTUMN OF 1557 the authorities were searching for heretics and burning them all over south-east England and the Midlands. They burned a gentlewoman, Joyce Lewis, of Mancetter in Warwickshire. She had been married in succession to two prosperous local gentlemen, had enjoyed wearing smart clothes, and had gone regularly to Mass; until she was so disgusted at the burning of Lawrence Saunders and her neighbour Robert Glover that she refused to attend Mass and adopted the Protestant doctrines for which they had suffered. She was burned in Litch-field. John Kurde, a shoemaker of Syresham in Northampton-shire, was burned in Northampton. They burned a man and his wife and two other men in the same fire in Islington.

They were particularly worried about the activities of George Eagles, who travelled all over south-east England contacting Protestants and organising them into congregations. Mary and her government thought that Eagles was very dangerous, be-cause he was creating a secret Protestant organisation. Eagles had no money and no occupation; he did not need much money, for he ate very little and drank only water. He walked around Norfolk, Suffolk, Essex and Kent, sleeping sometimes in the houses of friends and sometimes in the fields and woods. People called him George Trudge-over-the-World, because he walked everywhere.

The authorities were determined to catch him. They offered a reward of £20 to anyone who gave information leading to his arrest. This was enough to tempt an unskilled working man who would have to work for four years to earn £20.

On St Mary Magdalene's day (22 July) 1557 Eagles was in Colchester market hoping to contact some of his Protestant friends there. Someone who wanted the £20 reward recognised him and informed the authorities, who sent constables to the market to arrest him. But he was warned that they were coming, and ran out of the market. He hid first in a grove just outside Colchester, and then in a nearby cornfield, where the corn was high. He lay down in the corn, which completely hid him from view. The constables arrived at the cornfield and walked through part of it; but Eagles lay very still, and no one saw him.

One member of the party searching for Eagles was very eager to win the reward. He waited until all the other constables had left, and then climbed a tree which stood by the side of the cornfield. He had a good view of the field from the tree, but he could not see Eagles hidden in the corn. After a while Eagles, hearing no noise, thought that all the searchers had gone away. He stood up and looked, and as he saw no sign of anyone, he knelt in the corn and prayed, thanking God for having delivered him from his enemies. But when he stood up to look around and knelt in prayer, the man in the tree saw him. He went into the cornfield and seized Eagles, and took him to the prison in Colchester. From there Eagles was taken to Chelmsford to be examined by the JPs.

The authorities treated his case as high treason. He was charged under the name of 'George Eagles otherwise Trudge-over-the-World' with having prayed to God to change the Queen's heart or shorten her days. He admitted that he had prayed to God to change the Queen's heart, but denied that he had prayed that her days should be shortened. He was convicted of high treason, and sentenced to be hanged, drawn and quartered. The sentence was carried out in Chelmsford. Soon afterwards his sister was burned as a heretic in Rochester.

The man who had caught Eagles in the cornfield did not win the £20 for which he had hoped. He received only part of it, as he had to share it with the other searchers who had spotted Eagles in Colchester market.[1]

Another illegal Protestant organisation alarmed the government in the winter of 1557. The leader of the group was the Scottish Protestant, John Rough. He had taken his degree at St Andrews University in 1534. Soon afterwards he became involved in a bitter dispute with his brother about property, and, wishing to break with his family, he became a monk in the monastery of the Black Friars in Stirling. He was sent on a visit to Rome, but was shocked by the corruption and immorality there; and a second visit to Rome increased his disillusionment with the Catholic Church. On his return to Scotland he left his monastery and became a prominent figure in the Scottish Protestant movement.

In 1546 sixteen Scottish Protestant gentlemen, instigated and paid by Henry VIII, assassinated the anti-English Chancellor of Scotland, Cardinal Beaton, in St Andrews Castle and seized the castle. After the murder, Rough joined the murderers in the castle; and meeting his acquaintance John Knox in St Andrews, persuaded Knox that he too should join them. King Henry II of France sent a fleet to recapture the castle for the Catholic party. Before the fleet arrived, Rough left the castle, so he was not taken prisoner when the castle surrendered to the French. The gentlemen who had murdered Beaton were taken as prisoners to France. Some of them succeeded in escaping from their French prisons to England. Knox was forced to row as a galley-slave in the French galleys, until he was exchanged for French prisoners in England; but Rough had already escaped from Scotland into England. After living for a time in Carlisle, he was appointed vicar of a parish near Hull.

When Mary became Queen, he left England illegally without a passport, escaping with some difficulty from Dover, and managed to reach the Protestant city of Norden in Friesland. He had no money, so he and his wife earned their living by knitting stockings and hose and selling them to customers in Flanders and elsewhere in western Europe. When he needed more yarn for his knitting he decided to risk going to England to buy it, because yarn was cheaper there than on the continent. But he would hardly have taken such a risk if he had not already decided to organise the Protestants in England into secret congregations.

Whatever may have been his original reasons for going to England, as soon as he arrived in London on 10 November 1557 he set about organising a secret illegal Protestant congregation. The congregation changed their meeting place regularly, to make it more difficult for the authorities to find and arrest them. They usually met in inns in or near London. They elected Rough as their minister, and chose a well-educated and wealthy young man, Cuthbert Simpson, as deacon of the congregation. The deacon was entrusted with the very important and dangerous task of keeping a secret list of the members.

Soon after Rough arrived, he went to Smithfield to watch the burning of the London Protestants James and Margery Austoo. Both James and Margery were firm and refused to recant, but Margery did better than her husband in their arguments with Bonner, who examined them at his palace in Fulham and condemned them as heretics. Rough was deeply moved, emotionally, to see them burn, and said this to an old acquaintance from his former parish near Hull whom he met in the street in London.

A London Protestant, James Mearing and his wife Margaret, were members of the congregation. Rough and Simpson were worried about Margaret Mearing; they thought that she was indiscreet, and that because of her the authorities would hear of the existence of the congregation. The authorities did indeed know about Rough's congregation, and took a very serious view of it; they thought it was an even more dangerous seditious organisation than George Eagles' group. They sent an agent to infiltrate it and act as a spy and informer. The agent was a forty-year-old tailor from Buckinghamshire named Roger Serjeant. He succeeded in joining the congregation. No one suspected that he was sending reports to the government giving the names and describing the activities of the members.

On Friday 10 December 1557 the congregation held a secret meeting at the Saracen's Head inn in Islington. Rough raised the question of Margaret Mearing. He said that she was endangering the safety of the congregation, and proposed that she be excommunicated and expelled. Simpson supported Rough's proposal, and it was approved by the congregation. Rough then excommunicated her, and she was expelled, though she protested her innocence. None of the members knew that it was Roger Serjeant, not Margaret Mearing, who was the danger.

But two days later the authorities, acting on Serjeant's information, swooped on them. Constables came and arrested them all at the Saracen's Head, and took them to the Gatehouse prison in London. They were examined by Bonner. The authorities thought that Simpson, as the deacon of the congregation, was the most important prisoner. He succeeded in hiding or destroying his list of the members, and would not tell the authorities their names.

Bonner and the Privy Council treated the case as high treason. They sent Simpson to the Tower, and obtained a warrant from the Queen, in the proper form, allowing them to torture him on the rack to make him reveal the names. The torture of the rack consisted in stretching the victim's legs and arms until his limbs were wrenched out of joint. Simpson was racked for three hours. Three days later he was again racked twice, and they drove a sharp arrow into his hand; but he revealed nothing under torture. In the end they sent him back to Bonner's prison.

As soon as Margaret Mearing heard that Rough and his comrades had been arrested, she forgave them for having

Cuthbert Symson upon the rack

excommunicated and expelled her, and decided to do all she could to help. She bought some clean linen for Rough, and went to his prison at the Compter, pretending that she was his sister, and persuaded the prison officers to allow her to leave the linen for him. She then went to Serjeant's house, and asked him if Judas, who betrayed Christ, lived there. When he said no, she said that surely Judas's name was Roger Serjeant. A few days later she was arrested in the street and taken to join Rough in the Compter prison.

Although Simpson had been interrogated under torture as if he were a traitor, the government did not have Rough and the others hanged, drawn and quartered like Eagles, but proceeded against them as heretics. They were examined about their views on the Real Presence, and were accused of holding the same heretical opinions as Ridley, Latimer and Cranmer. Rough told Bonner the story of his life, including his youth in Scotland, and mentioned that he had become a Protestant because, after going twice to Rome, he had been disgusted with the corruption and immorality of the Papacy. This enraged Bonner, though he himself had once insulted the Pope to his face. 'Hast thou been in Rome', said Bonner, 'and seen our Holy Father the Pope, and dost thou blaspheme him after this sort?' Bonner thereupon pulled out part of Rough's beard, and burned his cheek for half an hour, telling him that he was burning his cheek in the morning and would burn the rest of him in the afternoon.

Bonner acted quickly in the case of Rough and Margaret Mearing. It was on Sunday 12 December that Rough and the others were seized at the Saracen's Head. Margaret Mearing was arrested on Friday 17 December. She and Rough were both examined and condemned by Bonner next day. Their differences had been forgotten and forgiven before they were burned together at Smithfield in the same fire on Wednesday 22 December.

Simpson and the other prisoners who had been arrested at the
Saracen's Head were held for much longer before they were
burned. It was not until 19 March that Simpson and two of his
colleagues, Hugh Foxe and John Devenish, were examined by
Bonner and questioned about their opinion of the Real Presence. Bonner put Simpson in the stocks, hoping that harsh
treatment would persuade him to recant; but he was not tortured
again. Meanwhile several of the others who had been arrested at
the Saracen's Head, including Margaret Mearing's husband
James, were pressurised into signing statements incriminating
Simpson and showing the extent of his activities as the deacon of
the congregation.

In the end, Bonner rather reluctantly condemned Simpson as
a heretic. He told people that he liked Simpson, and that if
Simpson had not been a heretic he would have admired the
courage that Simpson had shown when he was racked in the
Tower. 'Also in my house', said Bonner, 'he hath felt some
sorrow, and yet I never saw his patience broken'.

Cuthbert Simpson, Hugh Foxe and John Devenish were
burned together in the same fire at Smithfield on 28 March
1558.[2]

CHAPTER 15

Bonner's Way with Heretics

DESPITE ALL HER TROUBLES, Mary had one consolation in 1557: her husband made peace with the Pope. After the French defeat at St Quentin, and with Alba's army at the gates of Rome, Paul IV agreed to repudiate his alliance with France. Philip ordered Alba to go to the Pope and implore forgiveness on his knees for his sin in invading the Papal States. Alba obeyed Philip's orders, but told his friends that it was only with the greatest difficulty that he forced himself to submit to the humiliation.

The Duke of Guise had been unsuccessful in Italy, but he and Henry II had other plans. In the winter of 1557, while Philip's armies in the Netherlands were in winter quarters preparing for a campaign next summer, Guise was secretly preparing to launch an attack on Calais at a time when the English garrison there had as usual been temporarily reduced during the winter to save money, and the winter gales in the Channel would make it difficult for the English to send reinforcements.

The Marches of Calais had been held by the English for 210 years, since the town was captured by Edward III in 1347. The English territory stretched for about eight miles inland from the sea and for some twenty miles along the coast from the frontier with France at Marquise, half-way between Calais and Boulogne, to the Emperor's provinces in the Netherlands at Gravelines. Boulogne, which had been captured by Henry VIII in 1544, had been restored to France by the peace treaty of 1550.

Calais was important to England for political, economic and military reasons. It was all that remained of the extensive territories which the English had once held in France, and was the justification for the King of England using the title 'King of France' and quartering the French *fleur-de-lys* on his coat of arms. It was a centre of international trade between England, France, the Netherlands and other parts of western Europe. It was also an important military bridgehead across the Channel where the English could assemble an army before launching an invasion of France.

Although reports had been received both by Mary's government in London and by Philip in Brussels that the French were preparing an attack on Calais in midwinter, the English garrison and Philip's forces were taken completely by surprise when Guise's army invaded the Marches of Calais on New Year's Eve 1557. Within a week they had overrun the whole of the territory except for the fortress of Guisnes, and on 7 January 1558 Lord Wentworth, the Governor of Calais, surrendered the town to Guise, who allowed the English soldiers to leave after they had given up their arms and equipment. Guisnes held out for another three weeks before surrendering to Guise.

The loss of Calais was regarded in England as a great defeat and a national humiliation. It led to bitter recriminations between the English and their Spanish allies, and an intensification of the anti-Spanish feeling in England. The English complained that Emmanuel Philibert's army at Gravelines had not come to their aid in Calais. The Spaniards said that their forces in the Netherlands would have come if the English at Calais had held out a little longer, but that they had not expected the English to surrender Calais within a week and the whole territory within a month.

While the people resented the loss of Calais, Mary continued to burn heretics. They found a heretic at Haverfordwest in Pembrokeshire in Wales. William Nichol, whom John Foxe described as 'an honest good simple poor man', was thought by many people to be half-witted. For this reason his vague denunciations of the 'cruel kingdom of Antichrist' were overlooked for a time, until a zealous Catholic denounced him as a heretic. He was burned at Haverfordwest on 9 April 1558.

Heretics were burned in Bristol and Litchfield, though as usual most of the victims were in Suffolk, Essex, Kent and London. In the spring of 1558 about forty men and women were arrested when they were attending a secret Protestant service in a field near Islington. Some were released, but twenty-two of them were imprisoned in Newgate prison in London. The warden of the prison told them that they would be pardoned if they agreed to go to Mass. Seven of them accepted the offer, and two others died in prison. The remaining thirteen were burned, seven of them at Smithfield and six at Brentford in June and July 1558.

The seven who were burned in Smithfield aroused the sympathy of many of the spectators. Before they were burned, the sheriff read out a proclamation of Philip and Mary which warned the people that the King and Queen had forbidden the spectators to show sympathy for heretics who were being burned, and that anyone who did so would be arrested and flogged. The proclamation did not deter large sections of the crowd from praising the martyrs and denouncing the wickedness of burning them.

The bishops and their chancellors in the dioceses of Norwich, Ely and Rochester, and Nicholas Harpsfield and Dick of Dover in Pole's diocese of Canterbury, relentlessly pursued the government policy of burning heretics, energetically backed by the High Sheriffs and JPs. Bonner in his diocese of London went his own way, sometimes behaving with great brutality and sometimes with sudden kindness. He flogged heretics in his garden, hoping that this would frighten them into submission, but on other occasions he let them go free.

John Fetty was a poor tailor in Clerkenwell, just outside the city of London; he was aged forty-two. He was a Protestant, but his wife was a Catholic, and she denounced him as a heretic to the parish priest. Fetty was arrested and imprisoned in the tower at St Paul's Cathedral which was known as the 'Lollards' Tower' because heretics had often been imprisoned there. His wife then had a mental breakdown; in John Foxe's words, 'his wife (by the just judgment of God) was stricken mad and distract of her wits, which declared a marvellous example of the justice of God against such unfaithful and most unnatural treachery'. Fetty was still fond of his wife, and he was worried about what would happen to his two small children if he was held in prison and his wife went mad. So he begged the authorities to release him, so that he could look after her and the children. The authorities sympathised with his predicament and hers, and as they thought that he was not dangerous they freed him and told him to take his wife home.

After a few weeks his wife recovered her sanity, but was still indignant that Fetty was a heretic. She did not think that his kindness to her was enough to excuse his heresy, so she again denounced him as a heretic, this time to the local JP. Fetty was again arrested and sent to the Lollards' Tower, where he was placed in the stocks and given nothing to eat or drink except bread and water. The authorities placed a bowl beside him in the stocks, containing water, bread and a stone; the stone was placed there apparently in mockery, to remind him that he would get nothing to eat and drink apart from the bread and water, except the stone.

After Fetty had been in the prison for fifteen days, his son, who was aged eight or nine, came to visit him. When the boy arrived at the bishop's house he met a priest who was one of Bonner's chaplains and asked the way to the Lollards' Tower, explaining that he wished to visit his father who was imprisoned there. 'Thy father is a heretic', said the priest. The boy replied: 'My father is no heretic, but you are a heretic, for you have Balaam's mark'. The priest then took the child into Bonner's house, where he was severely beaten with whips and rods by the priests, so that he was covered in blood. Foxe admitted that he had no evidence that Bonner himself was responsible. He wrote that the priest 'carried him into the bishop's house, whether to the bishop or not, I know not, but like enough he did'.

Richard Cluney, the keeper of Bonner's prison, took the boy to see his father in the Lollards' Tower. The child ran to his father, and kneeling to him asked for his blessing. Fetty was shocked to see his child covered with wounds; he threw his arms around the boy and indignantly asked who had treated him so cruelly. Cluney then snatched the child away and took him back to Bonner's house. Some days later Fetty was taken to be examined by Bonner. Fetty told Bonner that he had treated the child, and was treating Fetty himself and the other Protestants, as cruelly as Caiaphas and the Jews had treated Christ. Bonner thereupon denounced Fetty as a wicked heretic, and threatened him with the direst punishments; but he released him, and told him to take his child home with him.

Fourteen days later the child died. Again Foxe admitted that he did not know the cause of his death, 'whether through this cruel scourging or any other infirmity I know not, therefore I refer the truth thereof unto the Lord, who knoweth all secrets'. But he thought that the eight-year-old boy should be included among the martyrs, and should also be considered to have saved his father's life, because neither Bonner nor anyone else took any further proceedings against Fetty, who died many years later in the reign of Elizabeth I.

By the summer of 1558 copies of the books of Knox, Goodman, Ponet and Gilby were secretly circulating in England. For some years the government had been seizing seditious publications and punishing those who were found in possession of them; but a much more severe decree was now promulgated. A proclamation in the name of King Philip and Queen Mary, dated 6 June 1558, stated that 'divers books filled both with heresy, sedition and treason' were being brought into England from foreign countries, and were also being secretly printed in

England. In these books, 'not only God is dishonoured but also
an encouragement given to disobey lawful princes and governors'. The King and Queen therefore proclaimed that anyone
finding a copy of one of these 'wicked and seditious books' must
immediately burn it without showing or reading it to anyone
else. Anyone found in possession of a copy of these books, or
who disobeyed this proclamation, would immediately be put to
death without trial under martial law.[1]

Thomas Benbridge was a gentleman who owned a substantial
property in Hampshire. He was a Protestant. He refused to go to
Mass, and did not hide his religious opinions. He was denounced
to John White, the Bishop of Winchester, who condemned him
as a heretic. He was taken to the stake to be burned at
Winchester at the end of July 1558. Sir Richard Pexall, the
High Sheriff of Hampshire, was in charge of the execution, and
Dr John Seton, a canon of Winchester, was present. Seton had
been Gardiner's chaplain, and one of the Catholic doctors who
had disputed against Ridley, Latimer and Cranmer in the
disputation on the Real Presence at Oxford in April 1554.

There were supporters and opponents of Benbridge in the
crowd. Seton urged Benbridge to recant, and told him that if he
recanted he would be pardoned; but Benbridge refused to
recant, and began to explain his attitude. The Catholics in
the crowd demanded that he be silenced; one of them shouted,
'Cut out his tongue!'

Pexall gave the order for the fire to be kindled. The faggots
had not been well laid, and at first the flames rose and burned
Benbridge's beard, but did not set him properly alight. While his
beard burned, Benbridge stood motionless in the flames; but
when the faggots lower down caught fire, and burned off his
legs, he screamed in pain and called out 'I recant!' Pexall ordered
the execution to proceed; but some of Benbridge's supporters
broke through the cordon of guards, put out the burning

faggots, and pulled Benbridge out of the flames. Pexall then stopped the execution. Benbridge could not stand, having lost his legs; but he was lifted on to a man's back. As he sat there, Seton brought him a recantation which he had written out in Latin, and Benbridge signed it on the back of the man who was carrying him. He was then taken off to the local prison.

Pexall reported what had happened to the Queen and the Privy Council. Mary was very angry. The Privy Council wrote to Pexall that the Queen was surprised that he should have stopped the execution because Benbridge had recanted. She ordered him to burn Benbridge again at the same place a week later, and then to appear before the Privy Council to explain his conduct. Benbridge, who still could not walk, was carried to the stake at Winchester and burned there at the beginning of August. Pexall was imprisoned for a short time in the Fleet prison in London, and was then released with a reprimand. Benbridge's supporters who had pulled him out of the fire were also imprisoned.[2]

John Milles was a hatmaker. He and his brother Robert were among the Protestants who had been arrested for holding a secret prayer meeting in the fields near Islington. Robert was one of the six who were burned in Brentford on 14 July 1558; John was sent to Bonner's house in Fulham. Bonner took a stick and struck Milles on the hand and under the chin. Afterwards Milles was given a severe beating by Bonner himself and several of his priests. Bonner said cheerfully to Milles, 'They call me bloody Bonner', and warned him to expect the worst from him.

Then Milles's wife arrived at Bonner's palace. She was pregnant, and in the ninth month; the baby was expected any day. She demanded to see her husband, and after gaining access to Bonner she told him that if she was not allowed to see Milles she would remain there and give birth to her baby in Bonner's house.

Bonner had Milles brought in, and told Milles that he was a wicked heretic whose obstinate heresy was endangering his wife's pregnancy; Bonner said that if she had a miscarriage it would be Milles's fault. He then told Milles to make the sign of the cross and say: '*In nomine Patris et Filii et Spiritu Sancti, Amen*'. Milles refused to make the sign of the cross, and said the words in English: 'In the name of the Father, and of the Son, and of the Holy Ghost, Amen'. Bonner told him to say the words in Latin. After a moment's hesitation, Milles decided that there would be nothing wrong in saying it in Latin, and did so. Bonner then told Milles to take his wife to some house in Fulham where she could have her baby, and to return to captivity in Bonner's house as soon as the baby was born. A friend of Milles had come to Bonner's house with Milles's wife, and was waiting outside. Bonner told him to go with Milles and make sure that Milles returned after the baby was born; if he did not bring Milles back, he as well as Milles would be punished.

The baby was born next day. Milles's friend did not bring him to Bonner; he disappeared and went into hiding. But Milles went back by himself to Bonner's house. Bonner handed him a document in Latin which Milles did not understand, and told him to sign it; it was doubtless some form of recantation. Milles thought that as he did not understand what the document contained, he could not be accused of betraying his principles if he signed it, and did so. Bonner told him to go home and rejoin his wife, and no further proceedings were taken against him.

Thomas Hinshaw was also whipped by Bonner. He was a young man aged nineteen or twenty, and apprenticed to a master in St Paul's Churchyard in London. He was another of the Protestants who was arrested at the prayer-meeting in the fields near Islington. He was imprisoned in Newgate and then sent to Fulham to be examined by Bonner. After Bonner had questioned him himself, he invited his secretary John Harpsfield (the brother of Nicholas Harpsfield) to take part in the interrogation of Hinshaw. Harpsfield called him a 'peevish boy'; Hinshaw accused Bonner and Harpsfield of working to maintain their 'dark and develish kingdom'.

Bonner ordered that Hinshaw should be taken out into the garden, where he was told to bend down over a bench, while Bonner and Harpsfield whipped him with rods. Foxe wrote that Bonner himself beat Hinshaw 'so long as the fat-paunched bishop could endure with breath, and till for weariness he was fain to cease'.

Hinshaw fell ill with a fever. Bonner sent him back to his master in St Paul's Churchyard till he had recovered from the fever, when he intended to examine him again. But Hinshaw's

Thomas Hinshaw scourged by Bonner in his orchard at Fulham

fever lasted for a year. By the time he had recovered Queen Mary had died, the persecution of heretics had stopped, and Hinshaw went free. He was the third of the three men whipped by Bonner who escaped with his life.[3]

CHAPTER 16

Two Journeys

MARY PROMISED HER PEOPLE that she would regain Calais. The first reaction to the disaster had been to strengthen her position. Her Parliament that met in January 1558 voted her more money than they had ever granted her before, as the nation united to avenge the national disgrace and drive the French out of Calais with the help of their Spanish allies, who would eagerly join them in the campaign next summer. But as the months passed by, and no move was made against the French in Calais, disillusionment began, and the bitterness against the Spaniards was renewed. In July the Spanish army in the Netherlands, under Count Egmont, won a great victory over the French at Gravelines; but they made no move to follow up their victory with an attempt to regain Calais.

When King Philip left England for the second time in July 1557 – no one knew that he would never again in his life set foot on English soil – he sent a new ambassador to England, Don Gómez Suárez de Figueroa, Count of Feria. Feria fell in love with Jane Dormer, one of Queen Mary's ladies-in-waiting. She came from an old Catholic family, and was devoted to Mary, both because she admired the Queen's zeal for the Catholic religion, and because Mary was a very kind mistress to her ladies-in-waiting. But though Feria was therefore personally in favour with Mary, he had been entrusted by Philip with the duty of ensuring that Mary did nothing to harm Elizabeth, and his instructions from Philip were to do all he could to win Elizabeth's goodwill in preparation for the day when she succeeded Mary as Queen.

Mary was ill. Although she was only forty-two, it was generally known that she would soon die. One after another the pillars of Catholic Europe died in 1558. Charles V, who had continued to play an important part in political affairs from the Spanish monastery to which he retired when he abdicated, died in September. His sister Mary of Hungary, the Regent of the Netherlands, died in October. Cardinal Pole's health was failing, and he would soon die. Of the English Catholic bishops, whom Mary had appointed to replace the heretical Protestant bishops who had been burned or deprived of their sees, Christopherson of Chichester, Bird of Chester, Griffin of Rochester and Hopton of Norwich would die before the end of 1558, though Pope Paul IV and King Henry II of France would survive till 1559, and Mary of Lorraine till 1560.

Elizabeth was living in her house at Hatfield, some twenty miles north of London. She still had to be cautious, but she could confidently wait for the Queen to die. She entered into a close relationship with William Cecil, though they were both careful not to publicise their friendship. Cecil had risen rapidly under Edward VI to be Secretary of State before he was thirty, and he was very influential under Somerset and Northumberland. When Mary became Queen he became a Catholic and went to Mass, but Mary was suspicious of him, and dismissed him from his office as Secretary of State. He was sent to escort Cardinal Pole from Brussels to London when Pole arrived as Papal Legate in November 1554, but his brilliant career under Edward VI received a setback, and he was employed only on comparatively unimportant duties. This gave him time to act as Elizabeth's agent in the management of her property. Neither Elizabeth nor Cecil let it be known that they were looking forward to collaborating in more important matters in the future.

Mary, ill and saddened by the loss of Calais and the growing anti-Spanish feeling in England, went on burning heretics. The authorities even found a heretic to burn in the diocese of Exeter,

Devon and Cornwall were strongly Catholic areas. The district had been the centre of the Catholic rising of 1549 against the introduction of Cranmer's Book of Common Prayer under Edward VI. It was not until thirty years later that Devon and Cornwall became centres of Protestantism after the local seamen had played the leading part in the struggle of Protestant England against Philip II's Catholic Spain.

An elderly man named Prest lived near Launceston in Cornwall. Both he and his grown-up children were good Catholics, but his wife, who was very small, rather fat, and aged fifty-four, was a Protestant. Their differences of opinion on religion were so great, and she was so disgusted by the aggressive Catholicism of her husband and children, and their joy at the restoration of the Catholic religion when Mary became Queen, that she decided to leave home. She wandered all over Devon and Cornwall, maintaining herself by earning her living, chiefly by her spinning. When people asked her how she could manage without money, she said that she would have no need of money when she was with God in Heaven.

Her husband, despite his disapproval of his wife's religious opinions, was fond of her, and he went and looked for her all over Devon. He found her and brought her back to Launceston; but as she continued to express strong Protestant views, denouncing the Mass, the neighbours reported her to the authorities in Exeter. After being imprisoned for a time in very harsh conditions in the jail at Launceston, she was sent to Exeter to be examined by John Turberville, the Bishop of Exeter. He and his officials who interrogated her told her that she was an ignorant woman; but she knew her Bible well, and could give the right chapter and verse for her assertions, and she persisted in denying the Real Presence. Her interrogators called her an Anabaptist, probably because of her contempt for property, which she often expressed.

Turberville was patient with her. After interrogating her, he released her; but as she persisted in proclaiming her Protestant opinions, and denouncing the Mass in public, she was again arrested and sent to him. Turberville offered to release her if she would recant and return to her husband. 'Nay, that I will not', she said, 'God forbid that I should lose the life eternal for this carnal and short life. I will never turn from my heavenly husband to my earthly husband, from the fellowship of angels to mortal children God is my father, God is my mother, God is my sister, my brother, my kinsman; God is my friend most faithful.'

In the end Turberville condemned her as a heretic. She was burned at the usual place of execution at Southernhay, just outside the walls of Exeter, on 4 November 1558. She was the only martyr to be burned in the diocese of Exeter and one of the last to suffer in Mary's reign.

The persecution in the diocese of Norwich was as fierce as ever. Alice Driver, who was aged about thirty, was the wife of an agricultural labourer at Grundisburgh in Suffolk. She had perhaps been in contact with someone who had read the books of Knox and Goodman, for she was heard comparing Queen Mary to Jezebel. She was prosecuted at the assizes and sentenced to have her ears cut off. She said that she willingly suffered the pain and ignominy for the sake of the truth. Soon afterwards she was condemned as a heretic by Bishop Hopton, and was burned at Ipswich in the same fire with Alexander Gooch, a thirty-six-year-old man from Woodbridge in Suffolk, on 4 November 1558.

By the beginning of November, rumours were spreading that the Queen was dying. Her ladies-in-waiting were very sad, and were saddened, too, to see her so overcome with grief. They asked her what was the reason for her sadness: was it because of the absence of her husband King Philip? 'Not only that,' she said, 'but when I am dead and opened, you will find Calais lying in my heart.'

In the diocese of Canterbury, five Protestants had been denounced to Cardinal Pole in the summer of 1558, and Pole had instigated proceedings against them. In due course they were condemned as heretics. John Cornford of Wrotham, Christopher Brown of Maidstone, John Herst of Ashford, and two women of Maidstone, old Kathleen Tynley and young Alice Snoth, were all in prison at Canterbury waiting to be burned.

Nicholas Harpsfield was in London, but he hurried down to Canterbury, travelling the sixty miles, which was usually a two-day journey, in one day. The story spread among the Protestants that he knew that the Queen was dying, that when she died the new Queen, who was herself a heretic, would stop the burning of heretics, and that he was determined that these five heretics in Canterbury should suffer their just punishment for their grievous sin, and should be burned before Queen Mary died. He arrived in time. On 10 November 1558 the five were burned in the same fire in Canterbury.

On that day the Spanish ambassador, the Count of Feria, was also making a journey. He rode twenty miles north from London to Brockett Hall near Hatfield to have dinner with the Lady Elizabeth, who was staying in the house of her neighbour and tenant, Sir John Brockett. He arrived in time for the midday dinner at the usual time of 11.30 a.m. He and Elizabeth engaged in very pleasant conversation during dinner, at which Lady Clinton, the wife of the Lord Admiral, Lord Clinton, and several other ladies were present. After dinner Elizabeth spoke to Feria alone except for the presence of one or two of her ladies who spoke only English, and did not understand what they said when they spoke French. Feria told her of King Philip's great regard for her, and of his wish to continue the alliance with England when she became Queen. She said that she greatly appreciated the friendship which Philip had shown her, that she too wished to continue the alliance with Spain, and that she would never make peace with France unless Calais was restored to England. But while they exchanged these friendly words, Feria was wondering what she would do when she became Queen, and she was wondering how Philip would react to what she did.

Mary was dying in St James's Palace in Westminster, and Pole was dying in Lambeth Palace. They both of them wrote to Elizabeth beseeching her to preserve the Catholic religion when she became Queen. She seems to have sent them an encouraging, but ambiguous, reply. Mary died early in the morning of Thursday, 17 November – a day that would be celebrated by Protestants for 150 years as 'Queen Elizabeth's Accession Day'. Pole died the same evening, twelve hours after Mary.

As soon as Mary died, some lords of the Council set out at once for Hatfield, eager to be the first to tell Elizabeth that she was now Queen. There is a tradition at Hatfield that they found her sitting under an oak tree which still stands today. It is surprising that she should have been sitting under a tree on a cold and foggy November day; perhaps she was taking a walk in the park and they came to her when she was standing under the tree.

Elizabeth reappointed to her Privy Council most of the lords who had been on Mary's Privy Council and who had dutifully persecuted Protestants; but she appointed William Cecil to be her Secretary of State.

After spending six days at Hatfield, Elizabeth rode towards London. The Lord Mayor and all the city officials, with a large escort of men-at-arms and attendants, came out to meet her at Highgate. The Bishop of London, Bonner, came with them. When Bonner knelt to kiss the Queen's hand, she snatched it away, giving him a look of hatred and disgust. It was her first public gesture showing what she would do as Queen.

The burnings stopped at once. There were some Protestants in London, and two in Salisbury, who had been condemned as heretics and were waiting to be burned; but after Mary died, no warrant was issued for their burning to take place. They were soon released, and died in their beds many years later.

Thomas Bryce could now complete his poem, *The Register*, which he would soon be able to publish.

> When last of all to take their leave
> At Canterbury they did consume
> Who constantly to Christ did cleave,
> Therefore were fried with fiery fume.
> But six days after these were put to death
> God sent us our Elizabeth.

It took a few weeks for news of Mary's death to reach the English Protestant refugees in Switzerland. When they heard of it, they did not conceal their joy; it was a deliverance, an act of God which had put an end to the four years of terror. Kethe promptly wrote a hymn, based on the 100th Psalm, to celebrate the happy news:

> All people that on earth do dwell,
> Sing to the Lord with cheerful voice.
> Him serve with mirth, his praise forth tell;
> Come ye before him, and rejoice.

CHAPTER 17

Foxe's Book of Martyrs

KETHE AND THE REVOLUTIONARY REFUGEES in Geneva called on all people that on earth do dwell to rejoice in Queen Mary's death; but Elizabeth in England adopted a very different attitude. In her first proclamation after she became Queen she stated that it had pleased God to vest the crown in her 'by calling to his mercy out of this mortal life, to our great grief, our dearest sister of noble memory', the late Queen Mary.

She also made it clear, by appointing most of Mary's council to be members of her own Privy Council, that no one would be punished, or even criticised, for having burned or tortured Protestants under Mary if they were again prepared to change their religion and serve Queen Elizabeth as they had served Henry VIII, Edward VI and Mary. Lord Rich, Sir John Baker, and Edmund Tyrrel need have no fear if they were prepared to be loyal subjects of Elizabeth. She would not allow the Protestants to take revenge on their persecutors, any more than she would allow them to criticise a Queen.

Even when the Protestants thought that they had strong legal grounds for taking proceedings against Mary's agents who had burned and tortured them, Elizabeth stopped them from doing so. The Protestants prosecuted the Sheriff in Guernsey who, when Perotine Massey gave birth to a baby when she was burning at the stake, had ordered that the baby be thrown back into the fire. The court held that as the baby had not been condemned as a heretic, the Sheriff was guilty of murder; but Elizabeth pardoned him.

Nearly all the noblemen and gentlemen were ready to serve

Elizabeth and to continue governing the country under a Protestant Queen; but Elizabeth knew that she had to move cautiously in introducing religious changes. Unlike Henry VIII, she was a Protestant; she did not believe in the Real Presence. But she knew that most of her subjects were still Catholics, who did not really oppose the burning of troublesome Protestant dissidents, but who also hated foreigners, including the Italian Pope and the Spaniards. Many of them thought that Mary had burned too many Protestants – more than twice the number in forty-five months than had been burned in the previous 150 years. But the great majority of the 283 people burned during her reign had suffered in south-east England – 78 of them had been burned in London and the vicinity (56 of them in Smithfield), 62 in Kent (nearly all of them in Canterbury), 39 in Essex, 23 in Sussex, 18 in Suffolk, 14 in Norfolk, 10 in Gloucestershire – and the remainder elsewhere in south-east England and in the Midlands, except three in Wales, one north of the Trent in Chester, and one west of Bristol in Exeter.[1] Most of the country was Catholic, and even in south-east England there were many Catholics. It was probably only in London and Kent that there was a majority of Protestants.

Like Somerset and Cranmer under Edward VI, and unlike Mary, Elizabeth insisted that there should be no change in religion until it was authorised by law under royal authority. On the first Sunday of her reign, 20 November, she appointed Dr William Bill to preach at Paul's Cross. He had been the Master of Trinity College, Cambridge, under Edward VI, and had been ejected from the office by the Catholic fellows of the college when Mary came to the throne; but nothing worse had happened to him during her reign, which he had spent living quietly in the country. Elizabeth told Bill to say, in his sermon, that the Protestants should not make any alteration in religion until the Queen authorised it.

But Elizabeth's tolerance, and her reluctance to permit the

Protestants to go too fast, had encouraged the Catholics to resist. The lords and gentlemen were prepared to change again and enforce the orders of a Protestant Queen; but the Catholic bishops and doctors were too confident. They had burned Protestants under Henry VIII, and had been subjected only to mild penalties under Edward VI. Under Mary they had let themselves go and had burned many more Protestants. They were not afraid that a young Queen of twenty-five, who was restraining the Protestants, would harm them. They were prepared to defy her, confident that she could not resist their pressure.

Bill, in urging the Protestants to make no move until the Queen permitted them to do so, had made a passing reference to Protestantism as the 'true religion'. Bishop Christopherson of Chichester, who on Elizabeth's instructions preached at Paul's Cross on the following Sunday, said that Protestantism was not the true religion, but heresy. Elizabeth informed him that he had been appointed to preach restraint, not to incite religious hatred, and ordered him to be confined in his house. She would probably have released him soon if he had not died.

Elizabeth allowed Mary to have a splendid Catholic funeral. Bishop White of Winchester preached the sermon at the funeral. He chose as his text: 'I praise the dead more than the living', and did not disguise the fact that he was favourably comparing the dead Queen Mary with the living Queen Elizabeth. Elizabeth placed him under house arrest, but released him after a few weeks.

At Christmas, Owen Oglethorpe, the Bishop of Carlisle, celebrated Mass for Elizabeth in her chapel royal at Whitehall. Oglethorpe was a Yorkshireman who had become President of Magdalen College, Oxford, and Dean of Windsor under Henry VIII. He had complied with government policy under Henry VIII and at first under Edward VI, but he was eventually deprived of his offices by Northumberland's government in 1552 because he was too sympathetic to Catholic doctrines.

Under Mary he was an active Catholic, disputing against Cranmer, Ridley and Latimer in the Oxford disputation of April 1554, and was appointed Bishop of Carlisle by Mary.

When Oglethorpe celebrated Mass for Elizabeth at Christmas 1558, she ordered him not to elevate the Host for adoration. He refused to comply with her instructions, and elevated it; so she walked out of the chapel. Any woman who had done this six weeks earlier would have been burned as a heretic.

Elizabeth's coronation was to take place on 15 January 1559. She had great difficulty in finding a bishop who was prepared to crown her. The see of Canterbury was vacant after Pole's death. Heath, the Archbishop of York, and all the other bishops refused to crown her because she was a heretic; but Oglethorpe was pressurised into reluctantly agreeing to do so. Before the coronation Elizabeth, in accordance with the usual tradition, went to the Tower, and on the day before the coronation, 14 January, she went in procession through the streets of London from the Tower to Westminster. The event turned into a great Protestant demonstration. The usual pageants along the route showed Henry VIII and his lawful wife Anne Boleyn, and in one pageant a book was displayed. Elizabeth asked what book it was, and when she was told it was an English Bible, she kissed it.

Elizabeth's first Parliament met in March 1559. She asked it, after some hesitation, to pass legislation repudiating Papal supremacy, and acknowledging the Queen, not as Supreme Head but as Supreme Governor of the Church of England. Another bill introduced the Protestant service of the Third Book of Common Prayer, and made it a criminal offence to celebrate or attend Mass, punishable by imprisonment for six months for the first offence, twelve months for the second offence, and for life for the third offence.

These bills were opposed by the bishops in the House of Lords, including Bonner. Despite his public humiliation by the Queen at Highgate, no measures had been taken against Bonner, who was at liberty and still Bishop of London; but a claim was brought against him by the tenants to whom Ridley had granted leases when he was Bishop of London, and who had been ejected from their properties by Bonner. They had been unable to obtain any redress from Bonner or from Mary in 1555; now they tried again. This time they were successful; the authorities, after investigating the case, ordered Bonner to pay them compensation. But this was the only action taken against him.

The bill abolishing Papal supremacy and recognising Elizabeth as Supreme Governor of the Church of England was passed after heated debates in both Houses of Parliament. It was strongly opposed in the House of Commons by Story, who had played so prominent a part in the interrogation of several heretics, as well as having been one of the counsel for the prosecution at Cranmer's trial. He was elected MP for Downton in Wiltshire. In the debate he vigorously defended the part he had played in persecuting heretics under Mary. 'I wish for my part that I had done more than I did', he said. 'I threw a faggot in the face of an earwig at the stake at Uxbridge as he was singing a psalm, and set a bushel of thorns under his feet . . . and I see nothing to be ashamed of, nor sorry for.' He said that he had often told the bishops in Queen Mary's time that they were persecuting the common people, 'chopping at twigs. But I wished to have chopped at the roots, which if they had done, this gear had not come now in question.' Everyone thought that by chopping at the roots, he meant that they should have burned the Lady Elizabeth, now the Queen.

The bill abolishing the Papal, and restoring the royal, supremacy passed the House of Lords by thirty-three votes to twelve with all the bishops and two temporal lords voting against it. The bill abolishing the Mass and imposing the Third Book of Common Prayer passed in the House of Lords by a majority of only three. The bishops refused to take the oath of supremacy. Even Oglethorpe refused; he now bitterly regretted that he had agreed to crown Elizabeth.

Bonner went further. On the day that the Third Book of Common Prayer came into force, he celebrated Mass in St Paul's Cathedral. He was arrested and sent to the Marshalsea prison. Several of the other bishops were also imprisoned. All of them were deprived of their sees and replaced by Protestant bishops, except Anthony Kitchin, the Bishop of Llandaff, who alone of them all agreed to recognise Elizabeth as Supreme Governor of the Church of England.

The see of Canterbury was vacant after Pole's death. Elizabeth appointed Matthew Parker to be the new archbishop. He was a Norfolk man who had held important positions at Cambridge University under Henry VIII and Edward VI, and had lived in hiding in England under Mary. None of Mary's bishops would agree to consecrate Parker as archbishop. They had to find three of the old Protestant bishops who had been deprived under Mary – Barlow, Scory and Coverdale – and John Hodgkin, the suffragan Bishop of Bedford, to consecrate him.

Parker was the kind of archbishop that Elizabeth wished to have. He hated the extremists and revolutionaries as much as she did. One of the most important effects of the persecution of Mary's reign had been to make a powerful section of the English Protestants reject the doctrine of Christian obedience and become revolutionaries. They became known as Puritans, because they wished to purify the Church of England by getting rid of the 'dregs of Popery', such as crucifixes and vestments, which Elizabeth wished to retain; for the word 'Puritan' in the sixteenth century did not have its modern meaning.

Elizabeth was determined not to allow the Puritans to gain control in England, but she was reluctantly forced to rely on their support in Scotland, France and the Netherlands. After many vacillations, and repeatedly changing her mind, she reluctantly allowed Cecil to persuade her to support the Protestant revolution which John Knox led in Scotland, and to risk war with France and Spain by sending an English army into Scotland to help the revolutionaries. In the 1570s she was persuaded, equally reluctantly, to help William the Silent and the Protestant revolutionaries in the Netherlands. Her extraordinary indecision, and hesitation, and her habit of repeatedly changing her mind, was not primarily due to any defect in her character, and was certainly not, as some people believed, because she was a woman, but because she was so reluctant to help the Puritans and the revolutionaries, but needed their support against Philip II and the French Catholics.

'Of all other, Knox's name, if it be not Goodman's, is most odious here', wrote Cecil. Goodman did not return to England after Mary's death, but went off from Geneva to help Knox's revolution in Scotland, which Archbishop Parker disliked as much as Elizabeth did. 'God keep us from such destruction as Knox have attempted in Scotland, the people to be orderers of things', wrote Parker. He was outraged by Goodman's doctrine, 'that it is lawful for any private individual subject to kill his sovereign if he think him to be a tyrant in his conscience'. He thought that if the tenant and the servant began 'to discuss what is tyranny, and to discuss whether his prince, his landlord, his master, is a tyrant, by his own fancy and collection supposed, what Lord of the Council shall ride quietly-minded in the streets among desperate beasts? What master shall be sure in his bed-chamber?'

As this was the attitude of Elizabeth and her favourite archbishop, it is not surprising that they were not unduly concerned over the sufferings of the martyrs from the lower classes of society who had been burned under Mary. But John Foxe thought that the people in England did not really recognise the sufferings of the martyrs and the courage that they had shown in enduring torture and death for the true religion. He decided to translate his Latin book about the martyrs, his *Rerum in Ecclesia gestarum* into English, and write a greatly extended version of it from the information which he could now obtain. Returning to

England in October 1559, he travelled around the country speaking to the survivors, to the friends of the victims, to the spectators who had been present when they were burned. As the events had all taken place within the last seven or eight years, the witnesses' memories of them were still fresh.

Foxe also took copies of the letters that the martyrs had written to their families and friends, and of the official records of their interrogations in the bishops' registers. He liked to give the names, occupations, age, and the town or village of origin of the martyrs, as well as the places and dates of their martyrdoms, and details of their trials, burnings and other sufferings; but he could not always find out all this information. Sometimes he found out that a martyr had been burned at some place on some date, but could not discover his name.

By 1563 he had published the first English edition of his *Acts and Monuments of these latter and perilous days touching matters of the Church*. It included all the passages that he had already published in Latin dealing with the sufferings of the early Christian martyrs and the Lollards and Protestants in England and Europe between 1401 and 1546, and the new material which he had now collected about the martyrs under Mary. The book had 1,721 pages and ran to 1,450,000 words. It immediately became popularly known as the *Book of Martyrs*. It was dedicated to the 'most Christian and renowned princess, Queen Elizabeth'. Foxe did not mention that while the martyrs were suffering bravely in the fire and refusing to recant, Elizabeth became a Catholic and went to Mass. Instead, he praised God for 'the miraculous preservation of the Lady Elizabeth, now Queen of England, from extreme calamity and danger of life in the time of Queen Mary her sister'.

After the *Book of Martyrs* was published, many people wrote to Foxe. Some pointed out minor errors in his book. Some gave him the additional information which he had so far been unable to find, such as the names of the martyrs to whom he had referred and information about them. He also read comments from Catholic opponents who had gone abroad and published their attacks on his book in Spanish territory. They found some mistakes in the book, and used these mistakes to try to discredit him, and to show that all his *Book of Martyrs* was lying propaganda. Thus in his account of the burning of the martyrs in Windsor Great Park in 1543 he wrote that four men of Windsor – Marbeck, Peerson, Testwood and Filmer – were sentenced to be burned but that Henry VIII pardoned Filmer, while Peerson, Testwood and Marbeck were burned. This was an error; in fact it was Marbeck who was pardoned, and Peerson, Testwood and Filmer were burned. The Catholic writers accused Foxe of lying in writing that Marbeck was a martyr when he was pardoned, and that this proved that the *Book of Martyrs* was propaganda lies.

The new information which Foxe received persuaded him to publish a second edition of the *Book of Martyrs* in 1570. By now the international political situation had changed. Relations between Philip II and Elizabeth had become much worse. Philip's governor of the Netherlands, the Duke of Alba, was placing an embargo on trade with England and seizing English ships in the Netherlands, and Elizabeth was retaliating much more effectively by an embargo on trade with the Netherlands and seizing Spanish property in England. After vacillating in her policy towards Mary, Queen of Scots, Elizabeth was holding Mary as a prisoner in England and supporting the Scottish Protestant lords who were ruling Scotland as regents for Mary's infant son, King James VI. A dangerous Catholic revolt had broken out in the North of England, led by Catholic noblemen who had celebrated Mass in Durham Cathedral; the revolt had been suppressed, and many rebels executed. After Pope Pius IV had tried for some years to avoid a final break with England, he had been succeeded by Pope Pius V who as Cardinal Michele Ghislieri had been a fierce persecutor of Protestant heretics. Pius V finally excommunicated and deposed Elizabeth and issued a

bull absolving her subjects from the duty to obey her. Meanwhile Jesuit missionaries were being sent from the Spanish
Netherlands to organise secret Catholic resistance to Elizabeth's
government. Elizabeth and Cecil were now prepared, as they
had not been in 1559 and 1563, to give official support to anti-
Catholic propaganda, and to use Foxe's *Book of Martyrs* to arouse
fear and hatred of Rome, the Pope and the Catholics in the
minds of the English people.

But there were some passages in the first edition of the *Book of
Martyrs* which Elizabeth did not like. Foxe had criticised Henry
VIII, especially his brutal behaviour at the trial of the Protestant
martyr Lambert before Lambert was burned in 1538. The
propaganda line of Elizabeth's government, appealing to English
nationalism and wishing to identify it with Protestantism, was
that Henry VIII was a great English King who had freed England
from the domination of an Italian Pope. Elizabeth did not wish
to emphasize the fact that Protestants had been burned for
denying the Real Presence, not only by a Queen who had
submitted to Rome and the Pope, but also by a great and
patriotic English King who had broken with Rome. So Foxe cut
out from his second edition of 1570 the passages which criticised
Henry VIII personally. He was allowed to write about all the
Protestant martyrs who had been burned in Henry's reign, but
their persecution was attributed to the fact that the well-mean-
ing King had been misled by Gardiner's advice. As Gardiner had
afterwards been prominently associated with the persecution of
Mary's reign after England had been reunited to Rome, Foxe
portrayed Gardiner as a Papist who had always secretly supported
the Pope, but in the reign of Henry VIII had concealed the fact
while deceiving Henry into carrying out a Papist policy of
burning Protestants who denied the Real Presence.

The second edition of Foxe's *Acts and Monuments*, which
everytone still called the *Book of Martyrs*, was published in 1570
with the errors in the first edition corrected, the additional

information inserted, and the criticism of Henry VIII removed. It was much longer than the 1563 edition. The page numbers run to 2,303, but in fact there are 2,335 pages and 3,150,000 words. It is nearly four times the length of the Bible, and the longest single work which has ever been published in the English language.

Cecil had decided to use this new edition as anti-Catholic propaganda. If anyone had any sympathy for Mary, Queen of Scots, who was being portrayed in foreign countries as an unhappy, ill-treated Queen unjustly imprisoned for years in England, or for the Jesuit missionaries and other Catholic agents who were tortured on the rack or hanged, drawn and quartered, then Foxe's *Book of Martyrs* would remind the people of what these Catholics had done to the Protestants when they were in power. Elizabeth's government ordered that a copy of the 1570 edition of the *Book of Martyrs*, fastened by a chain, should be placed in every cathedral, and a copy was also placed in many churches. The captains of the ships that sailed from Plymouth to the West Indies and South America to raid and plunder the Spanish towns and ships there and to fight the Spaniards at sea, were ordered to have a copy of Foxe's *Book of Martyrs* in the ship.

In some cases the Protestants were now able, after many years, to see their persecutors punished. By the time that the 1570 edition was published, Bonner had died in prison in the Marshalsea in 1567 after he had been imprisoned there for eight years. Nicholas Harpsfield was also arrested for his defiance of the royal authority, and was imprisoned in the Tower for sixteen years until he died there in 1575. The great persecutor, Story, suffered a more terrible punishment. After his speech in the House of Commons in which he said that he wished that the bishops had struck at the roots of heresy in Mary's reign, he was accused of sedition against the Queen and was arrested in his barrister's robes as he was leaving court on the Western Circuit; but he succeeded in escaping with the help of the Spanish ambassador and in reaching the Spanish Netherlands. Alba employed him there as a persecutor of heretics in the office of the Inquisition in Antwerp. One of his main duties was to make sure that no heretical books were brought into the Netherlands from England.

Elizabeth's agents laid a trap for Story. They reported that an English ship had arrived at Bergen-op-Zoom full of heretical Protestant literature which the English planned to smuggle into the Netherlands. Story went on board the ship to interrogate the crew and to search the ship to find the heretical literature. The ship's captain suddenly sailed away with Story on board before the Spanish authorities in Bergen-op-Zoom could stop him. When the ship landed at Yarmouth, Story was arrested and sent to London where he was prosecuted for high treason for having incited Alba to invade England and for instigating the Catholic rising in the North. He was convicted and sentenced to be hanged, drawn and quartered. Despite the protests of the Spanish ambassador the sentence was carried out. The Englishmen who had read about him in Foxe's *Book of Martyrs* felt that he had received his just deserts.

The *Book of Martyrs*, with the full force of government propaganda behind it, undoubtedly had a powerful effect on the English people, and is one of the few books which can be said to have changed the course of history. The 1570 edition was reprinted twice in Foxe's lifetime, in 1576 and 1583. Foxe was sad when Elizabeth's government burned three foreign Anabaptists at Smithfield in 1575, and interceded for them as unsuccessfully as he had interceded for Joan Bocher and George van Parris in the reign of Edward VI; but he could rejoice in the fact that the sufferings of the martyrs had not been in vain, and that God had sent Elizabeth to deliver England from Papist tyranny.

Foxe died in 1587. By then Philip II had offered a reward to anyone who assassinated a Protestant heretical ruler, and Catholic fanatics, acting on his proclamation, had assassinated William of Orange in the Netherlands and had unsuccessfully attempted to kill Elizabeth in England. They were caught and put to death by dreadful tortures. The Protestants felt little sympathy for them, for they had read the *Book of Martyrs*. In the year after Foxe died, English seamen defeated the Spanish Armada. All the English ships carried a copy of Foxe's *Book of Martyrs*, and their crews believed that they were fighting to save their country from a repetition of the horrors of Mary's reign if the Spaniards succeeded in invading and conquering England.

The 1570 edition of the *Book of Martyrs* was reprinted again in 1598 and four times during the seventeenth century. The people were continuosly reminded of what would happen if England was ever again ruled by a Catholic sovereign. By this time the Protestants were calling Mary 'Bloody Mary', a phrase which Foxe himself never used, for Elizabeth would not have liked it if he had used these words about a Queen. The *Book of Martyrs* was reprinted again in the eighteenth and nineteenth centuries, and in the United States in the twentieth century. These modern editions include the suppressed passages of the edition of 1563.

Today in most of the world, Catholics and Protestants do not wish to burn and torture each other, though there are countries like Northern Ireland where the two religions are bitterly divided by hatred and violence. The Catholic Church is no longer a persecuting Church. Pope John Paul II may sometimes make statements which progressive Roman Catholics do not like, but he is not in favour of burning Protestant heretics.

In 2001, when Catholics go to Mass while their friends attend a Protestant church or do not go to church at all, it seems extraordinary that Catholics in Mary's reign should have burned Protestants who did not believe in the Real Presence. But the Real Presence was the symbolic, not the real, cause why the heretics were burned. They were burned because they resisted the authority of a tyrannical government. Belief in the Real

Presence and Papal supremacy had been made the test of their obedience. The heretics were burned because the government would not allow the simple people, or the prominent dissident intellectuals, to advocate what they believed and not what the government ordered them to believe. They were burned because when they were confronted with the choice of submission or resistance, they chose resistance. It is clear that it was resistance to authority, and not belief in the Real Presence and Papal supremacy, which was the real reason for the persecution, because some of the worst persecutors were noblemen and gentlemen, sheriffs and JPs, who were laymen, not churchmen, who changed their religion whenever a new sovereign came to the throne, but who always strongly believed that everyone should be forced to submit to authority.

Foxe has sometimes been criticised by modern writers for having devoted such a large proportion of his book to the story of a few prominent martyrs, like Cranmer, Ridley, Bradford and others. But this was only because he had more information about them than about the poor husbandmen and capmakers, and because they wrote many more letters to their friends which Foxe was able to see. When he found that a comparatively obscure figure like Woodman of Warbleton had written many letters to his relatives and friends, he wrote many pages about him. But the length of his references to individual martyrs was not the important thing for Foxe. He named and praised the humble people who had died for the cause in which they believed, not knowing that anyone would remember them, that Foxe would write a book about them, that Queen Elizabeth and her government, for political reasons, would give the widest publicity to the book, and that it would be repeatedly reprinted for four hundred years to ensure that their sufferings and courage would always be remembered.

The ideas of the martyrs, and their language, seem strange to us today. Some of them were persecutors as well as martyrs, and had burned Anabaptists and Arians before they themselves were burned. But in one sense their sufferings still have very topical significance for us. The story of Bloody Mary's martyrs is a story of agricultural labourers, tailors, hatmakers and eminent intellectuals, of their wives and daughters, and their children, a story of young men and young women, of old men and old women, some of them blind and crippled, who would not submit to tyranny and preferred to die a terrible death for what they thought was right. It is also a story of rulers and their leading ministers who ordered that the martyrs should be burned because they thought it right to enforce the authority of the state, of politicians and local government officials who eagerly helped them in order to further their careers, of jailers, men-at-arms and constables who obeyed their orders to burn and torture the martyrs, and of members of the public who joined the hue and cry against a persecuted minority, who taunted, insulted and mocked them as they prepared for an agonising death.

It is right that Bloody Mary's martyrs should be remembered today, and we should be grateful to Foxe for his book. The intensity of Mary's persecution instigated the revolutionary ideas of Knox and the Puritans; and Foxe's praise of the common people who suffered under Mary helped to spread the first stirrings of the democratic ideas of the Puritans which would lead them to challenge the authority of Kings and Queens, and to the revolutionary actions of 1640 and 1649. In its Presbyterian form Puritanism was intolerant, suppressing all religions except Presbyterianism; but Cromwell's Independents were in favour of granting religious toleration except to Roman Catholics and Quakers. After the Revolution of 1688 the policy was established in Britain of toleration for all Christian religions but with discrimination against Roman Catholics, who were still regarded as a danger because of the memories of Bloody Mary; and in the nineteenth century religious disabilities were removed from

Roman Catholics, thanks to the efforts of men with liberal ideas who were more strongly opposed than anyone, to everything that Queen Mary had believed or done. But in the twentieth century the persecution of humble individuals by a tyrannical state has been seen on a scale that surpasses the worst persecutions of the sixteenth century; and despite the differences in opinions and language, the martyrs and the persecutors of the twentieth century resemble in many ways the martyrs and persecutors of Bloody Mary's reign.

Some years ago it was reported that a Roman Catholic woman in London, who insisted on remaining anonymous, had gone on a pilgrimage, walking barefoot to Smithfield to atone for the sins of her Catholic co-religionists in burning Protestants 450 years before. She need not have felt any guilt about the burning of the martyrs, and she had done nothing for which she needed to atone. It is not modern Roman Catholics, who have never harmed a Protestant and who advocate tolera- tion and liberal ideas, who should atone for the crimes of Queen Mary, Gardiner, Bonner, Story, Harpsfield, Rich and Tyrrell. But every ruler who has launched a policy of religious, racial, nationalist or political persecution; every politician and journalist who has incited and approved of it; every soldier and camp guard who has carried out his orders to impose the tyranny, like Pharoah's soldiers who were punished by being drowned in the Red Sea; and every member of the public who has cheered on the witchhunt against the victims of persecution, should walk barefoot to Smithfield to atone for the crimes of Bloody Mary and her accomplices.

Notes and Sources

1 – THE PERSECUTING CHURCH

1. See Jasper Ridley, *The Statesman and the Fanatic* pp. 31–2, 124, 126–8, 135–6, 253–8 and the contemporary authorities there cited.
2. More, *Works* viii, pp. 31–2.
3. Daniell, *William Tyndale*, points out that although 6 October has been accepted as the date of Tyndale's execution, there is no evidence of the exact date, though it was certainly in the first days of October 1536.

2 – HENRY VIII: THE BREAK WITH ROME

1. Morice, 'A Declaration concerning . . . Thomas Cranmer', in *Narratives of the Reformation* p. 239.
2. Foxe, *Acts and Monuments* v, p. 697.

3 – EDWARD VI: THE PROTESTANT REFORMATION

1. Bale, *Scriptorum Illustrium Maioris Brytannie* i, pp. 694–5.
2. Machyn, *Diary* 8, see also *Greyfriars Chronicle* p. 70.
3. For Mary's unsuccessful attempt to escape from England, see the correspondence of van der Delft, Charles V. Scheyfre, Mary of Hungary and d'Eecke, 2 May–4 September 1550, and Dubois' report (mid-July 1550) (*Span. Cal.* x, pp. 80–173).
4. *Acts of the Privy Council*, 29 August 1551.
5. For Foxe's talk with Rogers, see Mozley, *John Foxe and his Book* pp. 35–6.

4 – QUEEN MARY

1. Renard to Charles V, 28 and 31 October 1553 (*Span. Cal.* xi, pp. 319–24, 327–30).

5 – FIRST VICTIMS

1. Saunders had been to Eton and King's College, Cambridge; but he was persuaded by his widowed mother to leave the university and become a merchant. He soon

changed his mind and returned to his studies at Cambridge where he learned to speak Latin, Greek and Hebrew. He was ordained a priest, and under Edward VI was appointed reader at a college in Fotheringhay in Northamptonshire. When the college was suppressed he became reader in Litchfield Cathedral. He was appointed vicar of Church Langton in Leicestershire and was also given a benefice in London.

2. Foxe, vi, pp. 611–12, 641–2; Huggarde, *The Displaying of the Protestants* p. 64.
3. For the burning of Rowland Taylor, see Foxe vi, pp. 696–700.
4. For the burning of Hooper, see Foxe vi, pp. 652–8.
5. For the burning of Ferrar, see Foxe vi, pp. 3–26.

6 – THE SEARCH FOR HERETICS

1. For Marsh's case, see Fox vii, pp. 39–68.

7 – THE SUMMER OF 1555

1. Mary, Queen of Scots, the granddaughter of Henry VIII's elder sister Margaret, who had married King James IV of Scotland, was next after Elizabeth in the hereditary line of succession to the throne. The hereditary succession had been altered by Henry VIII's Will, which had excluded Margaret's descendants from the throne. Queen Mary Tudor had relied on this Will, and the Act of Parliament of 1544 which authorised it, to establish her claim to the throne and the illegality of Edward VI's Will, which gave the crown to Jane Grey; but the provisions of Henry VIII's Will, which stipulated that Queen Mary Tudor should not marry a foreigner and would have meant that she forfeited the crown when she married Philip of Spain, had been repealed by the Act of Mary Tudor's Parliament in October 1553.
2. For John and Robert Glover, see Foxe vii, pp. 384–401.
3. For Robert Samuel and Rose Nottingham, see Foxe vii, pp. 371–4.

8 – THE HERETICS AT OXFORD

1. For the trial, the last days, and the burning of Ridley and Latimer, see Foxe vii, pp. 518–83; Ridley, 'Last Farewell', (Ridley, *Works* pp. 395–418).

9 – MORE BURNINGS IN LONDON

1. For Philpot, see Foxe vii, pp. 605–714; Philpot, 'Apology for spitting upon an Arian' (*The Writings of John Philpot* pp. 294–318).

10 – THE GREAT MISCALCULATION

1. For Cranmer's trial, his recantations, his last days, his burning and the text of his recantations and his final speech, see Foxe viii, pp. 44–90; *Bislop Cranmer's Recantacyons* passim; 'All the Submissions and Recantations of Thomas Cranmer' in Cranmer, *Works* ii, pp. 563–6; *A Supplicacyon to the Quenes Maiestie*; MacCulloch, *Thomas Cranmer* pp. 573–605; Jasper Ridley, *Thomas Cranmer* pp. 376–408.

11 – THE UNPOPULAR QUEEN

1. During Edward VI's reign, Cranmer had invited the German Protestant theologian, Martin Bucer, to England and had appointed him as Regius Professor of Divinity at Cambrige. The German Protestant, Paulus Phagius, had also been a lecturer at Cambridge; and Peter Martyr (Pietro Marire Vermigli) had come from Zurich to be Regius Professor of Divinity at Oxford. Bucer and Phagius had both died in Cambridge, and Peter Martyr's wife had died in Oxford.
2. For Maundrell and Coberley, see Foxe viii, pp. 102–5.
3. *Acts of the Privy Council*, 4 January 1555/6.
4. Huggarde, *The Displaying of the Protestantes* pp. 64, 74, 77.
5. For Julins Palmer's case, see Foxe viii, pp. 202–18.
6. For the Guernsey martyrs, the murder of the baby, and Foxe's controversy with Hardinge, see Foxe viii, pp. 226–41; Hardinge, *A Rejoinder to M. Jewells Replie against the Sacrifice of the Masse* pp. 184.
7. For Joan Waste, see Foxe viii, pp. 247–50.

12 – THE CONTINUING PERSECUTION

1. The nineteenth Oecumenical Council of the Church, summoned at the insistence of the Emperor Charles V in order to remove the abuses in the Church and thus strengthen and unite the Church against heresy, was held intermittently at Trent in the Emperor's territory in Northern Italy between 1545 and 1563, with repeated adjournments caused by the wars in Europe and the conflict of interests between the Popes, the Emperor, France and the German Lutherans.
2. For Woodman, see Foxe viii, pp. 332–77.
3. P. Hughes, *The Reformation in England* ii, p. 271n.
4. For Rose Allin, see Foxe viii, pp. 306, 385–6, 391–2.

13 – THE REVOLUTIONARIES

1. Ponet, *A Shorte Treatise of Politke Puouuer* p. 159.
2. Volumes 3, 4 and 5 of the modern editions of Foxe's *Acts and Monuments*.
3. Volumes 1 and 2 of the modern editions of Foxe's *Acts and Monuments*.

4. Bryce, 'The Regester, in Farr, *Select Poetry of the Reign of Queen Elizabeth* I pp. 162–72.
5. For the passages discussed and cited from the works of Knox, Gilby, Kethe and Goodman referred to in this chapter, see Knox's *Works* vols 3 and 4, and Goodman, *How Superior Powers ought to be obeyed*; and see the marginal notes in the Geneva Bible.

14 – THE SECRET CONGREGATIONS

1. For George Eagles, see Foxe viii, pp. 393–7.
2. For Rough, Simpson and their congregation, see Foxe viii, pp. 443–61.

15 – BONNER'S WAY WITH HERETICS

1. Proclamation of Philip and Mary, 6 June 1558, in Foxe viii, p. 468.
2. For Benbridge's cae, see Foxe viii, pp. 490–2; *Acts of the Privy Council*, 1 August 1558.
3. For the three men whipped by Bonner, see Foxe viii, pp. 483–6, 510–13.

17 – FOXE'S BOOK OF MARTYRS

1. There is a difference of opinion among historians as to the precise number of martyrs burned in Mary Tudor's reign, and the places where they were burned. This is due to a discrepancy in the numbers given by John Foxe and in the list sent to Cecil, because of a confusion, in some cases, about the martyrs' names, with the result that some martyrs are mentioned twice under different names. The confusion has been made worse by the errors and omissions of the editors of the modern editions of Foxe's *Book of Martyrs*. For the conflicting figures, cf. Dixon, *History of the Church of England* iv, pp. 374n, 484–5n, 490n, 602–3n, 630–1n, 635–6n, 639n, 645n, 647n, 651–4n, 708–9n, 712n, 714–5n; Hughes, *The Reformation in England* ii, pp. 260–4; and in Dickens, *The English Reformation* p. 266.

Bibliography

Acts of the Privy Council of England (New Series), ed. J.R. Dasent (London, 1890–1907).

Allen J.W. *A History of Political Thought in the Sixteenth Century* (London, 1928).

Archaeologia Cantiane, being Transactions of the Kent Archaeological Society (London and elsewhere, 1858–1999

Aylmer, J. *An Harborrowe for Faithfull & Trew Subiectes agaynst the late blowne Blaste concerninge the Gouvernet of Women* (Strasbourg, 1559).

Bale, J. *Scriptorum Illustrium Maioris Brytannie* (Basle, 1557–9).

Baskerville, G. *English Monks and the Suppression of the Monasteries* (London, 1931).

Belloc, H. *Cranmer* (London, 1931).

Bishop Cranmer's Recantacyons, (Miscellanies of the Philobiblon Society, vol. xv (London, 1877–84).

Bradford, J. *The Writings of John Bradford, M.A.* (Cambridge, 1848–53)

Bryce, T. 'The Regester'. *see* Farr.

Burnet, G. *The History of the Reformation of the Church of England*, ed. N. Pocock (Oxford, 1865 edn., first published in 1679–1715).

Calender of Letters, Documents and State Papers relating to the Negotiations between England and Spain in Simancas and elsewhere, ed. P. de Goyangos, G. Mattingly, R. Tyler, etc. (London, 1862–1954, cited as *Span. Cal.*).

Calender of State Papers and manuscripts relating to English Affairs in the Archive of Venice, ed. R. Brown, C Bentinck, etc. (London, 1864–1947, referred to as *Ven. Cal.*)

Calender of State Papers (Domestic Series) of the reigns of Edward VI, Mary, Elizabeth, 1547–1580, preserved in the Public Record Office (London, 1856, cited as *Cal. St Pap. Dom., Edw.* VI, etc.)

Calender of State Papers (Domestic Series) of the Reign of Elizabeth 1601–1603 with Addenda 1547–1565 preserved in the Public Record Office, ed. H.A.F. Green (London, 1870, cited as *Cal. St. Pap. Dom., Edw. VI.* etc., vol. vi)

Calender of State Papers (Foreign Series) of the Reign of Edward VI 1547–1553 preserved in the Public Record Office, ed. W.B. Turnbull (London, 1861, cited as *Cal. For Pap., Edw. VI*).

Calender of State Papers (Foreign Series) of the Reign of Elizabeth 1558–1589 preserved in the Public record Office, ed. J. Stevenson, etc. (London, 1875–1950, cited as *Cal. For. Pap. Eliz.*).

Calender of State Papers (Foreign Series) of the Reign of Mary, preserved in the Public Record Office, ed. W.B. Turnbull (London, 1861, cited as *Cal. For. Pap. Mary*).

Calender of State Papers relating to English affairs preserved principally in Rome, ed. J. M. Rigg (London, 1916-26, cited as *Papal Cal.*).

Calvin, J. *Calvini opera* vols. xxix–lxxxvii of *Corpus Reformatorum*, ed. C.G. Brettsch-neider and H.F. Bindseil (Brundwick and Berlin, 1863–1900).

Camden Miscellany, vol.xxviii (Royal Historical Society, London, 1984).

The Catholic Encyclopaedia, ed. C.G. Hubermann, et al. (London, 1907–13).

Chambers, R.W. *Thomas More* (London, 1935).

Chester A.G. *Hugh Latimer, Apostle to the English* (Philadelphia, 1954).

Chronicle of Queen Jane and of Two Years of Queen Mary, ed. J. G. Nichols (London, 1850).

Collier, J. *The Ecclesiastical History of Great Britain* (London, 1840 edn., first published 1708–14).

Collinson, P. *Elizabethan Essays* (London, 1994)

Collinson, P. *The Elizabethan Puritan Movement* (London, 1967).

Collinson, P. *Godley People: Essays on English Protestantism and Puritanism* (London, 1983).

Constant, G. *The Reformation in England* (London, 1934–41).

Cooper, C.H. *Athenae Cantabrigienses* (Cambridge, 1858–61).

Coverdale, M. *The Writings and Translations of Myles Coverdale, Bishop of Exeter* (Cambridge, 1858-61).

Cranmer, T. *The Works of Thomas Cranmer*, ed. J.E. Cox (Cambridge, 1844–6).

Daniell, D. *William Tynedale: a Biography* (New Haven and London, 1994).

Dickens, A. G. *The English Reformation* (London, 1964).

Dictionary of National Biography (Oxford, 1885–1901).

Dixon, R. W. *History of the Church of England from the Abolition of the Roman Jurisdiction* (London, 1878–1902).

Edward VI 'The Journal of King Edward's Reign written with his own hand', in Burnet *The History of the Reformation of the Church of England* (Oxford, 1865).

Ellis, H. *Original Letters illustrative of English History* (London, 1824–46).

Erasmus, D. *Opus Epistolarum Des. Erasmi Eoterodami*, ed. P.S. Allen (Oxford, 1906–58).

Farr, E. *Select Poetry Chiefly Devotional of The Reign of Queen Elizabeth* (Cambridge, 1845).

Feria, G. S. de F. 'The Count of Feria's dispatch to Philip II of 14 November 1558', ed. and traslated by M.J. Rodriguez Salgado and Simon Adams, *see* Camden *Miscellany* vol. xxviii.

Foxe, J. The Book of Martyrs:

    Latin edn. *Commentarii rerum in ecclesia gestarum* (1st edn., Strasbourg, 1554; 2nd edn., Basle, 1559).

    1st English edn. *Actes and Monuments of these latter and perillous dayes touching matters of the Church* (London, 1563).

    2nd English edn. *The Eccleiasticqll History, contayning the Actes and Monuments of thynges passed in every Kynges tyme in this realm, especially in the Church of England* (London, 1570).

Foxe, J. *The Acts and Monuments of John Foxe*, ed. J. Prett (London, 1877, New York 1965).

Froude, J.A. *The History of England from the Fall of Wolsey to the Defeat of the Spanish Armada* (London, 1856–70).

Fuller, T. *Church History of Britain from the Birth of Jesus Christ until the year MDCXLVIII* (London, 1856–70).

Gachard, L.P. *Collection des Voyages des Souverains des Pays-Bas* (Brussels, 1876–82)

Gairdner, J. *The English Church in the Sixteenth Century from the Accession of Henry VIII to the Death of Mary* (London, 1902).

Gairdner, J. *Lollardy and the Reformation in England* (London, 1908–13).

Gardiner, S. *Letters of Stephen Gardiner*, ed. J.A. Muller (Cambridge, 1933)

Garrett, C. *The Marian Exciles* (Cambridge, 1938).

Gasquet, F.A., and Bishop, E. *Edward VI and the Book of Common Prayer* (London, 1890)

Geneva Bible: *The Bible and Holy Scriptures conteyned in the Olde and Newe With moste profitable annotations upon all the hard places and other things of great importance,* (1st edn., Geneva, 1560).

Gilby, A. *An Admonition to England and Scotland to bring them to repentance* (first published Geneva, 1558), *see* Knox, *Works*

Goodman, C. *How Superior Powers ought to be obeyed* (New York, 1931 edn., facsimile of 1st edn., Geneva, 1558).

Grand Dictornaire Universel du XIXe siècle, ed. P. Larousse (Paris, 1866–77).

Gratwick, A. E., and Whittick, C. *The Losely List of Sussex Martyrs*, in *Sussex Archaeological Collections* vol. 133 (Lewes, 1995).

Greyfriars Chronicle: *Chronicle of the Grey Friars of London*, ed. J.G. Nichols (London, 1848).

Guy, J. *Tudor England* (Oxford, 1988).

Hall, E. *Chronicle* (London, 1809 edn., first published in 1542).

The Harleian Miscellany (London, 1818–13).

Harpsfield, N. *A Treatise on the Preteded Divorce between Henry VIII and Catherine of Aragon* (London, 1878 edn.)

Harpsfield, N. *The lyfe and Death of Sir Thomas Moore, knight, sometyme Lord high Chancellor of England, written in the tyme of Queene Marie*, ed. E.V. Hitchcock and R.W. Chambers (Oxford, 1932)

Haynes, S. *A Collection of State Papers left by William Cecil, Lord Burghley* (London, 1740)

Hayward, Sir J. *Annals of the first four years of the reign of Queen Elizabeth* (London, 1840 edn., written c. 1590)

Heylin, P. *Ecclesia Restaurata* (Cambridge, 1849 edn., first published in 1661).

Historical Manuscripts, Reports of the Royal Commission on (London, 1870–1942)

Holinshed, R. *Chronicles of England, Scotland and Ireland* (London, 1807–8 edn., first published in 1578)

Hooper, J. *Early Writings of John Hooper* (Cambridge, 1843).

Hooper, J. *Later Writing as Bishop Hooper* (Cambridge, 1843).

House of Lords Journal, vol. i (London, 1509–78).

Hudson, W.S. *John Ponet (1516–1556), Advocate of Ltd Monarchy* (Chicago, 1942).

Huggarde, M. *The Displaying of the Protestantes* (London, 1556).

Hughes, P. *The Reformation in England* (London, 1950–3).

Kaulek, J. *Correspondance politique de M.M. de Castillon et de Marillac 1537–1542* (Paris, 1885).

Kitch, M.J. *Studies in Sussex Church History* (Lewes, 1981).

Knox, J *The works of John Knox*, ed. D. Laing (Edinburgh, 1846–64).

Latimer, H. *Sermons and Remains of Hugh Latimer* (Cambridge, 1844–5).

Leadam, I.S. 'A Narrative of the Pursuit of English Refugees in Germany under Queen Mary', in *Transactions of the Royal Historical Society*, New Series, vol. xi (London , 1897).

Legg, J. Wickham *Cranmer's Liturgical Projects* (London, 1915).

Legg, J. Wickham *The Sarum Missal* (Oxford, 1916).

Le Neve, J. *Fasti ecclesiae Anglicanae* (London, 1715 edn.)

Letters and Papers (Foreign and Domestic) of the Reign of King Henry VIII, ed. J Brewer and J Gairdner, (London, 1862–1910, cited as *L.P.*)

Lingard, J. *History of England from the first Invasion by the Romans to the Accesion of William and Mary in 1688* (5th edn. London, 1849, first published 1819–30)

Liturgies of Edward VI: The Two Liturgies, A.D. 1549 and A.D. 1552, ed. J. Ketley (Cambridge, 1844).

Loach, J. *Edward VI* (New Haven and London, 1999).

Loades, D. *Mary Tudor: A Life* (Oxford, 1989).

Loades, D. *The Reign of Mary Tudor* (London,1991).

Lower, M.A. *The Sussex Martyrs* (Lewes, 1851).

MacCulloch, D. *Thomas Cranmer: a Life* (New Haven and London, 1996).

Machyn, H. *The Diary of Henry Machyn, citizen and merchant taylor of London from A.D. 1550 to A.D. 1563*, ed. J.G. Nichols (London, 1848).

Maclure, M. *The Paul's Cross Sermons 1534–1642* (Toronto, 1958).

Maitland, S.R. *Essays on Subjects connected with the Reformation in England* (London, 1899 edn., first published in 1849).

Marshall, R.K. *John Knox* (Edinburgh, 2000).

Marshall, R.K. *Mary I* (London, 1993).

Martin, C. *Les Protestants Anglais réfugiés à Genève au temps de Calvin 1555–1560* (Geneva, 1993).

Merriman, R.B. *Life and Letters of Thomas Cromwell* (Oxford, 1902).

More, Sir T. *The Complete Works of St Thomas More*, ed. R.S. Sylvester, et al. (New Haven and London, 1963–79).

Morice, R. 'A declaration concernyng the Progeny of that most Reverent Father in God, Thomas Cranmer, late archebisshopp of Canterbury', in *Narratives of the Days of the Reformation*) (London, 1859).

Mozley, J.F. *John Foxe and his Book* (London, 1940).

Muller, J.R. *Stephen Gardiner and the Tudor Reaction* (London, 1926).

Mullinger, J.B. *The University of Cambridge*, (Cambridge, 1873, 1911).

Neale, J.E. *Elizabeth I and her Parliaments 1559–1581* (London, 1953).

Neale, J.E. *Queen Elizabeth I* (London, 1934).

Nichols, J.G., ed. *Narratives of the Days of the Reformation* (London, 1859).

Nichols, J.G. *Literary Remains of King Edward VI* (London, 1857).

Noailles, A. de *Ambassades de M. M. de Noaailles en Angleterre*, ed. A. de Vertot (Leyden, 1763).

Original Letters relative to the English Reformation, ed. H. Robinson (Cambridge, 1846–7).

Oxford City Records. Selections from the Records of the City of Oxford 1509–1583 (Oxford and London, 1880)

Parker, M. *Correspondence of Matthew Parker, Archbishop of Canterbury* (Cambridge, 1853).

Parker, M. *De Antiqvitate Britannicae Ecclesiae* (London, 1572).

Parsons, R. *A treatise of Three Conversions of England from Paganisme to Christian Religion* (St Omer, 1603–4).

Philpot, J. *An Apologie of John Philpot written for spittings vpon an Arrian, with and Invective against the Arrians (the very natural children of Antichrist)* (probably London, c. 1560).

Philpot, J. *The Examinations and Writings of John Philpot* (Cambridge, 1842).

Pole, R. *Epistolarum Reginaldi Poli S.R.E. Caardinalis,* ed. A.M. Quirini (Brixen, 1744–57).

Pollen, J. H. *Unpublished Documents relating to the English Martyrs*, ed. J.H. Pollen, S.J., (Catholic Record Society, London, 1908).

Ponet, J. 'A Shorte Treatise of Politike Pouuer', in Hudson, *John Ponet* (Chicago, 1942, facsimile of first edition, Strasbourg, 1556).

Porter, H.C. *Reformation and Reaction in Tudor Cambridge* (Cambridge, 1958).

Prescott, H.F.M. *Mary Tudor* (London, 1953 edn., first published in 1940).

Private Prayers of the Reign of Queen Elizabeth (Cambridge, 1851).

Read, C. *Lord Burghley and Queen Elizabeth* (New York, 1960).

Read, C. *Mr Secretary Cecil and Queen Elizabeth* (London, 1955).

Read, E. *Catherine, Duchess of Suffolk* (London, 1962).

Ridley, J. *Elizabeth I* (London, 1987).

Ridley, J. *Henry VIII* (London, 1984).

Ridley, J. *John Knox* (Oxford, 1968).

Ridley, J. *The Life and Times of Mary Tudor* (London, 1973).

Ridley, J. *Nicholas Ridley* (London, 1957).

Ridley, J. *The Statesman and the Fanatic, Thomas Wolsey and Thomas More* (London, 1982); sub. nom. *Statesman and Saint*, New York, 1983).

Ridley, J. *Thomas Cranmer* (Oxford, 1962)

Ridley, J. *The Tudor Age* (London, 1988).

Ridley, N. *The Works of Nicholas Ridley, D.D., Sometime Lord Bishop of London, Martyr 1555* (Cambridge, 1841).

Rogers, T. *History of Agriculture and Prices* (Oxford, 1872).

Roper, W. *The Mirrour of Vertue in Worldly Greatnes* (*The Life of Sir Thomas More*) (London, 1903 edn.)

Rose-Troup, F. *The Western Rebellion of 1549* (London, 1913).

Rymer, T. W. *Foedera, Conventiones, Literare, Et. Acta Publica inter Reges Angliae* (London, 1704–17).

Sanders, N. *The Rise and Growth of the Anglican Schism* (London, 1877 edn., first edn. Cologne 1585).

Selve, O. de *Correspondance politique de Odet de Selve*, ed. G. Lefèvre-Pontalis (Paris, 1888).

Seton-Watson, R.W. *A History of the Czechs and Slovaks* (London, 1943).

Smyth, C.H. *Cranmer and the Reformation under Edward VI* (Cambridge, 1926).

State Papers during the Reign of Henry VIII (London, 1821–52).

Statutes of the Realm (London, 1810–24).

Stow, J. *Annales, or a Generall Chronicle of England, begun by Iohn Stow, continued and augmented by Edmund Howes* (London, 1631).

Strype, J. *Annals of the Reformation and establishment of religion and other various occurences in the Church of England during Queen Elizabeth's happy reign* (Oxford, 1824 edn., first published in 1708–9, cited as *Annals of the Reformation*).

Strype, J. *Historical Memorials Ecclesiastical and Civil of Events under the Reign of Mary I* (Oxford, 1822 edn., first publdished in 1721, cited as *Ecclesiastical Memorials*).

Strype, J. *The Life of the Learned Sir Thomas Smith* (Cambridge, 1820 edn., first published 1698).

Strype, J. *Miscellaneous Writings and Letters of Thomas Cranmer*, ed. J Cox (Cambridge, 1840–6, first published in 1694, cited as Strype, *Cranmer*).

Sussex Notes and Queries, vol. I (Lewes, 1927).

'Thomas Cranmer 1489–1556', in *Three Commemorative Lectures Delivered at Lambeth Palace* (Westminster, 1956).

Townsend, G. *The Life and Defence of the Conduct and Principles of the Venerable and Calumniated Edmund Bonner Bishop of London* (London, 1842).

Troubles connected with the Prayer Book of 1549, ed. N. Pocock (London, 1884).

The Troubles at Frankfort (Zurich, 1575).

The Troubles of our Catholic Forefathers, related by themselves, ed. J. Morris (London, 1872–7)

Two London Chronicles from the Collections of John Stow, ed. C.L. Kingsford (London, 1910).

Tyler, R. *The Emperor Charles the Fifth* (London, 1956).

Tyndale, W. *Doctrinal Treatises and Introductions to different portions of the Holy Scriptures* (Cambridge, 1848, cited as Tyndale, *Works*).

Tyndale, W. *The Obedience of a Christian Man. see* Tynedale, *Works*, vol. 1.

Tytler, F.F. *England under the Reigns of Edward VI and Mary* (London, 1839).

Unpublished Documents Relating to the English Martyrs ed. J. H. Pollen (Catholic Record Society, London, 1908).

Valor Ecclesiasticus temporis Regi Henrici Octavi (London, 1810–34).

Weiss, C.H. *Papiers d'état du Cardinal de Granvelle* (Paris, 1841–52).

Wilkins, D. *Concilia Magnae Britanniae et Hiberniae a Synodo Verulamiensi A.D. CCCCXLVI ad Londinensem A.D. MDCCXVII* (London, 1737).

Williams, G.H. *The Radical Reformation* (London, 1962).

Wood, Anthony à *Athenae Oxoniensis, an Exact History of all the Writers and Bishops who have had their education in the University of Oxford. To which is added the Fasti or Annals of the said University* (London, 1813–20 edn., first published in 1691–2).

Wright, T. *Three chapters of Letters relating to the Suppression of the Monasteries* (London, 1843).

Wriothesley, C. *A Chronicle of England during the reigns of the Tudors from A.D. 1485 to 1559*, ed. W.D. Hamilton, (London, 1875–7 cited as Wriothesley's *Chronicle*).

Zurich Letters, comprising the correspondence of several English Bishops and others with some of the Helvetian Reformers during the reign of Queen Elizabeth (Cambridge, 1852–5).

Index

Numbers in *italic* refer to illustrations